D1104926

ECONOMIC PLANNING AND SOCIAL
JUSTICE IN DEVELOPING COUNTRIES

Economic Planning and Social Justice in Developing Countries

OZAY MEHMET

ST. MARTIN'S PRESS   NEW YORK

All rights reserved. For information write:
St. Martin's Press Inc., 175 Fifth Avenue, New York, N.Y. 10010
Printed in Great Britain
ISBN 0-312-23443-0
First published in the United States of America in 1978

Library of Congress Cataloging in Publication Data

Mehmet, Ozay
   Economic planning and social justice in developing
countries.

   Includes index.
      1. Underdeveloped areas – Economic policy. 2. Eco-
nomic development – Social aspects. I. Title.
HC59.7.M427 1978   338.9'009172'4   78-18797
ISBN 0-312-23443-0

CONTENTS

ACKNOWLEDGEMENTS

The conception of this study dates back to 1973 when I was involved in field-work in Africa on behalf of the International Labour Office and the International Development Association of the World Bank. In Uganda I witnessed the mass exodus of Asians expelled by Idi Amin. Previously, in 1969, I had been an observer of the race riots in Malaysia, and several years earlier I had seen the Greeks and Turks fighting in Cyprus. These, and less agonising field experiences elsewhere, led me step by step to question many of the basic assumptions of the (mostly neoclassical) theory of economic growth which I learnt first as a student and then as a teacher of economics. Why is there such a huge gap between the theory of development and the grim realities of developing countries? Why, after two decades of economic planning, do the problems of mass poverty, unemployment and inequality in the Third World remain unchecked, often causing conflict and division? Is it that the theories are wrong — that the Western economic model is inappropriate? Or, is it that the tool of planning has been misused — if so, by whom and how? What, if any, are the 'lessons' for the future? These are complex issues, largely at the 'frontier' of development studies. The answers to be found in the following pages are derived from one central hypothesis: that regular economic planning (as defined in this study) *is an effective, non-violent alternative path to development with social justice.*

Many debts of gratitude have been accumulated during the preparation of the study. I have profited from numerous discussions with students and colleagues at the universities of Windsor, Toronto and Ottawa, and I have learnt a great deal from friendships forged in Malaysia, Uganda, Somalia, Liberia, Guyana and elsewhere, as well as in Geneva and Washington. But I alone must be held responsible for all opinions expressed in the study. I would like to acknowledge my thanks to the following for their help and advice during the long months of research and writing: B. Higgins, R. Zind, J. Nellis, A. Ames, G. Abonyi, G. Helleiner, J. Holland, D. Dawson, J. Buttrick, M. Yudelman, I. Adelman, N. Meltz, S. and J. Nagata, R.S. Milne and M. Crener. I owe special thanks to A.J. Kerr whose constant encouragement was an inspiration throughout. But above all, I wish to thank my wife, Karen Ann, and my sons Sean and Erin, for their patience and understanding.

O. Mehmet
February 1978

PREFACE

Benjamin Higgins

When Keynes's *General Theory* was published some four decades ago, it was hailed as the beginning of a revolution in economics. And indeed it seemed for a time that the analytical framework provided in that shattering book would permit the conversion of economics from a rather rarefied exercise in social astronomy, with economists as observers of the system rather than intervenors in it, into a quantified, operational and highly skilled profession, with economists acting almost as social engineers. Alas, it is all too apparent today that the Keynesian theoretical framework, even in its neo-Keynesian elaborations, is much too general and much too simple to serve as the sole guide to policy formulation. Even in the advanced countries for which the Keynesian system was designed, it does not provide satisfactory solutions for the really pressing problems of the post-war era: simultaneous unemployment and inflation; balance of payments crises; regional disparities; inequalities among social, ethnic and linguistic groups; pollution; congestion and urban blight; growing shortages of energy and other non-renewable resources. But in the less developed countries, where the main problems still lie on the supply side rather than on the side of management of effective demand, Keynesian economics is proving even more unsatisfactory. It was of course tried, in virtually all non-socialist LDCs, development being equated with growth and growth with capital accumulation. But as we all know now, even high rates of growth (of national income) do not guarantee development, in the sense of widespread and deep improvements of welfare of poor people in poor countries. Moreover, today even rapid growth eludes many LDCs.

The disappointing results of the two development decades have led to disillusionment, not only with regard to Keynes's *General Theory* as a basis for development planning and policy, but with general theories as a whole. There is a strong tendency among development economists today to disaggregate – by region, by sector, by enterprise, by community. Development economists today are happy to find theories applicable to some number of similar cases; the search for a general theory has been abandoned for a while – perhaps for ever, as economists increasingly think of themselves less as 'social engineers' and more as 'social doctors', seeking to diagnose and cure maladies; the medical doctor does not need a 'general theory of health'. Professor Ozay Mehmet's book is very much in line with these trends.

Another aspect of the new approach to development planning and policy is a 'return to the laboratory' in the sense of making on-the-spot case studies. Here too Professor Mehmet is in tune with the times. His five case-studies, drawn from the three major geographic groupings of developing countries (Asia, Africa and Latin America) are the very core of his analysis. To be sure, in the final chapters of his book he manages to generalise; but at the same time he leaves his readers highly conscious of the differences among his cases as well as of their similarities.

Professor Mehmet's welfare economics is also in line with recent thought. He does not waste much time worrying about how to move from individual orderings of wants to a social welfare function; he is quite happy to make value judgements of his own as to what is good for society, and these value judgements conform to those which have recently gained widespread and official public support. His approach is consonant both with the Unified Approach to Development Policy and Planning, so warmly embraced by the UN General Assembly and by nearly all members of the United Nations 'family', and with the more recent Basic Needs Approach recommended by the World Employment Conference. He sees no inherent conflict between equity and efficiency, and proposes a comprehensive employment policy as a vehicle for equalisation as well as growth. He is less concerned with capital accumulation than with malnutrition, illiteracy, land tenure and urban slums. There is a remnant of the Pareto principle in all this, however; his system of egalitarian planning and reform is designed to make *everyone* better off, although of course the gains of the poor will be substantially greater than the gains of the rich. It is this application of the Pareto principle that allows him to feel optimistic about egalitarian planning as a form of 'non-violent revolution'. He recognises that his proposals will encounter resistance, even if no group loses in terms of absolute economic welfare, since there are implicit in his system shifts in political power structure and in social status. But he ends on an optimistic note.

There is another idea in the book, one that appears also in my book with Jean Downing Higgins, which will appear at about the same time as this one, an idea that is in the air in development circles, not yet entirely crystallised. This is the idea of the development plan, and of a process of planning from below, as a new and major element in the political organisation of democratic countries (or of countries wishing to become more democratic). Professor Mehmet was born in a developing country, which may be why he got to this idea more directly than I did. The intellectuals of LDCs are less bound than we are to ideologies associated with European powers, whether eighteenth-century liberalism and *laissez-faire* economics or Soviet-bloc Marxism, and thus more free to think for themselves. They have understood for some time that when it comes to development planning and policy, 'plan or no plan', or even 'socialism *v.* capitalism', are not the real issues. There is no need to choose between a 'market economy' and a 'centrally planned economy'. Indeed these terms, used by the United Nations to group countries for statistical purposes, are really misnomers. All countries use the market as source of information and a guide to decision-making, and, in varying degrees, as a mechanism for allocating resources and distributing goods and services. And all governments do some central planning.

But planners with experience in developing countries know that the information provided by the market, detailed and sensitive as it may be in reflecting changes in taste and technology, is not enough. The established political processes, such as periodic elections in parliamentary democracies or the intra-party shifts of power by which the 'people's democracies' change their leadership and their policies, provide another source of information; but when it comes to detailed decisions regarding content of a development plan and choice among policy options, this information is vague and blunt. The planners and politicians of developing countries are well aware of the fact that in today's world of mutual vulnerability, mistakes in plans or policies can be extremely expensive, if not disastrous. They are therefore eagerly seeking new channels for information flows that will be more sharply pointed towards social needs than either the market or the established political processes can be.

Out of Asia, and particularly out of the UN Centre for Regional Development in Nagoya, comes the concept of 'the barefoot planner', roughly analogous to Mao's 'barefoot doctors', in the sense that both expressions imply continuous contact of highly trained professionals with the target population whose welfare is to be improved. Instead of sitting in air-conditioned offices in the capital city, constructing econometric models and running them through the computer, as many development planners have done and as some must continue to do, the 'barefoot planner' would be especially trained to conduct a continuous dialogue with peasants and workers, to discover their values, traditions, hopes and aspirations; and to raise the level of expectations of this target population if it is significantly below what it is technically possible to attain. They would also be trained to spot problems in need of solving and opportunities for carrying out development projects that will solve such problems at the community level – such as the rusted gate that prevents use of the irrigation system of Rivière Barette in Haiti, something no planner sitting in Port au Prince would have discovered. In this fashion a whole new stream of information can be channelled to the model-builders and to the politicians, supplementing both the market and the existing political process. Both the DRIPP project in Haiti and the Pahang Tenggara project in Malaysia operated very much in this fashion. It is becoming increasingly common practice to conduct project planning in constant contact with the community to be served the project.

Our of Latin America comes the concept of 'Desarrollismo' (or in Brazil, Desenvolvimentismo) as an economic, social and political philosophy in its own right, an alternative to both *laissez-faire* liberalism and to Marxist socialism. Planned development becomes the most important single unifying force in the society, as we have seen above. 'Rally round the Plan' replaces 'Rally round the Flag' as a battle cry. For a society to rally around the plan, however, the plan must reflect the wishes and aspirations of the members of this society; and there will normally be some conflicts of interest among social groups. One function of the plan, therefore, is to resolve these inter-group conflicts in the best possible manner. One of the functions of the 'barefoot planner' is to spot potential sources of conflict and resistance, measure their strength, and report accordingly to the central planners and the politicians. This additional information can then be used in formulating the plan. Conflict resolution is a major task of development planning.

But if development planning can provide new channels of information to make government, and the entire economic organisation, more efficient; if it can serve as a unifying force; if it can become an instrument of conflict resolution; if it can serve as an integrated economic, social and political philosophy; if it can contribute significantly to achievement of the aspirations of all mankind: why then limit it to developing countries? The answer is: no reason at all. Once it is accepted that 'development' really means improvement in social welfare, and that 'development planning' can improve the whole organisation of society so as to bring such improvement, then 'development theory' becomes the whole of social science and 'development planning' the whole of social philosophy. No society is so perfect that it has no need of knowledge as to how best it can be improved.

There is obviously much in all this new emphasis on 'bottom-up' planning that needs clarification and solidification. We are, after all, talking about a new political and social philosophy, a new 'third option'. There are obvious risks in a political system which leans heavily on professional intermediaries between people and their elected representatives. Professor Mehmet makes a radical proposal to the effect that not only should planners be in direct contact with the target population whose welfare is to be improved, but foreign aid agencies also should bypass the host government and go straight to the target population they wish to serve — to me, a very attractive proposal indeed. But there is more to be said on both sides of these issues; let us hope that Professor Mehmet's book stimulates the debate that it deserves to launch.

Part One

ECONOMIC GROWTH WITHOUT SOCIAL JUSTICE

1 WHAT WAS WRONG WITH POST-WAR ECONOMIC PLANNING IN LDCS?

During the two decades following the Second World War economic planning in the less developed countries (LDCs) became highly fashionable. By 1970 there hardly existed an LDC without some kind of Development Plan.[1] Usually prepared at the urging of, and with technical assistance from, the international aid agencies and Western donors, these documents aspired to a set of highly ambitious targets, predicated on the expectation of generous foreign aid funds from Western sources, principally the USA and the United Nations. For their part, Western aid-givers were motivated by a multiplicity of objectives, partly humanitarian, partly commercial and partly military in nature.[2] A dominant rationalisation was the 'widening gap' theory. Its central argument was that while the advanced, industrialised countries of the West were attaining higher standards of living, the underdeveloped countries of the Third World were becoming poorer.[3]

Western prescriptions to narrow the 'widening gap' called for massive aid programmes to finance development projects in the poor countries of Asia, Africa and Latin America. After all, if the Marshall Plan could help bring about the miracle of post-war reconstruction in Western Europe, why not attempt the same experiment in other parts of the world?

However, Western aid to the Third World did not come unconditionally. It came as an instrument of the 'Cold War', to defend a capitalist ideology increasingly threatened globally by a Communist alternative. It came to transplant an American or Western way of life in an age of 'rising expectations'. Above all, it came to foster a process of rapid industrialisation built on technology and know-how imported directly from the West.

Scarcely any attempt was made to adapt these Western formulae to the environments and circumstances of the LDCs. The appropriateness or the capacity of the political and social institutions of these countries to absorb large inflows of foreign funds, or to manage a controlled process of rapid change, were rarely taken into account. The efficiency of the governmental machinery and bureaucracy to implement and monitor large-scale development projects was seldom questioned. Neither was the moral commitment of the political leadership to economic and industrial development doubted. It was as if there existed only one single constraint on industrial expansion: capital shortage. Given generous foreign aid programmes, rapid industrial take-off was merely a matter of time.

W.W. Rostow, the proponent of the take-off theory, proposed a foreign aid strategy to contain Communism, arguing that one or two decades of aid might be adequate to transform a stagnant, low-income LDC into one progressing along a steady growth path.[4] The 'Big Push' theorists, guided by Rosenstein-Rodan, argued that to achieve maximum impact of scarce development funds, all resources should be concentrated on industrialisation since the 'growth poles' were only to be found in the manufacturing and non-agricultural sectors.[5] In fact, inflationary financing could well be utilised, either through forced savings or merely by printing more money, since a higher level of national output was only a few years ahead. For this reason, all other social needs and reforms (such as educational and manpower development, administrative modernisation, agrarian development) could be postponed until industrialisation was sufficiently advanced to become a self-sustaining process. In short, industrialisation, with Western aid and technology, was the panacea to break the poverty trap in which the poor countries of the Third World found themselves, owing to their large and stagnant 'subsistence' sectors. Income maximisation via industrialisation became the universal target of economic planning. Equitable income distribution, while generally acknowledged as a desirable objective, was sacrificed to the immediate goal of maximising the gross national product (GNP). In the idiom of the period, there was no point in becoming concerned about distribution when there was practically nothing to distribute.

Model-Building and Macro-Planning

Model-building was the indispensable tool of planners and economists involved in the design of development plans. Models afforded the means for the application of economic theories to the practical task of planning.

The typical development plan in the early post-war period was a macro model based on certain key aggregate relationships between employment, output and investment.[6] Derived from the Keynesian income and employment theory, originally by Harrod and Domar, these macro models related aggregate output to the stock of capital by the capital-output ratio.[7] The UN took the initiative to popularise macro-planning based on the crucial capital-output ratio. Thus, it was declared in 1955:

> The rate of economic growth may be analytically considered as
> being the function of two factors: (a) the rate of capital formation
> and (b) the capital/output ratio; accordingly development policies
> may be described as aiming to increase the former, reduce the
> latter, or do both.[8]

Another group of UN experts stated: 'After estimating the current
rate of savings, the *crucial* question will be what amount of net
national output can be expected from investment to be made on the
basis of the estimated savings.'[9] Naturally, these declarations were
consistent with the general opinion in the economics profession at the
time that the bottleneck resource in the development process was
capital. As Lewis had expressed it:

> The central problem in the theory of economic growth is to
> understand the process by which a community is converted from
> being a 5 percent to a 12 percent saver – with all the changes in
> attitudes, in institutions and in techniques which accompany
> this conversion.[10]

The macro models were logically complete constructions designed for
internal consistency. The need for consistency was obvious: to avoid
resource bottlenecks or surpluses in the process of growth. In fact,
the principle of formal consistency implied zero substitution in factor
use. This proved to be highly damaging in the implementation stage
since, even in closed economies, there are always alternative techniques
of production, such as more or less labour-intensive and more or less
capital-intensive methods. For example, different proportions of
bricks, cement and steel could be used in the building and
construction projects. The range of alternative techniques would be
even greater in the case of open economies linked to the world economy
through international trade. Consequently, there might be significant
departures in the implementation stage from the theoretical assumptions
and fixed input-output relations presumed in the planning stage.
Strict adherence to the original plan procedures would, doubtless,
create an intolerable degree of inflexibility and might cause waste and
inefficiency – contrary to original objectives.

The Indian planning experience based on a 'grand strategy' is a good
example of macro model-building. This strategy was heavily influenced

by the macro-economic theories of C.P. Mahalanobis[11] involving
sequential inter-industry flows and optimal timing. The basic
Mahalanobis idea was that the growth process should be carefully
integrated and the growth of each sector phased over time to achieve
optimal sectoral linkage and interdependence. Thus, the first sector to
be developed was heavy industry, centred around the creation of an
Indian iron and steel industry. This was necessary to increase the
domestic supply of producer goods which subsequently would be
needed to develop consumer-goods industries.

The early five-year Indian plans were drafted in line with the 'grand
strategy' theories. While heavy industrialisation was given top priority,
agricultural production lagged and imports of food as well as
machinery increased rapidly, leading to a severe balance of payments
crisis, and a slow-down in the rate of economic growth. The
major lesson of the Indian experience with the 'grand design'
approach is that the planners and policy-makers can neglect rural areas
and food production only at their peril.[12]

A national plan is only as good as the quality and quantity of
information on which it is based. Effective macro-planning requires
national accounts covering production, employment, prices, incomes
and balance of payments, as well as detailed inter-industry relationships.
A fundamental weakness of planning efforts in the post-war years was
the lack of adequate and reliable data. Some LDCs did not even possess
vital statistics about population, let alone GNP and detailed input-
output relationships. In such cases, the bolder planners simply indulged
in 'planning without facts',[13] making guesstimates on more or less
arbitrary assumptions. A striking example of this is Somalia's *First
Five-Year Plan, 1963-67.* To quote the candid admission of the
planners:

> The methodology of planning for the Somali Republic does not
> follow the usual pattern based on the Gross National Product
> (GNP) approach, for the simple reason that information about GNP
> is not available. Certain other necessary data is either not available
> at all, or if available, is unreliable and incomplete. This is true of
> population, birth and death rates, age distribution, immigration
> and emigration, labour force, employment and unemployment,
> wages and salaries, areas under different crops, agricultural
> production, yields of different crops, agricultural holdings,
> livestock population, livestock products, livestock trade, forestry,
> fisheries, small-scale and handicraft industries, building construction,

electricity, wholesale and retail trade, price indices, road transport, education, health, personal income and housing.[14]

Yet the lack of accurate information was seldom considered sufficient reason to refrain from constructing some of the most sophisticated mathematical models then fashionable in the Western planning circles. For example, in a large number of Third World countries elaborate input-output tables were constructed, with most of the cells either filled with zero or hypothetical figures.[15] Under such conditions, it was only inevitable that planning would prove, at best, to be an educational exercise, albeit a highly expensive and wasteful one.

In the proliferation of plans in LDCs,[16] international aid agencies as well as rich donor countries played a key role. Preparation of comprehensive plans, however weak the underlying assumptions and statistical bases, was necessitated by the demands of donors wishing to see aid funds well utilised within the context of a rational pattern. Most plans were made not out of a domestic necessity, nor out of genuine desire on the part of governments dedicated to rapid social and economic development, but simply to obtain foreign aid.[17] In fact, the provision of aid from the World Bank and UN was usually contingent upon the existence of a plan. LDCs lacking plans, but desiring to meet this requirement, extensively utilised the services of expatriate planning experts, sometimes by direct contract but more generally through technical assistance programmes. On occasion the planning exercises were carried to such absurd lengths that

the construction of plans [became] an exercise for foreigners by foreigners. The recent plan in the Sudan for example, was largely prepared by two foreign technicians and the document was written and printed in English (Government of the Sudan, Economic Planning Secretariat, *The Ten Year Plan of Economic and Social Development* 1961/2 – 1970/1, 1963). Once the plan was prepared, the planning organization was disbanded and planning ceased.[18]

The Sudan case may not be the most representative example, but it clearly demonstrates the degree of unrealism which characterised much of the planning efforts in the 1950s and 1960s. Ambitious and abstract models of economic growth were formulated speedily based on aggregative theories developed in the West, usually by expatriate planners. Little or no attention was paid to social, institutional and political realities, and the appropriateness of the existing bureaucratic machinery to handle a process of rapid transformation was seldom adequately considered.

Industrialisation and Employment

In recent years the general enthusiasm for industrialisation in LDCs has been declining for a variety of reasons. One principal reason is its failure to create a sufficient number of jobs to absorb a rapidly expanding population and labour force in an age of 'rising expectations'. The data presented in Table 1.1 show that while several LDCs achieved quite impressive aggregate rates of growth of manufacturing output during the 1950s and 1960s, manufacturing employment increased, on the average, at only about 50 per cent of the output growth rate. In some countries the level of employment in manufacturing actually declined. For example, in Thailand during 1960-9, while the output of the manufacturing sector registered an impressive 10.7 per cent expansion, employment in this sector fell by 12.0 per cent. In Algeria it fell by no less than 27 per cent. What these figures imply is that the productivity gains of industrial growth were the result of highly capital-intensive Western technology utilised in modern sectors. Coupled with the relatively small size of these modern sectors (see column 3, Table 1.1), the drive for industrialisation was clearly an inappropriate strategy of providing adequate opportunity for productive employment for all job-seekers.

Sadly, but quite aptly, there is an expanding population of 'marginal men'[19] in LDCs now — the survivors of the post-war population explosion reaching adulthood only to find that they cannot play a productive role simply because there are no employment openings for them. The resulting frustration and idleness represent both social and economic waste, while also posing as constant threats to political stability.

Conflicting Employment and Income Objectives: A Critique of the Neoclassical Growth Theory

Economic planning in the post-war period was primarily based on the assumptions and prescriptions of the neoclassical growth theory.[20] This theory assumed that, far from being conflicting, the employment and incomes objectives of growth (both desirable) are in the end mutually reinforcing. In the early stages of growth there may be unemployment, but this is temporary and is bound to disappear once growth accelerates. At a comparatively early stage of the debate about

Table 1.1: Growth of Manufacturing Employment and Output in LDCs, 1960-9

Regions/Countries	(Col. 1) ΔE_M (1960-9)	(Col. 2) ΔO_M (1960-9)	(Col. 3) EM/L_T (1970)
E. Africa			
Ethiopia	6.4^a	12.8	—
Zambia	10.5^b	13.8^b	—
W. Africa			
Ghana	6.3^c	10.6	8.6
Nigeria	5.7^d	14.1	—
Asia			
Korea	13.0^a	18.4	13.2
W. Malaysia	8.1^e	8.6	8.7
Pakistan	2.6^d	12.3	9.5
Philippines	5.3	6.1	11.4
Singapore	17.4^a	17.7^e	13.9
Thailand	-12.0^c	10.7	3.4
Middle East and North Africa			
Algeria	-27.0^e	-0.5	6.4
Egypt	0.7^f	11.2	12.9
Iran	9.8^d	11.2	16.7
Iraq	7.7^a	5.2	9.5
Israel	5.1	12.1	23.2
Tunisia	7.8^a	4.1	9.5
Turkey	5.2^b	14.5	7.1
Latin America			
Brazil	1.1^g	6.5	1.7.8
Chile	4.2^c	4.8	23.2
Colombia	3.0	5.9^b	12.8
Costa Rica	2.8^d	8.9	11.5
Dominican Republic	1.1^b	1.7^b	8.2
Ecuador	6.0	11.4	14.0
Panama	11.1	12.9^b	7.6

a. 1963-9	d. 1963-8	g. 1959-69
b. 1960-8	e. 1966-9	
c. 1963-7	f. 1966-8	

$\Delta E_M, \Delta O_M$: annual growth rate of manufacturing employment and output during 1960-9 (unless otherwise stated). E_M, manufacturing employment, covers all persons working for the establishment, except working proprietors, active business partners, unpaid family workers and home-workers. O_M, manufacturing output, gross value added. L_T is total labour force.

Source: D. Morawetz, 'Employment Implications of Industrialisation in Developing Countries: A Survey', *The Economic Journal*, Vol.84 (September 1974), Table I.

development planning. Charles Bettelheim expressed the overwhelming body of formal opinion when he wrote: *'The aim of increasing employment per se* is hardly an *economic aim.'*[21] He went on to argue as follows:

> Unemployment is an essentially transitory phenomenon, a legacy of the past, a consequence of relative economic backwardness and of a low rate of investment (which itself is a result of the use of low productive techniques). Unemployment can be overcome in a relatively short time, provided that the investible surplus is fully mobilised and regularly increased through investment in techniques. . .to achieve a sufficiently high level of productivity. . .A consequence of the short-term and transitory character of the unemployment problem is that it would be wrong to prepare an investment programme which would aim mainly at solving this temporary problem.[22]

Bettelheim's rather optimistic view was derived formally from the neoclassical theory of economic growth. This theory, based on Western experience, was formulated on the assumption that there is a positive, historical relationship between the expansion of output and the growth of employment, reflecting the fact that labour is a vital factor of production. This point is also at the crux of the argument, recently repeated with considerable effect, by Stewart and Streeten, who concluded that 'the path which maximizes the growth of output will also maximize the growth of employment'.[23]

However, the realities of the LDCs — mounting unemployment and 'population explosion' coupled with the amazing growth of labour productivity made possible by capital-intensive technology transferred from the West — are difficult to reconcile with theoretical formalism. It is highly questionable that a theory of growth, based on certain restricted assumptions such as homogeneous inputs, perfect factor mobility and high elasticity of substitution, can provide an adequate foundation for planning and economic policy in LDCs, many of which possess unique institutional and structural features.

The neoclassical growth theory was developed in the West, and it obviously reflected Western perspectives. For historical and cultural reasons, the Western countries manifested a smaller divergence between private and social net benefits of economic growth than is apparently the case in many LDCs today. Countries in Western Europe have been ethnically and linguistically more homogeneous and far more attached to the material objectives of the Protestant ethic; and, at least from the nineteenth century on, they have implemented a variety of political, economic and legal reforms at home to promote growth with fairer income distribution. In addition, colonialism and mercantilist foreign trade have played their part in ensuring that rapid economic growth was accompanied with conditions of virtually full employment of labour.

On the other hand, the position of LDCs today is in many respects fundamentally different. Typically they are plural societies, divided along tribal or ethnic lines. Often institutions and social values are seriously at variance with the assumptions of the neoclassical growth theory. For example, it is quite normal for the rich to keep their savings in foreign bank accounts, partly out of fear of political instability and partly to finance a style of living which involves extensive and costly trips overseas. The literature on the 'flight of capital' and such practices as 'over-invoicing' imports and 'under-invoicing' exports provides telling evidence of this problem.[24] The implication is that the national saving-income ratio need not rise, as predicted by the neoclassical theory, as a result of greater income concentration at the top induced by deliberate government policy. On the other hand, whenever the rich do invest in LDCs, they generally prefer projects which are 'hedged' against inflation and possess low social priority, e.g. high-rise luxury apartments and real estate in choice urban locations. While highly profitable from a private standpoint, such projects are socially counter-productive inasmuch as the beneficiaries are the landlords, speculators and the affluent who can afford high rents.

The experience of LDCs with 'infant industry' development is another important area of concern. Evidence from many developing countries shows that the new industrialists are typically the wealthy and privileged families with kinship links to politicians and officials controlling the decision-making process. Through influence-peddling, they are able to obtain state subsidies, tariff protection and profitable government contracts. Operating as actual or virtual monopolies, without domestic or foreign competition, these new, protected industrialists have little incentive to improve productive efficiency. Nor is there any motive for ploughing back any of the profits realised from these 'no-fail' ventures. Data in Table 1.2 provide highly interesting evidence regarding the extent of disguised subsidy extended to new industries in a number of LDCs. We shall explore this problem in greater detail in the case-study of Pakistan in Chapter 7. Little, Scitovsky and Scott, after surveying industrialisation in seven LDCs, have concluded:

> In all the countries reviewed the main feature. . .has been the creation of an internal market protected by high custom duties and import quotas. . .these countries have now reached the stage where policies that are followed to promote import-substitution are proving to be harmful for the economic development of these countries. Industrialisation sheltered by high level of protection has led to the creation of high-cost enterprises. . .[25]

In the long run productive efficiency of 'infant industries' may be raised to tolerable levels, but the waiting period in many LDCs is certain to be painfully long and costly. This follows from the fact that those who are benefiting from income concentration are also members of political elites which control the bureaucracy and the state, and they would be inclined to preserve the elitist growth pattern.

The Disguised Unemployment Hypothesis: Fallacy of Two-Sector Models of Growth

In his celebrated 1954 article, W.A. Lewis[26] used Joan Robinson's concept of disguised unemployment[27] to advance a theory of economic development in LDCs for rapid industrialisation. The basic proposal was to transfer surplus labour from peasant sectors in which marginal physical productivity (MPP) of labour was assumed to be 'negligible, zero, or even negative'[28] for employment in the modern sector in industrial or infrastructural projects. The social cost involved would be practically zero, given the assumption of zero or negative MPP. Agricultural output need not fall while industrial output would increase. In this sense, labour supply to the modern sector would be unlimited so long as disguised unemployment prevailed.

Although a number of empirical studies[29] challenged the existence of zero or negative MPP of labour, the Lewis two-sector model and its variants[30] became highly popular amongst development planners. In plan after plan, one finds references to disguised unemployment as the most abundant asset available for rapid growth, and its utilisation in the modern sector as a deliberate policy aim. The unrealism of these two-sector models is evidenced by their failure to take into account the effects of seasonal fluctuations in farming activities on labour supply as well as a wide range of institutional

Table 1.2: Some Examples of Nominal and Effective Tariffs on Manufactures in Developing Countries

| | | Percentage | |
		Nominal Tariff Rate	Effective Tariff Rate[a]
Argentina	1953	38	55
	1958	141	162
Brazil	1966	99	118
	1966	53	58
	1966	96	113
Chile	1961	111	182
India	1961	—	313
Korea	1963-5	36	40
Malaysia	1963	9	8
	1965	10	11
	1965	2	− 6
Mexico	1960	22	27
	1960	39	61
	1960	24	26
Pakistan	1963-4	93	271
	1963-4 (i)	53	95
	(ii)	42	45
	1963-4	85	271
Philippines	1961	46	49
	1961-5	41	71
	1965	25	61
Taiwan	1965	29	48
	1966	30	33
Tanzania	1963-6	26	37
Turkey (overall)	1960s	44	65
	1965		
Refrigeration units		62	80
Electric motors		71	66
Ammonium nitrate fertiliser		71	186
Superphosphate fertiliser		27	925
Truck tyres		131	170
Plastic		102	916
Electric cables		82	147

Source: D.T. Healey, 'Development Policy: New Thinking About an Interpretation', *Journal of Economic Literature,* Vol.X, No.2, September 1972, p.762. Several sources are used.

a. Based on the formula:

$$e_i = \frac{t_i - \sum_j a_{ji} t_j}{V_i}$$

where

e_i = effective tariff rate on commodity i;

t_i ≠ nominal rate of tariff on commodity;

a_{ji} = the material input coefficient, i.e. material inputs as a proportion of the value of output, both measured at world prices;

t_j = nominal rate of tariff on material inputs;

V_i = value added as a proportion of the price of commodity i, at world prices.

determinants of labour utilisation in LDCs. For example, it can be shown[31] that the modern and traditional sectors are highly inter-dependent in terms of cash remittances from the wage-earners in the modern sector to their dependants in the traditional sector who are thus maintained as disguised unemployed. When such features as the seasonality of farming activities and inter-sectoral cash remittances are incorporated into a model of disguised unemployment, there would, in fact, be one unified employment market mechanism manifesting a trade-off between open unemployment in the modern sector and disguised unemployment in the traditional sector.

In retrospect, it is evident that the two-sector growth models were based on the principle of draining rural resources into urban sectors.[32] Since only the latter were regarded as the 'leading' sectors, it was felt necessary and desirable to transfer quantities of labour, as well as food and funds for financing urban-based industries. Accordingly, several policy instruments were designed, such as disguised taxes on rural areas, inflationary financing and forced saving, to squeeze resources from rural sectors. In this way, industrialisation has resulted in a rural-urban disequilibrium, and all its attendant social and political problems.

In the final analysis, the amazing thing about neoclassical theories and assumptions utilised in development planning in LDCs is not that they were applied so uncritically, but that they were relied upon for as long as a quarter of a century.

The Efficiency/Equity Trade-Off in Economic Growth

Western economics is characterised by a fundamental split between two major themes: efficiency in production and equity in the distribution of that product. The principle of efficiency, derived from the notion of a rational, 'economic man' with limited funds facing a perfectly competitive market operating according to Adam Smith's famous 'invisible hand' doctrine, ensures in theory that scarce resources are utilised in their most profitable uses. The pursuit of profit maximisation may create income differentials amongst citizens or it may cause unequally distributed opportunities, but these are deemed necessary — indeed, desirable — in order to act as incentives, in the form of rewards and penalties, for promoting a level of aggregate output which is both the largest possible and rapidly growing.

Yet, these same differentials may violate the principle of equity, derived from humanistic and egalitarian tradition and proclaimed in constitutional and political institutions guaranteeing universally distributed rights, duties and privileges to all individuals. The most efficiently working market-place may result in a degree of deprivation and poverty that conflicts with such basic human values as dignity, equality and fairness. The ultimate test for any process of social and economic development is that it should serve both the efficiency and equity objectives. At many points along the growth path, these two objectives may conflict with each other. For example, anti-poverty policies designed to shift income to the low-income groups to reduce economic inequality may also tend to weaken incentives for investment and growth. However, the equity and efficiency are not necessarily always conflicting. This is especially so in most LDCs with large volumes of unemployed or underemployed labour, potentially available for productive utilisation that would both increase the level of national output and the income share of the poor.

In the post-war planning and industrialisation drives in LDCs, a most unfortunate strategy choice was made, usually with active donor encouragement: equity was sacrificed for the sake of efficiency. Equitable income distribution, while generally acknowledged as a desirable objective, was traded for the immediate goal of maximising the gross national product. In the idiom of the period, there was no point in becoming concerned about distribution when there was practically nothing to distribute. It was essential to 'postpone' or delay equity considerations until some more favourable future date.

The planning trade-off in favour of efficiency was responsible for what has aptly been described as the 'hot pursuit of GNP'.[33] The evidence now accumulating, and analysed in the following chapters, clearly demonstrates that the preoccupation with efficiency objectives has been a failure. To be sure, industrialisation has helped to attract branch plants of multinational corporations in modern sectors, utilising Western investment funds and techniques of production. But only in rare cases did post-war industrialisation lead to the general improvement in the living standards of the majority of inhabitants. Usually, growth of GNP has been accompanied with greater income concentration in the top layer of the socio-economic pyramid with mass poverty at the bottom.

Economic Growth, Social Justice and Egalitarian Development

A process of economic growth which worsens social and economic inequalities is elitist and morally indefensible. It is growth without equity. It is against the ideals of social or distributive justice, which are broader in scope than the concepts of legal and political justice. The latter proclaim equality of all before the law and grant equal political rights, including one man, one vote. As will be discussed in Chapter 8, social justice goes beyond this, proclaiming the idea of a fair distribution of economic and social benefits as well as costs. Derived from historical egalitarian principles and typically enshrined in the constitutions of nations as well as in the United Nations Declaration of Universal Human Rights and other Conventions,[34] the search for social justice has been a driving force behind man's long struggle for a better life for all.

The 'dismal science' of economics is by no means silent on the subject. The general normative guidelines of social justice for economic policy can be derived from the axioms of welfare economics.[35] This, for example, is the idea behind the famous Compensation Principle formulated by a number of economists such as Kaldor, Hicks, Little and Scitovsky. According to this doctrine, an economic policy measure (e.g. a development project) which met the efficiency conditions would be judged socially justified on equity grounds as well if it increased the standard of living of at least one individual while harming no one; however, if there occurs a welfare loss for some individuals while benefiting others, then the gainers ought to be *potentially* capable of compensating the losers. For practical policy purposes, this may not be a very helpful yardstick, since it does not require *actual* compensation. Nevertheless, there is a strong presumption that the interests of the losers should be safeguarded in some appropriate way. This fact is emphasised in a recent theory of justice as fairness advanced by John Rawls.[36] His conception of justice rests on two basic principles:

> the first requires equality in the assignment of basic rights and duties, while the second holds that social and economic inequalities, for example inequalities of wealth and authority, are just only if they result in compensating benefits for everyone, and in particular for the least advantaged members of society. These principles rule out justifying institutions on the grounds that the hardships of some are offset by a great good in the aggregate. It may be expedient but it is not just that some should have less in order that others may prosper. But there is no injustice in the greater benefits earned by a few provided that the situation of persons not so fortunate is thereby improved.[37]

Regrettably, the concept of social justice had no practical relevance in
the process of post-war growth in most LDCs. This does not mean
that planning objectives totally ignored egalitarian ideals. On the
contrary, national plan documents almost always contained long
and ambitious lists of promises, quite in keeping with social justice,
included in preambles. But these were mostly for 'window-dressing'
purposes. The following two examples from Pakistan and India were
typical:

> The nation aspires to a standard of living for all its people as
> high as can be achieved with the resources available to it; equitable
> distribution of wealth; education of all in accordance with their
> talents; victory over disease; adequate facilities for transport
> and communication so that the nation may be effectively unified
> economically and socially.[38]

Indian planners expressed similar objectives: 'ever since Independence,
two main aims have guided India's planned development — to build
up by democratic means a rapidly expanding and technologically
progressive economy and a social order based on justice and
offering equal opportunity to every citizen.'[39]

These and similar lofty aims were abandoned during the
implementation and execution stages of plans. It is a central argument
of this book that this happened mainly because of the elite
management of planning and economic policy in LDCs. As discussed
in Part Two, domestic elites generally control the political system
and the economic decision-making machinery of these countries. In
the post-war period, these elites were successful in influencing the
allocation of planned investment expenditures and channelling them
into projects calculated to augment their own wealth, status
and power.

Income concentration at the top socio-economic stratum was
achieved through a growth strategy that actively encouraged the
expansion of property income at the expense of employment income.
Property income accrues primarily to asset-holding groups, such as
landlords, industrialists and owners of fixed capital and cash balances.
These assets earn dividends, interest, rent and other forms of property
income. Employment income, on the other hand, accrues to wage- and
salary-earners. Since the post-war growth in LDCs was based on capital-
intensive industrialisation, it seriously limited the growth of jobs and
employment income, while the priority accorded to capital formation

greatly enhanced the share of property income. In view of the fact that wealth assets are heavily concentrated at the top, it follows that income maximisation through industrialisation in LDCs was a process creating greater income inequality.

It is important to be clear about the politics of income distribution. In LDCs, and to a lesser extent in advanced countries, income shares are determined more in the political arena than in a competitive market-place according to the 'invisible hand'. In the political arena of LDCs the privileged and wealthy elites dominate the political system and the bureaucracy. As a result, they can control the budget, the public expenditure and the economic policy, including the substance and implementation of economic plans. In the general enthusiasm for rapid industrialisation in the Third World, the efficiency and the appropriateness of the prevailing *status quo* were seldom questioned. Planners simply assumed that the political and administrative machinery, as well as the will of the ruling classes, were favourably attuned to the requirements of planned development. Since, however, virtually no LDC possessed efficient administrative machinery, and since the political system was generally elitist, it was inevitable that the growth of GNP and new wealth would be inequitably distributed, widening the gap between the elites and the masses.

Western donors, economists and planners cannot avoid a major moral responsibility for the negative consequences of economic growth in LDCs. After all, they actively participated in the process of spreading and popularising economic planning in these countries. Preoccupied with GNP maximisation, these participants generally ignored the distributive effects of growth. As a leading exponent of economic planning explicitly declared in a standard textbook on the subject: 'Our subject matter is growth [i.e. growth of output per head of population] *and not distribution*'[40] (emphasis added).

Western aid donors, including the United Nations and its affiliated agencies, bear an especial burden of responsibility. The original technical assistance programme of the UN system was designed precisely in order to promote human rights in accordance with the principles of legal, political and social justice.[41] For reasons of international diplomacy, the UN as well as foreign aid donors have chosen to turn a 'blind eye' to the problems of elitist growth and widening socio-economic inequalities within LDCs, while the rich countries relied on 'aid rather than trade' policies.

The experience gained during the last quarter-century regarding

the abuses of economic planning and policy in developing nations
can and should serve as a valuable guide for future action to promote
social justice. This study advocates the concept of egalitarian planning
as a tool for levelling incomes, expanding employment and
meeting the basic needs of the bulk of the LDC populations.[42] Part
Three is devoted to a detailed discussion of the general principles and
some policy instruments of egalitarian planning. But it would be
impossible to achieve economic and social development in LDCs
consistent with social justice unless there were appropriate reforms
in the political and economic institutions as well. As Rawls has
pointed out, 'it is necessary to set the social and economic process
within the surroundings of suitable political and legal institutions.
Without these background institutions the outcome of the distributive
process will not be just.'[43] Some of the key elements of a more
egalitarian economic planning, based on a decentralised pro-rural
approach, will be discussed, beginning in Chapter 8. First, however, it
is necessary to document and analyse the dimensions of the post-war
process of growth without social justice. The following three chapters
will discuss the global evidence on such issues as income distribution,
absolute poverty and the unemployment crisis, while Part Two will be
devoted to five case-studies, based on Malaysia, Liberia, Pakistan,
Brazil and Uganda.

Notes

1. According to the latest edition of the catalogue of Inter Documentation
Company, AG, of Switzerland, which lists all existing national Development Plans,
there are no less than 323 plans, all prepared since 1951.

2. Lester B. Pearson *et al., Partners in Development* (Praeger, New York,
1969).

3. B. Ward, L. D'Anjou and J.D. Runnals (eds.), *The Widening Gap:
Development in the 1970's* (New York and London, Columbia University Press,
1971); L.J. Zimmerman, *Poor Lands, Rich Lands: The Widening Gap* (Random
House, New York, 1965); G. Myrdal, *Rich Land and Poor Land* (Harper, New York,
1965); A Shonfield, *The Attack on World Poverty* (Chatto and Windus, London,
1961); G. Ránis (ed.), *The Gap Between Rich and Poor Nations* (Macmillan,
London, 1972).

4. W.W. Rostow, *Stages of Economic Growth* (Cambridge University Press,
1960); Maxwell Graduate School of Citizenship and Public Affairs, Syracuse
University, *The Operational Aspects of US Foreign Policy*, 86th Congress, 1st
Session, Senate Committee on Foreign Relations, Committee Print, Study No.6,
11 November 1959.

5. P.N. Rosenstein-Rodan, 'Problems of Industrialisation of Eastern and
South-Eastern Europe', *Economic Journal*, Vol.53 (June-September 1943)
reprinted in A.N. Agarwala and S.P. Singh (eds.), *The Economics of*

Underdevelopment (Oxford University Press, New York, 1963); *idem,* 'Notes on the Theory of the Big Push', in H.S. Ellis and H.C. Wallich (eds.), *Economic Development for Latin America* (St. Martin's Press, New York, 1961). The following is a short-list of the earlier textbooks on development: W.A. Lewis, *The Theory of Economic Growth* (Unwin University Books, London, 1955); G.M. Meier, *Leading Issues in Development Economics, Selected Materials and Commentary* (Oxford University Press, New York, 1964); C.P. Kindleberger, *Economic Development* (McGraw-Hill, New York, 1958); A.O. Hirschman, *The Strategy of Growth* (Yale University Press, New Haven, Conn., 1958); S. Kuznets, *Six Lectures on Economic Growth* (Free Press, New York, 1959); H. Leibenstein, *Economic Backwardness and Economic Growth* (John Wiley, New York, 1957); E.E. Hagen, *The Economics of Development* (Richard D. Irwin, Homewood, Ill., 1968); B. Higgins, *Economic Development: Problems, Principles and Policies,* rev. ed. (Norton, New York, 1969).

    6. There is a vast volume of literature on planning in LDCs ranging from individual country studies in journals and books to the actual development plan documents published by the governments of LDCs. Country studies are presented in A. Waterston, *Development Planning, Lessons of Experience* (Oxford University Press, London, 1966); G.F. Papenek (ed.), *Development Policy – Theory and Practice* (Harvard University Press, Cambridge, Mass., 1968); M.F. Milikan (ed.), *National Economic Planning* (Colombia University Press, 1967); H.S. Ellis (ed.), *Economic Development for Latin America* (Macmillan, 1961). Also, see the individual country studies undertaken by the IBRD, numbering more than twenty. On the theory and techniques of planning, see C. Bettelheim, *Studies in the Theory of Planning* (Asia Publishing House, New York, 1959); J. Tinbergen, *Development Planning* (Weidenfeld and Nicolson, London, 1967); *idem, Central Planning* (Yale University Press, New Haven, Conn., 1964); J.C. Fei and G. Ranis, *Development of the Labor Surplus Economy: Theory and Policy* (Richard D. Irwin, Homewood, Ill., 1964); H.B. Chennery and P.G. Clark, *Interindustry Economics* (John Wiley, New York, 1959); UN, ECAFE, *Programming Techniques for Development Planning* (Bangkok, 1960). Textbook treatment of development is presented in references cited in footnote 5.

    7. In algebraic terms where Y = national income, K = capital, I = investment, S = savings, and changes are denoted by d, the growth rate $G = dY/Y$, the saving ratio $s| = S/Y$ and (under equilibrium I = S)

$$= I/Y$$

Also, $dK = I$, and
the incremental capital/output ratio $k = dK/dY = I/Y$
Since, $dY/Y = (I/Y)/(I/dY)$, therefore, $G = s/k$.
The original H-D model was presented in R.F. Harrod, *Toward a Dynamic Economics* (St Martin's, New York, 1948), and E.D. Domar, 'Capital Expansion, Rate of Growth and Employment', *Econometrica* (April 1946), pp.137-47.

    8. UN, ECAFE, 'Economic Development and Planning in Asia and the Far East', *Economic Bulletin for Asia and the Far East,* Vol.VI, No.3 (November 1955), Bangkok, pp.25-6.

    9. UN, *Programming Techniques,* 1960, pp.10-11.

    10. Lewis, *The Theory of Economic Growth,* pp.225-6.

    11. 'The Approach of Operational Research to Planning', *Sankhya,* Vol.16 (1955).

    12. On Indian planning, see W.B. Reddaway, *The Development of the Indian Economy* (Allen and Unwin, London, 1962); J.P. Lewis, *Quiet Crisis in India* (Brooking Institution, Washington, 1962).

    13. W. Stolper, *Planning without Facts* (Harvard University Press, Cambridge, Mass., 1967). A critical appraisal of planning in Asia is given in G. Myrdal, *Asian Drama* (Pantheon, New York, 1968), Appendix 3.

14. Somali Republic, *First Five-Year Plan, 1963-1967* (Mogadiscio, Somalia, 1963), p.25. For an evaluation of the success of this plan, see O. Mehmet, 'Effectiveness of Foreign Aid — The Case of|Somalia', *Journal of Modern African Studies,* Vol.9, No.1 (1971), pp.31-47.

15. A.H. Conrad, 'Econometric Models in Development Planning — Pakistan, Argentina, Liberia', in Papanek, *Development Policy — Theory and Practice;* A.T. Peacock and D. Doser, 'Input-Output Analysis in an Underdeveloped Country: A Case Study', *Review of Economic Studies* (October 1957).

16. The Draft Outline of a five-year plan published by the Planning Commission of the Government of India in July 1951 was the first comprehensive national planning document for an LDC. Since then, no less than 323 plans have been prepared. See the catalogue of Inter Documentation Company, AG, Switzerland.

17. R. Vernon, 'Comprehensive Model-Building in the Planning Process: The Case of the Less Developed Countries', *Economic Journal* (March 1966).

18. K.B. Griffin and J.L. Enos, *Planning Development* (Addison-Wesley, London, 1970), pp.20-1.

19. J.P. Grant, ' "Marginal Men": The Global Unemployment Crisis', *Foreign Affairs,* Vol.50, No.1 (October 1971).

20. This theory crystallises the contributions of several economists, past and present. Its conceptual roots extend back to the writings of Adam Smith, Malthus, Ricardo, Marx and Keynes. The post-Keynesian growth model, formulated by Harrod-Domar (for a summary, see Kindleberger, *Economic Development,* Chapter 3), was the starting-point for most neoclassical model-builders relying on aggregate input-output relationships. For a survey of the writings of leading model-builders such as Kaldor, Solow, Robinson, Kahn, Hahn and Matthews, *inter alia,* see A.K. Sen (ed.), *Growth Economics* (Penguin, Harmondsworth, 1970). The most comprehensive statement of the neoclassical growth model is J.E. Meade, *A Neo-Classical Theory of Growth* (Allen and Unwin, 1961).

21. *Studies in the Theory of Planning* (Asia Publishing House, New York, 1961), p.294.

22. Ibid., pp.430-1.

23. F. Stewart and P. Streeten, 'Conflicts Between Output and Employment Objectives in Developing Countries', *Oxford Economics Papers,* Vol.23, No.2 (July 1971), p.166.

24. There is a revealing discussion of corruption in Myrdal, *Rich Land and Poor Land,* Chapter 20. Also, see M.J. Esman, *Administration and Development in Malaysia* (Cornell University Press, Ithaca, New York, 1972); F.W. Riggs, *Thailand: The Modernization of a Bureaucratic Policy* (East-West Center Press, Honolulu, 1966); T.V. Benitez, *The Politics of Malawi* (The Asian Center, U.P., Curzon City, 1969).

25. I. Little, T. Scitovsky, M. Scott, *Industry and Trade in Some Developing Countries, A Comparative Study* (Oxford University Press for the OECD Development Center, 1970), pp.xvii-xviii.

26. W.A. Lewis, 'Economic Development with Unlimited Supplies of Labour', *The Manchester School,* Vol. 22 (May 1954). Reprinted in A.N. Agarwala and S.P. Singh, *The Economics of Underdevelopment* (Oxford University Press, New York, 1963), pp.400-49.

27. Joan Robinson, 'Disguised Unemployment', *The Economic Journal.* Vol. 46 (June 1936), coined the term 'disguised unemployment' to explain the differences between the productivity of workers in their normal occupations, consistent with their abilities and training, and in inferior jobs which they might be forced to accept during periods of cyclical unemployment in industrialised countries. Subsequently, the concept was applied to the

unemployment problems of LDCs.

28. Ibid., p.402.

29. B. Hansen, 'Marginal Productivity Wage Theory and Subsistence Wage Theory in Egyptian Agriculture'. *Journal of Development Studies*, Vol.2 (July 1966), pp.367-99; T.W. Schultz, *Transforming Traditional Agriculture* (Yale University Press, New Haven, 1964); M. Paglin, 'Surplus Agricultural Labour and Development: Facts and Theories', *American Economic Review*, Vol.55 (September 1965).

30. G. Ranis and J.C.H. Fei, *Development of the Labor Surplus Economy* (Richard D. Irwin Inc., Homewood, Ill., 1964); 'A Theory of Economic Development', *American Economic Review*, Vol.51 (September 1961).

31. O. Mehmet, 'Disguised Unemployment and Agricultural Development', *Canadian Journal of Agricultural Economics*, Vol.19, No.1 (July 1971); *idem*, 'A Note on Unemployment and Labor Migration in LDCs; A Diagrammatic Illustration', *American Journal of Agricultural Economics*, Vol.58, No.2 (May 1976).

32. See Chapter 11 for an elaboration of this matter.

33. Mahbub ul Haq, 'Employment in the 1970's: A New Perspective', *International Development Review*, Vol. XIII, No.4 (1971).

34. For example, see Arthur H. Robertson, *Human Rights in the World* (Manchester University Press, Manchester, 1972), which includes, *inter alia*, the United Nations Covenant on Human Rights. Regarding the role of international organisations in the promotion of human rights, see Rosalind S. Pollock, *The Individual's Rights and International Organisations* (Smith College, Mass., 1966). See also the UN publications dealing with human rights, e.g. *Yearbook on Human Rights*.

35. For a survey of the extensive literature on normative economics see E.J. Mishan, 'A Survey of Welfare Economics 1939-1959', *Economic Journal* Vol.70, No.278 (1960), reprinted in *idem, Welfare Economics, Five Introductory Essays* (Random House, New York, 1964).

36. *A Theory of Justice* (Harvard University Press, Cambridge, Mass., 1971).

37. Ibid., pp.14-15.

38. Government of Pakistan, Planning Commission, *The Second Five Year Plan* (1960-5) (Karachi, 1960), p.1.

39. Government of India, Planning Commission, *Third Five Year Plan* (New Delhi, 1961), p.4.

40. Lewis, *Theory of Economic Growth*, p.9. In fairness to Lewis, however, it must be added that this quote should not be construed as implying that Lewis was indifferent or opposed to distribution as a planning objective. Even his early writings, e.g. *The Principles of Economic Planning* (Unwin, London, 1949), provide evidence to the contrary. Nevertheless, the Lewis quote does reflect the general intellectual thinking at the time on growth and income.

41. Robertson, *Human Rights in the World*.

42. In recent years 'Basic Needs' (BN) strategy has gained widespread acceptance. The 1976 World Employment Conference, sponsored by the ILO, defined BN as follows: (1) adequate food, clothing and shelter; (2) education and health; (3) basic human rights; (4) employment as a means and an end; and (5) improved quality of employment. See ILO, *Employment, Growth and Basic Needs: A One World Problem*, Report of the Director General (Geneva, 1976), p.32. The BN strategy is also strongly endorsed by the World Bank. It is a strategy very close to our concept of egalitarian development.

43. Rawls, *A Theory of Justice*, p.275.

2 DISTRIBUTION EFFECTS OF GROWTH: THE EVIDENCE

'Our subject matter is growth and not distribution'
— W.A. Lewis

Planned economic growth in LDCs during the post-war period was regarded as a deliberate attempt at maximising income *per capita* subject to financial and resource constraints. Levelling of incomes amongst persons, ethnic groups or regions was only paid lip-service. Significantly, employment creation was generally believed to be ultimately reconcilable with the primary objective of income maximisation.

In the early 1960s some observers began to realise that planned economic growth in LDCs does not work in the expected manner. The first disturbing signs suggested that while the income objective of growth might be achieved, employment generation was disappointingly meagre.[1] By the mid-1960s empirical evidence on industrialisation in many LDCs pointed strongly to a structural conflict between the income and employment targets. For example, during the decade 1955-65 manufacturing employment in a large number of LDCs had increased, on average, at about 50 per cent of the rate of output. In several countries, such as Pakistan, Egypt and Turkey, employment generation was only minimal despite rapid growth of population and labour force; and in countries like Thailand employment in the 1960s declined in absolute terms. Yet, in all of these countries, very impressive rates of output growth were achieved (Table 1.1, p.23). This kind of evidence, against the backdrop of the 'population explosion', tended to demonstrate that, far from being mutually reinforcing, the employment and income goals of planned growth are seriously conflicting.

At the same time, an even more disappointing body of evidence regarding the distributive effects of post-war growth began to accumulate. This new evidence indicated that industrialisation in LDCs often leads to increased poverty and deprivation for the masses while augmenting the economic and political power of the entrenched interests and ruling elites. Data on income distribution, admittedly imperfect, show that in several LDCs the real income of no less than 60 per cent of the population has declined, sometimes in absolute terms as well as relatively, while the income share of wealthiest groups increased.

Increased inequality in the size distribution of income was intellectually justified by economists and planners in the early stages of development planning with the traditional argument that measures to promote fairer sharing of national income in the take-off stage would be prejudicial to growth of output due to its depressive effects on saving, investment, technology and incentives.[2] This intellectual bias against distribution, however, merely strengthened the status and power of the entrenched and emerging elites who were generally inclined to utilise this new instrument of national planning, together with the inflows of foreign aid funds which accompanied it, for self-aggrandisement and to preserve the *status quo*. In a real sense, post-war planning has often worked to create social injustice and greater inequalities.

The rest of this chapter will attempt to document these negative effects of post-war growth experience in LDCs.

The Concept of Poverty and Measurement of Income Inequality

Empirical analysis of poverty in LDCs is a complicated issue. There are two major difficulties: first, the lack of reliable and adequate data on income distribution, especially as regards the personal or size distribution, and second, the conceptual ambiguities associated with defining and measuring relative and absolute poverty. The former problem can be attributed to the fact that during much of the post-war planning efforts, top priority was assigned to the compilation of national accounting data, such as gross national product, trade and balance of payments statistics, etc. In those relatively few cases when attempts were made to collect income distribution data, it was for the purpose of describing the functional distribution of income, which is not very helpful so far as the study of poverty is concerned. For the latter purpose, data from surveys of family expenditure and budgets would be required — something which comparatively few LDCs, and then only in recent years, began to collect.

The principal conceptual obstacle in the way of an objective analysis of poverty and income inequality is that there exists no satisfactory theory of the *size* distribution of income, comparable to the marginal productivity theory which underlies the *functional* income distribution. The various measures of income inequality (such as the Gini coefficient, the Lorenz curve, the lognormal method, and the Theil index) all suffer from inconsistencies and may lead to contradictory conclusions, as demonstrated by Atkinson, Champernowne, Radanive and others.[3] It must be conceded, therefore, that such a concept as 'the optimum distribution' is a practical impossibility, and planning and policy have to rely on second-best solutions. We shall discuss these matters further in Chapter 8.

In recent years, there has been a marked improvement in the availability of data on income distribution in LDCs. While still subject to several shortcomings, the growing evidence throws important light on the question of who benefited from post-war economic growth? Almost invariably, the new data indicate that (1) incomes are more unequally distributed between persons in LDCs than in advanced countries, and (2) for most LDCs the process of post-war growth has actually worsened income inequality.

A Review of Evidence of Growing Inequality

A pioneering study of the problem of growing inequality in LDCs is the work of Adelman and Morris (AM): *Economic Growth and Social Equity in Developing Countries,*[4] representing several years of investigation of this problem.[5] AM utilised multivariate techniques in order to accommodate the impact of a host of social, political and institutional factors, not normally quantified, on the process of economic growth. AM's primary concern was the explanation of the variance in relative income shares in terms of 35 independent variables ranging from the level of GNP to 'the degree of social tension', 'the extent of leadership commitment to economic development', etc. These subjective variables were converted into numerical scores, on a cardinal scale ranging from 0 to 100, by a series of admittedly arbitrary grading tests which, subsequently, were validated by a group of 30 independent experts involved in planning work in LDCs.

The results of the AM study, shown in Table 2.1, indicate that those who have derived the most benefit from post-war economic growth have been those already in the wealthiest income groups. On the whole, the richest 5 per cent of the population received an income share of 30 per cent. In fact, in several LDCs, including Libya, Peru, Gabon, Tanzania, Rhodesia and Colombia, the top 5 per cent received over 40 per cent of the total income. On the other hand, the poorest 60 per cent had an average income share of only 26 per cent — i.e. a little over 40 per cent of what their share would have been under perfect income distribution. In one extreme case (viz. Libya) this group received just 2 per cent of total income.

Adelman and Morris believe that maldistribution of income in LDCs

Table 2.1: Income Distribution Estimates (percentage shares by population groups)

Country	0-40 per cent	40-60 per cent	0-60 per cent	60-80 per cent	80-100 per cent	95-100 per cent
(1) Argentina	17.30	13.10	30.40	17.60	52.00	29.40
(2) Bolivia	12.90	13.70	26.60	14.30	59.10	35.70
(3) Brazil	12.50	10.20	22.70	15.80	61.50	38.40
(4) Burma	23.00	13.00	36.00	15.50	48.50	28.21
(5) Ceylon	13.66	13.81	27.47	20.22	52.31	18.38
(6) Chad	23.00	12.00	35.00	22.00	43.00	23.00
(7) Chile	15.00	12.00	27.00	20.70	52.30	22.60
(8) Colombia	7.30	9.70	17.00	16.06	68.06	40.36
(9) Costa Rica	13.30	12.10	25.40	14.60	60.00	35.00
(10) Dahomey	18.00	12.00	30.00	20.00	50.00	32.00
(11) Ecuador	16.90	13.50	30.40	15.60	54.00	33.70
(12) El Salvador	12.30	11.30	23.60	15.00	61.40	33.00
(13) Gabon	8.00	7.00	15.00	14.00	71.00	47.00
(14) Greece	21.30	12.30	34.10	16.40	49.50	23.00
(15) India	20.00	16.00	36.00	22.00	42.00	20.00
(16) Iraq	8.00	8.00	16.00	16.00	68.00	34.00
(17) Israel	16.00	17.00	33.00	23.90	43.10	16.80
(18) Ivory Coast	18.00	12.00	30.00	15.00	55.00	29.00
(19) Jamaica	8.20	10.80	19.00	19.50	61.50	31.20
(20) Japan	15.30	15.80	31.10	22.90	46.00	14.80
(21) Lebanon	7.20	15.80	23.00	16.00	61.00	34.00
(22) Libya	.50	1.28	1.78	8.72	89.50	46.20
(23) Malagasy	14.00	9.00	23.00	18.00	59.00	37.00
(24) Mexico	10.50	11.25	21.75	20.21	58.04	28.52
(25) Morocco	14.50	7.70	22.20	12.40	65.40	20.60
(26) Niger	23.00	12.00	35.00	23.00	42.00	23.00
(27) Nigeria	14.00	9.00	23.00	16.10	60.90	38.38
(28) Pakistan	17.50	15.50	33.00	22.00	45.00	20.00
(29) Panama	14.30	13.80	28.10	15.20	56.70	34.50
(30) Peru	8.80	8.30	17.10	15.30	67.60	48.30
(31) Philippines	12.70	12.00	24.70	19.50	55.80	27.50
(32) Rhodesia	12.00	8.00	20.00	15.00	65.00	40.00
(33) Senegal	10.00	10.00	20.00	16.00	64.00	36.00
(34) Sierra Leone	10.10	9.10	19.20	16.70	64.10	33.80
(35) South Africa	6.11	10.16	16.27	26.37	57.36	39.30
(36) Sudan	15.00	14.30	29.30	22.60	48.10	17.10
(37) Surinam	22.26	14.74	37.00	20.60	42.40	15.10
(38) Taiwan	14.20	14.80	29.00	19.00	52.00	24.10
(39) Tanzania	19.50	9.75	29.25	9.75	61.00	42.90
(40) Trinidad and Tobago	9.42	9.10	18.52	24.48	57.00	26.60
(41) Tunisia	10.62	9.95	20.57	14.43	65.00	22.40
(42) Venezuela	13.40	16.60	30.00	22.90	47.10	23.20
(43) Zambia	15.85	11.10	26.95	15.95	57.10	37.50

Source: I. Adelman and C.T. Morris, *Economic Growth and Social Equity in Developing Countries* (Stanford University Press, California, 1973). Sources of materials used by Adelman and Morris are listed on pp.244-8 of their book. Their statistical methodology is explained in great length, in Chapters 2 and 3.

stems from 'socio-economic dualism' reflecting unequal allocation of political, economic and social opportunities in those countries. Their analysis points to the fact that the most significant independent variables explaining increased inequality of incomes are the rate of improvement of human resources, direct government activity, the degree of political participation and a reduction in socio-economic dualism. Their overall conclusion on the impact of post-war economic growth in LDCs is that

> development is accompanied by an absolute as well as a relative decline in the average income of the very poor (p.189).

> hundreds of millions of desperately poor people throughout the world have been hurt rather than helped by economic development. Unless their destinies become a major and explicit focus of development policy in the 1970's and 1980's, economic development may serve merely to promote social injustice (p.192).

The AM findings have been criticised by a number of observers. Deepak Lal has argued that AM have used cross-sectional data to derive conclusions as if they were based on time series.[6] Rayner has challenged the appropriateness of factor analysis employed by AM on the ground that this technique treats all independent variables equally, for example by assigning equal weights on GNP and such non-economic variables as 'the degree of social tension'.[7] Brookins has argued that AM have basically used ordinal data as if they were cardinal and, therefore, their 'scores' are in fact invalid.[8] Adelman and Morris have attempted to rebut these arguments, and have rigorously defended the validity of both their methods and empirical findings.[9]

What adds credibility to the AM arguments and findings is that there is supporting evidence from other sources and studies. Two other major sources of supporting evidence are the World Bank and the International Labour Organization. Felix Paukert of the ILO produced cross-sectional data on income distribution in 56 countries classified according to GDP *per capita*.[10] The results for 37 LDCs with less than US $500 GDP *per capita* are summarised in Table 2.2. A comparison of the income share of the richest 20 per cent population with that of the poorest 20 per cent clearly demonstrates a widening degree of income inequality as the level of GDP *per capita* rises. Thus, for the set of 9 LDCs having under $100 *per capita*, the inequality ratio is 7.2; it rises to 10.7 for the 8 countries having an average GDP *per capita* of $101-$200, and reaches 12.7 for the 9 countries with a GDP *per capita* of between $301 and $500. For the whole set of these 37 LDCs, Paukert found that the poorest 60 per cent of the population received an average of 26.2 per cent of income (compared with 26 per cent in AM), while the richest 5 per cent enjoyed an average of 29 per cent (as compared with AM's 30 per cent).

The World Bank study[11] is also based on cross-sectional data. It was designed to explain the variation in income shares of the top 20 per cent, middle 40 per cent, and the bottom 40 per cent income recipients. Summarising the findings of the study, Hollis Chenery states that: 'It is now clear that more than a decade of rapid growth in underdeveloped countries has been of little or no benefit to perhaps a third of their population.'[12] One of the members of the World Bank study group, Ahluwalia, states that: 'The average income share of the lowest 40 per cent ... amounts to about 12.5 per cent, but there is considerable variation about this average.'[13]

The World Bank Team regards income concentration in LDCs as evidence following the historical experience of advanced countries to the effect that in the early stages of economic growth there is increased income inequality.[14] While the political aspects of distribution are discussed,[15] it is concluded that any egalitarian measures must be fully acceptable to ruling elites controlling the political and governmental institutions, for otherwise they are

Table 2.2: Group Averages of Size Distribution of Personal Income Before Tax in 37 LDCs* by Income and Level of GDP/Head, in the Neighbourhood of 1965

Group of LDCs by Level of GDP/Head	(1) Poorest 20 per cent	(2) Poorest 60 per cent	(3) Richest 20 per cent	(4) Richest 5 per cent	(3) (1)
Under $100 (n=9)	7.0	30.1	50.5	29.1	7.2
$101 — 200 (n=8)	5.3	25.9	56.5	24.9	10.7
$201 — 300 (n=11)	4.8	24.1	57.7	32.0	12.0
$301 — 500 (n=9)	4.5	24.7	57.4	30.0	12.7
Arithmetic mean (n=37)	5.4	26.2	55.5	29.0	10.3

*Those with GDP/head less than $500.

Source: Felix Paukert, 'Income Distribution at Different Levels of Development: A Survey of Evidence', *International Labour Review,* Vol.108 (August-September 1973), Table 6.

doomed to failure since the elites are not motivated by enlightened self-interest to go along with schemes of income transfers from the affluent and powerful groups to the poor and politically weak masses. Thereupon, the central theme of the study shifts to the identification of possible redistribution strategies for the benefit of target groups that would be politically acceptable to the ruling elites. The preferred strategy is based on a proposal to divert no more than 2 per cent or 3 per cent of GNP towards the target groups.[16] The choice of these orders of magnitude rests on the presumption that such a limited redistribution would place a minimal burden on the elites. The study then examines in considerable detail the various policy interventions (e.g. land reform, educational investment, factor pricing) to promote the welfare of the target groups.

The Bank approach is obviously a compromise solution, dictated by considerations of international diplomacy. It is drawn on the assumption that the existing political machinery, controlled by ruling elites, can be utilised to achieve egalitarian objectives, provided only that they are implemented in sufficiently small doses. This is highly doubtful. Arthur Okun's Leaky Bucket Experiment[17] is even more relevant to the corrupt and highly imperfect world of the LDCs than it is to the USA welfare programmes. Thus, the existing elites can be expected to divert public expenditures to their own benefit, even when these funds are earmarked for projects designed to improve the condition of the poor and underprivileged groups. The obvious implication is that political reform – though not necessarily by violent revolution – is an essential precondition for egalitarian growth. This is a topic discussed in greater detail in Chapter 8.

Time Series Evidence

Since we are concerned with the distributive effects of post-war growth, it is not sufficient to rely on cross-sectional data. Unfortunately, historical evidence on income distribution is available for comparatively few LDCs.[18] These studies, too, are finding evidence of growing income inequality. One such country is Brazil, which will be examined in greater detail in Chapter 7. An empirical study comparing 1960 and 1970 income distribution[19] found that the principal gainers of the Brazilian economic growth were those in the top 5 per cent income group, while the bottom 80 per cent suffered a relative decline, especially the underprivileged urban groups. Increased Brazilian poverty during this decade stemmed from economic policies unconcerned about equity and distribution. Tax concessions and investment incentives were a boon to those with property incomes and tax liabilities, while the post-1964 deflationary measures reduced real wages of the working poor. Elitist education, health and social policies also tended to contribute toward widening income inequalities in the Brazilian society. Increased reliance on foreign investment during the 'economic miracle' beginning in the late 1960s was also accompanied by greater external dependency and net financial outflows.

Mexico is another interesting example. During 1950-63 the Mexican average income *per capita* increased by an impressive 47 per cent — a fact which encouraged several observers to refer to another case of economic 'miracle'. In fact, however, Roger D. Hansen has shown how the Mexican self-serving elite was able to mastermind the political and economic decision-making in order to derive the major gains from this growth.[20] As a result, the richest 20 per cent were able to increase their income share from 20 per cent to 32 per cent between 1950 and 1963. On the other hand, the poorest 60 per cent of the nation received 21.5 per cent of the total income in 1963, compared with 24.6 per cent in 1950.[21]

The experience of other LDCs for which the necessary data is available is summarised in Table 2.3. Countries such as India, South Korea, Malaysia and Thailand, as well as several Latin American countries, demonstrate strong evidence of increased income inequality accompanying rapid GNP growth. It is important to add, however, that in a few cases (usually smaller LDCs, but none the less as diverse as Taiwan and Singapore), the evidence indicates reduced inequality, thanks to deliberate redistributive policies adopted. The experience of these countries is extremely important, inasmuch as it demonstrates that widening inequality in income shares is not a necessary condition of rapid growth in its early stages; given appropriate policies and proper management of economic planning, the two objectives could be simultaneously pursued.

For the majority of LDCs, the post-war industrialisation experience shows that there is no automatic trickling-down of the benefits of growth across the entire nation; in fact, growth tends to lead to income concentration at the top with greater poverty at the bottom of the socio-economic pyramid. This, in turn, implies that income shares in LDCs are determined less in the market-place than in the political arena. More specifically, *political* power concentration may be an important determinant of income and wealth concentration in

Table 2.3: Size Distribution of Income in Selected Countries,
1950-70

Country	Year	R_1	R_2	Gini Ratio
Argentina	1953	11.5	6.7	0.41
	1959	14.0	7.9	0.46
	1961	13.4	9.6	0.43
Hong Kong	1966		12.3	
	1971		8.3	
India	1953/4			0.40
	1961/4			0.46
Malaysia, West	1957/8	15.8	8.7	0.43
	1967/8	21.6	12.3	0.51
	1970	34.3	14.1	
Mexico	1950	18.1	9.8	0.53
	1957	27.5	14.0	0.55
	1963	32.5	17.0	0.54
Puerto Rico	1953	15.7	8.9	0.42
	1963	21.0	9.2	0.45
Taiwan	1953			0.55
	1965			0.32
Thailand	1962/3			0.50
	1968/9			0.55

a. R_1 = ratio of the income share of the top decile to that of the bottom decile.

b. R_2 = ratio of the income share of the top quintile to that of the bottom quintile.

Sources: These measures of inequality are based on T.H. Oshima, 'Income
Inequality and Economic Growth: The Postwar Experience of Asian
Countries', *Malayan Economic Review* (October 1970). Argentina, Mexico and
Puerto Rico data are from R. Weisskoff, 'Income Distribution and Economic
Growth in Puerto Rico, Argentina and Mexico', *Review of Income and Wealth*,
No.4 (December 1970), p.312. Malaysian data are from L.L. Lim, 'Income
Distribution in West Malaysia' in *Income Distribution, Employment and
Economic Development in South East and East Asia* (The Japanese Economic
Research Center, Tokyo, and The Council for Asian Manpower Studies, Manila,
July 1975), Vol.I, p.184. The remaining data from *idem*, Vol.I, p.304, except
Hong Kong, which is from Vol.II, p.624.

the hands of the privileged few, and of mass poverty. The next chapter will present a wide range of data about absolute poverty in LDCs, which demonstrate that there is a high correlation between poverty and lack of political power amongst the masses.

Is the Experience of Developed Countries Relevant?

Economists have studied the relationship of economic growth and income distribution in industrialised countries for a long time. For example, Kuznets and others[22] have found strong evidence of a relative deterioration in the position of low-income groups in England, the USA, Germany and other developed countries during their drive to maturity. Subsequently, economic development brought about a levelling of income distribution, especially following the adoption of progressive reforms designed to narrow the income disparities between the rich and poor. These reforms have ranged from regulations affecting employment conditions, public education, housing, health and welfare, progressive taxation, to reforms in the political and legal system.

The experience of the advanced countries, at first sight, would tend to suggest that there is no cause for alarm about the growing inequality in today's LDCs. It is tempting to believe that they are merely going through the same stages of growth as the advanced countries did in earlier periods. Once economic development places LDCs into more advanced stages, then we can expect income distribution to become fairer. As we have already noted, this has been the typical intellectual rationalisation employed in the post-war industrialisation drive.

Unfortunately, however, economic history of advanced countries may not repeat itself in LDCs. Some, such as Brazil, have been involved in the growth process and in international trade for several centuries. Several emerging LDCs in Africa and elsewhere may require an intolerably long period before signs of greater equality may be detected. Even then, institutional reforms in the political systems would be unavoidable. After all, this is what happened in industrialised countries: in early stages of industrial expansion, they introduced such reforms as universal suffrage, freedom of association, speech, etc., equal legal and political rights, followed by equality of opportunity for such public goods and services as education.

Today, in most LDCs the political and governmental machinery is dominated by self-seeking elites and privileged classes. In the post-war period, these groups have successfully utilised economic planning and foreign aid for their enrichment and have effectively resisted egalitarian reforms likely to weaken their dominance of the *status quo.* There is little hope that in future they may *voluntarily* introduce redistributive programmes in aid of the poor. First, however, it is necessary to understand their impact on the planning process.

Elites, Social Ownership of Resources and the Planning Process

Economic planning is a *dynamic* process, and static or partial equilibrium models leave out vitally important social and political dimensions of the process. This is especially true in so far as the impact of LDC elites on post-war planning is concerned. There is a vast volume of literature on these elites by sociologists, political scientists and anthropologists,[23] but economists have generally ignored their influence,[24] partly owing to their preoccupation with static models, but also because of a professional belief in the validity of the 'trickle-down' effects of the growth process. Both of these reasons now require critical reappraisal in view of the stubbornness of the inequality and poverty problems.

Neo-Marxist interpretations of socio-economic stratification are useful in analysing the relations between elites and masses, and in studying the correlation between income concentration on the one hand, and political power distribution and social ownership of assets and resources on the other.[25] But *correlation* is not the same thing as *causality,* and it is practically impossible to determine whether it is the concentration of political power in few hands which causes income and wealth accumulation at the top with mass poverty at the bottom, or whether political power is achieved as a result of an elitist process of accumulation of productive assets. There is ample evidence from LDCs to support both hypotheses: thus, in many countries which participated in the 'Green Revolution', large-scale, mechanised farming techniques (as we shall observe in subsequent chapters) led to the emergence of new groups of wealthy farmers (many of whom used to be marginal peasants until recently) and their subsequent acquisition of higher social status and political power within the provincial polity. On the other hand, there is widespread evidence pointing towards the *possession* of political power as the principal explanation for the accumulation of income and wealth at the top. Liberia, Malaysia and Brazil, discussed in Part Two, are cases in point.

Accumulation of wealth and the road to political power have to be studied as part of a complex, dynamic process. Static and partial equilibrium models of the pricing mechanism, or the Marxist structuralist theories of *class*, provide an inadequate theoretical framework. At the present time, there is no settled theory or unified approach for a non-controversial study of poverty and inequality in LDCs. The analysis below is primarily eclectic, borrowing, in varying proportions, from neo-Marxist, structuralist and market theories.

Turning to the role of elites in the planning process, we begin with the following two propositions: (1) elitism implies concentration, *inter alia,* of power and influence over decision-making in few hands; and (2) when economic planning decisions on what to produce, how to produce, where to produce and for whom to produce are made under elitist conditions, income generation and distribution will be *biased* in favour of groups influencing those decisions. Conversely, individuals and groups excluded from the decision-making process will be 'losers', their 'loss' reflected in a greater income inequality and poverty.

Who are the elites? Since our concern here is not taxonomy, it is sufficient to note that there are numerous kinds of elites which can be classified according to function (military, professional and bureaucratic), geographic location (urban, provincial and local) or historical origin (feudalistic, aristocratic and despotic). Our interest lies in the way in which elites *bias* the consequences of economic planning. What are the sources of this bias? How is it created?

The principal source of elite bias over planning and economic decisions is to be found in the social ownership of assets and productive resources. It can be said that there is a positive correlation between the degree of this bias and the extent to which ownership of land, capital, cash balances and other assets are concentrated in distinct social groups and classes. In Latin America, where there is a long history of high income and wealth concentration at the top, elites successfully utilised post-war economic planning as a technique of enrichment and self-aggrandisement.[26] In the newly independent countries of Africa and Asia, political independence set the stage for the emergence of new elites, sometimes (e.g. Malaysia) by a relatively simple replacement of a colonial elite, while economic planning gave these elites the chance to acquire new and expanding portfolios of assets. In both situations, a circular pattern is discernible in that ownership and control of productive resources eased the way to power, and the exercise of power created further elitist wealth accumulation.

Planning is no more and no less than a specific instrument of decision-making. It is an integral part of the political and bureaucratic system. But the inherent, exclusive characteristic of elites implies a convergence in few hands of all sorts of decision-making authority: those relating to budget expenditures, taxation, government contracts, trade licensing, regulation of banking and financial institutions, tariff and fiscal policies, planning priorities, as well as decisions ostensibly non-economic in nature, e.g. foreign relations or national security. Elites which control the decision-making process are easily able to bias the decisions taken. Thus, during the post-war drive for industrialisation, when building import-replacing home industries was a highly fashionable growth strategy, tariff protection, justified on various grounds of national interest, helped members of elites to acquire monopolistic enterprises, sometimes in partnership with multi-national corporations. In the African pattern of military elitism, the survival motive has tended to compel the supremacy of military expenditure over all other needs,[27] while in the case of the despotic and dynastic elites of the Middle East, traditionalism has been utilised as a means of keeping the masses in a state of political underdevelopment.[28] In all these cases, post-war economic planning has worked largely as a façade or a veil disguising the elite management of the growth process. The tragic case of the overthrow of Haile Selassie of Ethiopia[29] is a reminder of the potential risks and dangers of an oppressive and out-dated elitism.

Elites typically consist of cliques of families or social groups within some sort of extended family network. Their kinship ties are preserved through marriages of convenience, church affiliations, social clubs and/or business partnerships. These close ties represent a most effective, though informal, means of promoting and monopolising political power, which, in turn, is utilised for wealth accumulation and income concentration, typically through elite manipulation of public expenditure and economic policies. Thus, wealth accumulation may be regarded as a reward for the possession and exercise of political power. Whoever holds political power has an opportunity for wealth accumulation for the duration. The ruling class realises that its continued affluence is dependent upon its political survival, not on its economic performance, as for example, on undertaking a certain rate of capital formation. Thus, it is interested in status-promoting forms of conspicuous consumption, not thrift and saving; it is interested in forging political deals and alliances, not entrepreneurial risk-taking.

Political survival may often require negative role-playing. If the provision of universal education, designed to cure illiteracy, is also likely to raise the political consciousness of the masses, then the political elite will resist educational reform as a matter of survival. If doing this causes a manpower shortage, the elite can rely on imports of expatriate personnel. If the formation of farmer co-operatives is likely to lead to political activity, the elite can prevent the creation of such institutions. If domestic merchants and entrepreneurs tend to become too affluent and powerful for the elite, it may attempt, by fair or foul means, to contain or destroy the business class, and rely instead on foreign firms willing to respect and enhance its political supremacy.

In Part Two, we shall examine the influence of elites on post-war economic planning and policy in five LDCs: Malaysia, Liberia, Pakistan, Brazil and Uganda. These five countries have been selected, not because they are 'typical' (if there is such a country), but, on the contrary because they represent an illustrative sample of a diversity of cases: large and small, new and old, plural, dependent, dualistic, etc. No claim at comprehensive coverage of all alternative forms of elitism in LDCs is made; nor is any inference to be drawn that elite management of the economy in other countries follows the pattern of these five countries. Each LDC is very much a special case, deserving study on its own merits.

Yet, elite superstructures underscore the fundamental inequity of post-war growth and industrialisation in LDCs: they exercise decisive control and management over the planning process, ensuring that it remains an elitist instrument. In this context, planning and economic policy may act merely as a mechanism of domination and exploitation for the benefit of few over many.

Elitist economic planning demonstrates the validity of Rawls's exhortation, cited at the end of the preceding chapter, to the effect that when income growth takes place within and through a political and bureaucratic system, controlled by a small minority, the growth process will serve the interest of this privileged minority, while harming the majority. Furthermore, this social injustice, could be entirely consistent with otherwise impressive rates of increase in GNP *per capita.*

In retrospect, it was a serious planning mistake or a calculated elite strategy to have ignored the distributive effects of post-war industrial programmes. As we have already noted, pressure for planning in LDCs came from donor countries wishing to see their aid funds efficiently utilised within a rational development perspective, and from international aid agencies interested in promoting a global programming and budgeting procedure for the allocation of limited aid funds. The moral commitment of the leaders in LDCs and the adequacy of the political, bureaucratic and social institutions in these countries to cope with planned economic growth were seldom taken into account by the outside planners. In this favourable aid and planning climate, the elites successfully channelled development expenditures for self-aggrandisement and self-enrichment.

There are significant lessons to be learnt from the mistakes of the post-war planning experience. The cardinal truism is that economic development is intrinsically linked to social and political transformation, and that egalitarian reforms in domestic institutions are necessary and integral parts of an economic development process which serves both the efficiency and equity objectives. To accelerate social and economic progress in the Third World requires major institutional reforms for wider popular participation in the political and economic decision-making process. Only then can economic planning become an instrument for improving the standard of living of the people, instead of serving the interests of the ruling classes. At the same time, it is necessary that economists and planners, both foreign and local, begin to put the welfare of human beings before physical or financial targets, such as a dogmatic maximisation of GNP. Instead of being preoccupied with the ways and means of achieving the fastest possible growth rate of national production, they should also devote attention to the question of who benefits from that production. Equitable economic growth need not necessarily conflict with efficient growth. There would be strong presumption of such a conflict if a strategy of income redistribution were simply to consist of transfers of purchasing power from the wealthy to the poor. But, this need not be the case. For example, agrarian development, discussed in Chapter 11, would be capable of raising the income share of the rural poor while also raising the productivity and employability of these poverty groups. Similarly, investment in human resources could be regarded as a special case of 'infant industry' justifying large-scale expenditure. Such an approach would expand manpower development and employment creation in LDCs now suffering from chronic unemployment and underemployment. We shall discuss these issues in Chapter 4, and again in Chapters 9 and 10.

The Distributive Effects of Foreign Investment

Along with the domestic elites, there was a second major category of gainers from post-war economic growth in LDCs: foreign investors and multinational corporations. In fact, often the elites and foreign interests acted as partners in a mutually profitable scheme of industrialisation. Direct private investment funds, as well as foreign aid, were eagerly sought by various LDCs through a variety of fiscal and commercial incentives. Little or no consideration was given to the fact that capital inflows would cause outflows of dividends, profits and other forms of remittances.

In recent years, the role of multinational firms in LDCs has received much public attention in the wake of business scandals involving extensive bribery and corruption disclosures, as well as the CIA's spy activities in Chile and elsewhere.[30] In fact, however, the role of multinational firms in LDCs is fundamentally linked to dualistic and/or dependent economies. The 'modern' sectors of these countries are dominated by the branch plants of Western corporations, with particular concentration in mining, petroleum and manufacturing industries. Utilising highly sophisticated techniques transferred from the West, these firms' primary objective is maximum global profits. We have already noted that their contribution in terms of job creation has been limited. Often, too, they have been involved in domestic politics in order to protect their assets from possible nationalisation or expropriation.

According to the data in Table 2.4, the outstanding stock of direct foreign investment in LDCs in 1970 was about US $40 billion, and the reported after-tax earnings of US manufacturing affiliates averaged about 12 per cent in 1969.[31] The latter figure is most likely understated owing to undeclared profits realised through transfer pricing and other indirect means. The average corporate income taxes in most LDCs are of the order of 50 per cent, including withholding taxes on dividends, but this nominal rate is effectively reduced by tax holidays and other concessions. Assuming a 40 per cent effective tax rate, a 12 per cent after-tax return on foreign equity investment of $40 billion is equivalent to 20 per cent before-tax earnings, or a total of $8.0 billion. This implies an 8 per cent tax revenue for the host LDC treasury, or $3.2 billion. The amount accruing to foreign interests would be $4.8 billion — a sum representing 60 per cent of total official aid inflows from Western donors to LDCs (see Table 2.4).

Postponing for the moment the question of the efficiency of the use

Table 2.4: Returns on Direct Foreign Investment in LDCs and
Official Aid Inflows, 1970 (amounts in US billion dollars)

(1)	Outstanding stock of direct foreign investment		40
(2)	Before-tax earnings (at 20 per cent)		8
	2(i) Share of host-country Treasury (8 per cent)	3.2	
	2 (ii) after-tax return to foreign interest (12 per cent)	4.8	
(3)	Total official aid inflow to LDCs[a]		8

a. Includes grants and net loans.

Sources: Cols. 1 and 2: Based on Grant L. Reuber, *Private Foreign Investment
in Development* (Clarendon Press, Oxford, 1973), p.25; Col. 3: OECD,
Development Assistance 1971 Review (December 1972, Paris).

of foreign borrowing and the associated social costs in LDCs, the
benefits of income generated by foreign direct investment mostly accrue
to investors and creditors outside the LDCs. So far as local tax revenues
are concerned, these benefit primarily the wealthy and powerful
groups, judging from the evidence on income distribution presented
earlier. Additionally, where foreign borrowing has been undertaken for
political and non-economic reasons (for example, to finance
prestige projects, military purchases, or to increase the supply of
'luxury goods'), then the social costs of such investment will clearly
exceed social benefits at least from the standpoint of the majority of
citizens.

Table 2.5 presents United Nations data based on a group of 41 LDCs
regarding net inflow of direct foreign investment during 1965-70.[32] It
will be seen that the percentage of inflows to outflows dropped sharply
from 42 per cent to 30 per cent for the group as a whole. In Asia it
dropped from 32 per cent to just 8 per cent, in Africa from 48 per
cent to 27 per cent. Only in the Western hemisphere was an increase
registered. These trends indicate a rapid growth in the level of foreign
indebtedness of LDCs as a result of their industrialisation drive. While
there may be corresponding advantages, for example due to the
training of skilled indigenous workers and savings in terms of research
and development costs, it is highly doubtful that these have been
sufficiently large to compensate for the rising volume of service costs
of foreign borrowing.

Even in the case of official aid funds, the magnitude of benefit
to the recipient country is much less than it was initially thought to be
— in fact, it is likely that in many cases foreign aid inflows may

Table 2.5: Inflow of Foreign Direct Investment as a Percentage of
Outflow of Income on Accumulated Post-Direct-Investment in
Selected LDCs by Regions, 1965-70[a]

Region	No. of Countries	1965	1970
Africa	9	0.48[b]	0.27
Western hemisphere	22	0.50	0.59
Asia and West Asia	10	0.32	0.08
Total	41	0.42[b]	0.30

a. All statistics — inflows and outflows — are in gross figures.
b. Excluding Algeria.

Source: United Nations, *Multinational Corporations in World Development*,
    ST/ECA/190, Department of Economics and Social Affairs (New York, 1973),
    Table 42, pp.192-3.

actually tend to reduce domestic saving and investment by encouraging
consumption and imports which otherwise would not have taken place.[33]
More simply put, foreign aid funds may cause unnecessary and
superfluous spending (e.g. on luxury imports), no doubt on the part
of the members of the elites and ruling classes. As in the case of direct
foreign investment inflows, foreign aid to LDCs, even when provided
on concessional terms, has resulted in severe problems of debt burdens
for most countries.[34]

Disguised Taxes and Price Distortions

Increased foreign indebtedness was not the only consequence of
industrialisation in LDCs. The creation of 'infant industries' in enclave
sectors was associated with significant distributional effects resulting
from deliberate fiscal and credit policies designed to stimulate the
growth of domestic import-substitution industries, sheltered by high
tariffs and over-valued currencies. These preferential policies created
inequitable tax burdens and serious distortions in domestic price
structures. In Pakistan, for example, import-substitution policies
caused the ratio of domestic manufacturing to farm prices to be
twice as high as international prices.[35] The redistribution of income
from farming to manufacturing industries generated in the process
has been estimated at about $500 million per annum during 1951-64
or 11 per cent to 13 per cent of the potential income of the farming
sector if world prices had prevailed. In other words, distorted domestic
terms of trade represented a disguised tax of 11 per cent to 13 per cent

on farm incomes. It is important to note that most of this disguised tax fell on farmers in East Pakistan, while most of the new industries were located in West Pakistan,[36] this unfair tax shift being caused by the disproportionate political power of West Pakistani landlords.[37]

A similar estimate for Argentina showed that her protectionist industrialisation programme during 1947-55 redistributed income in favour of the manufacturing sector in an amount equivalent to a tax on farm incomes of between 30 per cent and 40 per cent.[38] Argentina subsequently eased this policy so that by the 1960s the redistribution process reflected only a mere 5-6 per cent tax on agriculture. In the case of Pakistan, however, the extent of disguised tax on agriculture, and its disproportionate burden on East Pakistan, continued to increase until the eventual break-up of the country.

Evidence similar to Pakistan's and Argentina's is also available from several other LDCs with comparable protectionist policies, such as Brazil, Mexico and India.[39]

Financial Dualism

Tax and credit policies in LDCs giving preferential treatment to foreign and new enterprises in the enclave sector fit Myint's model of 'financial dualism'.[40] In previously colonial areas, such as Malaysia (described in Chapter 5), this phenomenon has long roots in colonial economic policies generally favouring expatriate planters and entrepreneurs. During the post-war industrialisation drive virtually every LDC offered the potential multinational investor a wide-ranging set of tax and credit concessions and guarantees, including the right to transfer profits, dividends and interest; freedom from double taxation; accelerated depreciation allowances; and facilities for the immigration and employment of expatriate personnel.[41]

The social costs of these concessions fell disproportionately on the poorer segments of the population, as we have pointed out above. Seen in this light, the multinational firms participating in post-war industrialisation of developing nations differed little, if any, from their predecessors in the old, colonial system of international trade, as some economists have argued.[42] We shall return to this theme in Chapter 5 in the context of Malaysia, and again in Chapter 12 in our discussion of the New International Economic Order.

The preferential treatment of multinational firms in the post-war industrialisation drive of LDCs represented one aspect of financial dualism. It also had a second dimension, one which involved

discriminatory and selective concessions extended to privileged and
well connected families who emerged as the new class of indigenous
entrepreneurs. The members of this new class were often themselves
active politicians or partners of the political elite leadership. Therefore,
they were quite capable of influencing the legislative and the legal
process to promote laws and regulations designed to enhance their
interests and status. One interesting case is Mexico. Since the 1930s,
Mexican GNP had grown at more than 6 per cent annually, giving rise
to another case of 'economic miracle'. In fact, this growth was
accompanied by growing inequalities between the 'haves' and the
'have-nots'. Thus, thanks in a large measure to the elite control of the
labour unions, money wage-rates were kept at such low levels that they
lagged behind the inflation rate, causing a decline in real wages and the
income share of the workers. On the other hand, a biased political
system provided the Mexican entrepreneurial class with a sheltered
domestic market thanks to an elaborate system of import licensing and
tax credits for up to ten years on new investments. Devaluation of the
peso in 1949 and again in 1954 provided additional protection for the
Mexican industrialists. Finally, direct investment subsidies at such
nominal rates of interest were provided that 'the cost of borrowing
may even have reached negative levels during the inflationary years of
the late 1940s and early 1950s'.[43] As a result of these favourable
measures, the incomes and profits of the entrepreneurial class
increased rapidly relative to the masses. By the early 1960s the Mexican
income distribution was more inequitable than it was before 1940.

Pakistan is another important example. We shall study it in some
detail in Chapter 7. Government subsidies and grants there helped to
create large industrial monopolies owned and controlled by a handful
of families. As Papanek noted:

> Sixteen families controlled firms with one-quarter, and 60 families
> firms with nearly one-half, of all sales of manufacturing units. In
> short, the number of entrepreneurs required to start a rapid
> process of industrialisation in a country with a population of
> 100 million was about 100.[44]

In conclusion, it is evident that post-war industrialisation in most LDCs
has failed to improve the living standards of a significant bulk of the
inhabitants. It has been designed and managed in such a way that it
benefited domestic elites and foreign interests. Thus, economic
planning worked more as a tool spreading inequality than as a means of

raising the economic welfare of the masses, in spite of lofty promises declared in so many five-year plans.

Notes

1. For early warning signs on this, see ILO, *Employment Objectives in Economic Development*, Studies and Reports, New Series, No. 62 (Geneva, 1962), and *idem, Employment and Economic Growth*, Studies and Reports, New Series, No.67 (Geneva, 1964). For early empirical studies on this subject, see Michael P. Todaro, 'An Analysis of Industrialisation, Employment and Unemployment in Less Developed Countries', *Yale Economic Essays*, Vol. 8, No.2 (Fall 1968); Werner Baer and Michel Herve, 'Employment and Industrialisation in Developing Countries', *Quarterly Journal of Economics*, Vol.80, No.1 (February 1966).

2. Recent surveys of the relevant literature are: W.R. Cline, 'Distribution and Development: A Survey of Literature', *Journal of Development Economics*, Vol.1, No.4 (February 1975); Deepak Lal, 'Distribution and Development: A Review Article', *World Development*, Vol.4, No.9 (1976).

3. A.B. Atkinson, 'On the Measurement of Inequality', *Journal of Economic Theory*, Vol.2 (September 1970); D.G. Champernowne, 'A Comparison of Measures of Income Distribution', *Economic Journal*, Vol.84 (December 1974); K.R. Radanive, 'Patterns of Income Distribution in India 1953-4 to 1959-60', *Bulletin of Oxford University Institute of Economics and Statistics* (August 1968).

4. I. Adelman and C.T. Morris, *Economic Growth and Social Equity in Developing Countries* (Stanford University Press, Stanford, California, 1973).

5. Earlier studies of Adelman and Morris include: *Society, Politics and Economic Development* (Johns Hopkins Press, Baltimore, 1967); 'Performance Criteria for Evaluating Economic Development Potential: An Operational Approach', *Quarterly Journal of Economics*, Vol. LXXXII (May 1968).

6. Lal, 'Distribution and Development'.

7. A.C. Rayner, 'The Use of Multivariate Analysis in Development Theory: A Critique of the Approach Adopted by Adelman and Morris', *Quarterly Journal of Economics*, Vol. LXXXIV (November 1970), pp.638-47.

8. Oscar T. Brookins, 'Factor Analysis and Gross National Product: A Comment', *Quarterly Journal of Economics*, Vol. LXXXIV (November 1970), pp.648-50.

9. 'Factor Analysis and Gross National Product: A Reply', *Quarterly Journal of Economics*, Vol. LXXXIV (November 1970), pp.651-62.

10. 'Income Distribution at Different Levels of Development: A Survey of Evidence', *International Labour Review*, Vol.108 (August-September 1973).

11. Hollis Chennery *et al.*, *Redistribution with Growth* (Oxford University Press for the World Bank, London, 1974).

12. Ibid., p.xiii.

13. Ibid., p.7.

14. Ibid., p.xiv.

15. Ibid., pp.53-6.

16. Ibid., p.56.

17. *Equality and Efficiency, The Big Tradeoff* (The Brookings Institution, Washington, D.C., 1975), pp.91-5.

18. A useful source is S. Jain, *Size Distribution of Income: A Compilation of Data* (A World Bank Study) (Washington, D.C., 1976). Note that 'time series'

are actually inter-temporal comparisons.

19. A. Fishlow, 'Brazilian Size Distribution of Income', *American Economic Review, Papers and Proceedings,* Vol. LXII, No.2 (May 1972).

20. *The Politics of Mexican Development* (Johns Hopkins Press, Baltimore, 1971).

21. Ibid., Table 4-1, p.75.

22. S. Kuznets, 'Economic Growth and Income Inequality', *American Economic Review*, Vol.65 (1965); J. Zimmerman, *Poor Lands, Rich Lands: The Widening Gap* (Random House, New York, 1965), Chapter 5.

23. Studies of elites by political scientists include: H.B. Lasswell *et al.*, *The Comparative Study of Elites* (Stanford University Press, Stanford, California, 1952); R.E. Agpolo, *The Political Elite and the People* (University of the Philippines, Manila, 1972); F.W. Riggs, *Administration in Developing Countries* (Houghton Mifflin, Boston, 1964).

24. Some notable exceptions include E.E. Hagen, *On the Theory of Social Change* (Dorsey, Homewood, 1962); G. Myrdal, *Asian Drama* (Pantheon, New York, 1968).

25. C. Elliott assisted by F. de Morsier, *Patterns of Poverty in the Third World: A Study of Social and Economic Stratification* (Praeger, New York, 1975); S. Gellar, *Structural Changes and Colonial Dependency, Senegal 1885-1947* (Sage Research Papers in the Social Sciences, Series No. 90-036, London, 1976); S. Amir, *L'Afrique de l'ouest bloquée* (Paris, Editions de Minuit, 1971); A.G. Frank, *Capitalism and Underdevelopment in Latin America* (Monthly Review, New York, 1967).

26. Kalman H. Silvert, *The Conflict Society: Reaction and Revolution in Latin America* (Harper and Row, New York, 1968); Raul Prebish, *Change and Development: Latin America's Great Task* (Inter-American Development Bank, Washington, D.C., 1970).

27. Cf. S.K. Panta-Brick (ed.), *Nigerian Politics and Military Rule, Prelude to Civil War* (University of London, The Althone Press, 1970); R. Higgott and F. Fuglestead, 'The 1974 Coup d'Etat in Niger', *Journal of Modern African Studies,* Vol.13, No.3 (1975).

28. Marvin Zonis, *The Political Elite of Iran* (Princeton University Press, Princeton, New Jersey, 1971).

29. Robert L. Hess, *Ethiopia: The Modernization of Autocracy* (Cornell University Press, Ithaca, New York, 1970); Donald N. Levince, *Wax and Gold: Tradition and Innovation in Ethiopian Culture* (Chicago University Press, Chicago, 1965).

30. A highly informative discussion of pay-offs by American firms is given in Y. Kugel and G. Gruenberg, 'International Payoffs: Where We Are and How We Got There', *Challenge* (September-October 1976). See also the special report in *Newsweek* of 23 February 1976 regarding the Lockheed pay-off scandal.

31. Grant L. Reuber, *Private Foreign Investment in Development* (Clarendon Press, Oxford, 1973), p.25.

32. United Nations, *Multinational Corporation in World Development,* ST/ECA/190 (New York, 1973).

33. K.B. Griffin and J.L. Enos, 'Foreign Assistance: Objectives and Consequences', *Economic Development and Cultural Change* (April 1970); G.F. Papanek, 'The Effect of Aid and Other Resource Transfers on Savings and Growth in Less Developed Countries', *Economic Journal* (September 1975).

34. Lester B. Pearson *et al., Partners in Development, Report of the Commission on International Development* (Praeger, New York, 1969).

35. I. Little, T. Scitovsky and M. Scott, *Industry and Trade in Some Developing Countries, A Comparative Study* (Oxford University Press for the OECD Development Center, 1970), p.42.

36. S.R. Lewis, *Pakistan, Industrialization and Trade Policies* (Oxford University Press, London, 1970).

37. See the informative article by Talukder Maniruzzaman, 'Group Interests in Pakistan Politics 1947-58', *Pacific Affairs* (Summer 1966).

38. Little *et al., Industry and Trade in Some Developing Countries*, pp.42-3.

39. Ibid.

40. H. Myint, *The Economics of the Developing Countries* (Hutchison University Library, London, 1964), esp. pp.69-84.

41. B. Higgins, *Economic Development, Problems, Principles and Policies*, rev. ed. (Norton, New York, 1969), pp.568-74.

42. The 'Center/Periphery' thesis of the structuralists is detailed in R. Prebisch, 'The Economic Development of Latin America and its Principal Problems', *Economic Bulletin for Latin America*, Vol.7 (February 1962). Also see P. Baran, *The Political Economy of Growth* (Monthly Review Press, New York, 1957).

43. Hansen, *The Politics of Mexican Development*, p.49.

44. G.F. Papanek, 'Pakistan's Industrial Entrepreneurs – Education, Occupational Background, and Finance' in Walter P. Falcon and Gustaf F. Papanek (eds.), *Development Policy II – The Pakistan Experience* (Harvard University Press, Cambridge, Mass., 1971), p.238.

3 ABSOLUTE POVERTY: MEASUREMENT AND IDENTIFICATION

Statistics of income distribution, discussed in the preceding chapter, demonstrating growing inequality between the affluent elites and underprivileged masses, cannot adequately describe the extent of social injustice associated with post-war industrialisation in LDCs. As we have seen, the size distribution of income is useful for the study of *relative* poverty. It must be supplemented with a further analysis of *absolute* poverty. According to the latter concept, poverty is a multi-faceted, sub-standard human condition characterised by deprivation or deficiency in a number of basic needs such as food, shelter and clothing, as well as such opportunities for self-improvement as education, medical care and employment. The major conceptual requirement for the study of *absolute* poverty is the definition of 'poverty lines'[1] or 'minimum levels' of income or consumption of these basic needs. Once the 'poverty lines' are determined, the population below these lines would then constitute the poor. The practical task of measuring absolute poverty in LDCs is beset by a number of inherent difficulties of international comparisons.[2]

In this chapter we shall adopt the common usage of regarding absolute poverty as a multi-faceted condition, and we shall examine income and several other socio-economic criteria, relying, wherever appropriate, on international poverty lines and standards.

The Income Criterion

The most comprehensive study in recent years of global absolute poverty was the one undertaken by the World Bank discussed in Chapter 2. It is particularly valuable for the light it throws on the rural/urban aspects of absolute poverty in LDCs. Of the 1.7 billion population covered, no less than 835 million were estimated to fall below the poverty line of US $75 per annum (Table 3.1).

The poverty of the Third World was particularly acute in Asia, where 57 per cent of the population had an average *per capita* income of under $75 per annum. By comparison, 46 per cent of Africans were below the poverty line. The continent with the least incidence of poverty was America, with an overall poor population of only 19 per cent; no doubt mostly concentrated in South and Central America

Table 3.1: Estimated Extent of Rural/Urban Poverty in LDCs, 1969

Population	Total	Rural	Urban
Combined Population of LDCs (m)	1,700	1,225	475
(Per cent)	100	72	28
'Poor' Population with income under $75/capita per annum	835	695	140
(Per cent)	100	83	17
under $50/capita per annum	560	480	80
(Per cent)	100	86	14

Source: Derived from *Rural Development, Sector Policy Paper*, World Bank, February 1975, Annexes 1 and 2, p.79.

(Table 3.2).

Evidently, global poverty is primarily an Asian dilemma. In fact, we can be even more specific: if we isolate just four Asian countries, viz. India, Pakistan, Indonesia and Bangladesh, two out of every three inhabitants live in deprivation, surviving on less than $75 per head. In fact, almost half the combined population of these countries lives on under $50 per person.[3]

We can be more exact about the incidence of absolute poverty in LDCs. It is, first and foremost a rural problem, although, as we shall see, it is also acute in urban 'ghettos'. However, despite rapid migration to urban centres during the 1950s and 1960s, the bulk of the population of developing countries still resides in rural areas. What is more, they will continue to do so for generations to come. In 1969, 1.2 billion or 72 per cent of the total population of LDCs lived in rural areas compared with 475 million in urban centres (Table 3.1). No less than 83 per cent of the poor population with under $75 *per capita* income was rural. If we define poverty in terms of the $50 criterion, then 86 per cent of the aggregate poor population was rural.

There is an important difference in the area distribution of poverty in Asia and Africa on the one hand and America on the other. Whereas 85 per cent of the total poor population in Asia and Africa resides in rural areas, in America there is a more even distribution, with 60 per cent of the poor living in rural areas and 40 per cent in urban centres (Table 3.2).

Before proceeding further, it is important to note that rural

Table 3.2: Incidence of Global Poverty, By Regions, 1969 (in millions)

Region	Population			'Poor' Population[b]		
	Total	Rural	Urban	Total	Rural	Urban
LDCs in Africa	360	280	80	165	140	15
LDCs in America	260	120	140	50	30	20
LDCs in Asia	1,080	855	225	620	525	95
Total LDCs	1,700	1,255	475	835	695	140
Four Asian LDCs[a]	765	625	140	510	435	75

a. India, Pakistan, Indonesia and Bangladesh.
b. Population with under $75/capita p.a.
Source: *Rural Development,* Annexes 1, 2, 3, pp.79, 80.

income levels may tend to overstate the severity of poverty in those
areas. This is due to the fact that in many LDCs non-monetary
productive activities in the peasant and subsistence sectors (not
normally included in the computation of national accounts) represent a
significant proportion of output.[4] These non-monetary activities
relate partly to production for own consumption of crops and
livestock by farmers, and partly to the construction of dwellings,
storage and transportation facilities as well as the manufacture of
simple tools and implements. In addition, non-cash activities may
cover barter-type transactions undertaken within a tribal, or
subsistence economy. To the extent that these types of productive
activities are excluded from income levels, the incidence and severity
of poverty would be overstated. For example, under the 1964 United
Nations system of national accounting (SNA)[5] much of these
non-monetary activities were ignored from the calculations of GNP and
GDP in LDCs. However, in the revised SNA a broader definition of
income is recommended in order to include non-monetary activities.[6]
Nevertheless, evaluation of these activities on the basis of imputed
costs or indirect prices is by no means easy and, in all likelihood,
such estimates would be subject to significant margins of error.

Despite these pricing problems, the magnitude of rural poverty
and deprivation in LDCs is too large to be affected significantly
by conceptual or measurement problems. The great majority — and in
some countries almost the totality — of rural populations live in
conditions of abject poverty. As we shall see presently, they lack
adequate food, medical care, social services and housing. In many
LDCs, especially in Latin American republics, over 50 per cent of

the entire rural population are landless peasants, depending for their livelihood on the whims and fancies of rich landlords and the generosity of their relatives and family members.

Nutritional Deficiencies

The United Nations Food and Agriculture Organization (FAO) has long been involved with the problem of measuring standard nutritional requirements on the basis of daily *per capita* diets of calories, proteins and other food nutrients essential for healthy and productive existence. These standards are difficult to measure due to the differential effects of climatic factors and work conditions as well as personal and sex differences of individuals in different countries and regions. For example, the FAO standard calorie requirements for a 'reference man' weighing 143 lbs are 2,800, 3,200 and 4,400 respectively, if he did sedentary, light and heavy work in a warm climate. The protein requirement ranges from 40 to 80 grams, depending on quality.[7] For convenience of comparisons, FAO has also computed estimates of *average* calorie and protein requirements for all ages, body weights, climates and kinds of work as well as for both sexes. For the LDCs combined, the *per capita* daily average is 2,284 calories and 38.4 grams of protein.[8]

Using these average nutritional requirements, it can be demonstrated that more than 50 per cent of the population in many LDCs suffers from malnutrition and food deficiencies, and that most of the malnourished are the poor. Some relevant data for a group of LDCs is presented in Table 3.3. The case of Brazil is particularly revealing because Brazil is by no means among the poorest LDCs. In fact, in terms of *national* nutritional standards, it exceeds the FAO averages for both proteins and calories. But there are wide discrepancies in the nutritional standards of the socio-economic groups. Thus, no less than 57.6 per cent of the urban families and 35.2 per cent of those in rural areas suffered from significant diet caloric deficiency. All these families were in the lowest income groups. By contrast, families in the top income groups enjoyed more than twice the average calorie intake of those in the bottom income group.

In the Malagasy Republic, 65.7 per cent of families were below the average FAO daily calorie requirement, and a further 27.7 per cent were only marginally above it. These 93.4 per cent of families were at the lower end of the income pyramid. The evidence from India, Tunisia and other LDCs supports the fact of major nutritional deficiencies among the poor (especially among the poorest) groups.[9]

Table 3.3: Nutrition Levels by Income Classes, in Some LDCs

Family Group/ Expenditure Group	Percentages of families	Calorie Intake Cals. *(per capita)*	Protein Intake Grams *(per capita)*
Latin America			
Brazil (1960/1)			
Annual family income (new cruzeiros per year)			
Urban areas			
under 100	4.16	1,315	35.6
100-249	21.94	1,788	49.1
250-499	31.48	2,227	66.9
500-1,199	30.54	2,830	95.7
1,200 and over	11.88	3,569	119.9
Total average		2,345	73.2
Rural areas			
under 100	7.94	1,755	50.0
100-249	27.30	2,267	64.9
250-499	29.68	2,577	75.9
500-1,199	24.56	3,144	95.4
1,200 and over	10.52	3,674	116.6
Total average		2,083	80.6
India (1958)			
Maharashtra State			
Expenditure *per capita* (in rupees)			
Urban and rural areas			
0-11	21.3	1,340	37.9
11-18	18.9	2,020	56.6
18-34	20.7	2,485	69.0
34 and over	39.1	3,340	85.7
Total average		2,100	59.7
Africa			
Malagasy Republic (1962)			
Income per family per year (in francs)			
1-20	54.7	2,154	47.3
20-40	27.7	2,292	54.1
40-80	11.0	2,256	53.6
80-130	3.8	2,359	61.2
130-190	1.5	2,350	59.1
190-390	0.8	2,342	64.6
390-590	0.3	2,456	65.4
Other classes	0.2		

Table 3.3 Cont'd

Family Group/ Expenditure Group	Percentages of families	Calorie Intake Cals. *(per capita)*	Protein Intake Grams *(per capita)*
Tunisia (1965/7)			
Income per person in rural areas (in dinars)			
Less than 20	8.2	1,782	
20-32	16.2	2,157	
32-53	30.8	2,525	
53-102	32.4	2,825	
102-200	10.9	3,215	
200 and over	1.5	3,150	

Source: Computed from David Turnham, *The Employment Problem in Less Developed Countries: A Review of Evidence,* Development Centre Studies, Employment Series No.1 (Paris, OECD, 1971), pp.90-1.

The problem of malnutrition among the bulk of the population of LDCs has obvious implications for healthy living as well as productive employment. Invariably, the low-income groups are the undernourished as well. Thus, they are effectively caught in a vicious circle of poverty in which low productivity and malnutrition are both the cause and effect of inadequate income; yet, income is the only means of breaking out of the poverty trap. Protein and calorie deficiencies lead to mental and physical handicaps, which in turn lead to sickness and unemployment, which result in substandard levels of income. In this tragic cycle whereby malnutrition reinforces poverty and poverty breeds malnutrition, there is a permanent and growing population of 'marginal men'[10] who are the survivors of the post-war population explosion. They have now reached adulthood only to find out that they cannot play any productive role and are, therefore, condemned to a life of misery and deprivation.

The poverty trap in LDCs is particularly tragic for its effects on children. Medical and clinical evidence from many countries points to a strong positive correlation between malnutrition among children, and long-term damage to the brain, nervous system and the body.[11] Food deficiencies in the childhood years permanently reduce the body's resistance to disease and parasitical infliction in subsequent years. Over time, the result is a steadily expanding army of dependent population, unable to work and feed itself. It can only be supported at a heavy social cost, at the expense of future economic development.

None of the above is inconsistent with the fact that, in most instances, inadequate food, low nutritive content and insufficient income are self-inflicted in the sense that they result from illiteracy, inertia and religious and social taboo, as well as ignorance.[12] But the realisation of this is a clear proof of the fact that post-war industrialisation has merely worked to confer increased wealth and comfort for the elite groups at the top while bringing misery and poverty for the masses.

The Anti-Rural Bias of Industrialisation

The process of post-war industrialisation in LDCs generally worsened the disparities between the rural and urban areas because of the phenomenon of 'Urban Bias'.[13] Most of the development projects, including schools, housing and other social capital formation, were concentrated in urban centres. Furthermore, and as we have already seen, preferential tax and credit policies and inflationary financing designed to encourage the creation of home industries seriously drained rural resources and surpluses. For several LDCs available evidence suggests that rural incomes have lagged relative to industrial sectors, although in terms of average nutritional standards the position of the urban poor was often inferior when compared with their rural counterparts (see Table 3.3).

The anti-rural bias of the post-war planning in LDCs can be demonstrated with reference to social security programmes, education and health services as well as in terms of the effects of the so-called 'Green Revolution'.

Social Security

The extent of social security coverage has an important bearing on living standards since protected individuals are automatically guaranteed a substitute income (e.g. under an employment insurance scheme) or some form of benefit (e.g. medical care). The post-war period has seen a tremendous growth of social security in industrialised countries, both in terms of protected population as well as in terms of contingency benefits. In some LDCs, too, there has been considerable progress. However, these benefits (including statutory pensions, old age, invalidity and death, medical care) have been limited to a small fraction of the economically active population, mostly concentrated in urban labour forces. So far as the rural sectors (where the majority of inhabitants reside) are concerned, virtually no progress has been made. Thus, a recent world-wide survey undertaken by the International Labour Organization concluded:

> It is only too common for social security systems to exclude the agricultural sector. Only in Europe and a handful of industrialised countries in Asia and America are farmers protected. Elsewhere little, if anything, has been done. . .It is no exaggeration to say that social security concerns barely one agricultural worker in ten in the world at large, and the figure is even lower in the less industrialised regions.[14]

Rural Illiteracy

Illiteracy is alarmingly high in most rural areas of LDCs, no doubt due to lack of schooling opportunity. In the urban areas of Brazil, Mexico and Venezuela, for example, the literacy rate is between 70 and 80 per cent, but it is less than 20 per cent in the rural areas.

Illiteracy in Argentina, where it might be expected to decline, is

apparently becoming a permanent feature of country life not only
because of the difficulties encountered in providing rural
education but also because of actual discouragement on the part of
local landowners.[15]

In Latin America as a whole, the average illiteracy rate is about 45 per
cent, but it rises to 70 per cent in south-east Asia, to 75 per cent
in the Middle East, to 80 per cent in India and Africa, and is as high
as 95 per cent in the greater part of Africa south of the Sahara. Given
that the literate population is concentrated in urban centres, these
figures strongly suggest that in many rural communities in the
Third World, there is hardly a single person who can read and write.
A truly nation-wide system of education is still lacking in many LDCs,
with the rural areas lagging behind urban centres both in terms of
quantity and quality (Table 3.4). We shall return to the problem of
educational restructuring in Chapter 10.

Table 3.4: Availability of Primary Schools in Urban and Rural Areas

Percentage of the total number of primary schools in each category
(urban and rural) which offer a complete number of grades

	Number of Countries	Complete Urban Schools as a Percentage of Total Urban Schools	Complete Rural Schools as a Percentage of Total Rural Schools
Countries by GNP *per capita*			
Up to $120 (excluding India)	9	53	36
India	1	57	49
$121 − 250	7	72	32
$251 − 750	16	77	62
$751 − 1,500	2	89	56
Over $1,500	6	100	99
By Major Regions			
Africa	16	79	54
Asia (excluding India)	9	94	66
India	1	57	49
Latin America	10	88	34
Europe	5	98	99

Source: *Rural Development*, Annex 7, p.84.

Health and Medical Care

Medical and hospital facilities are another important sphere of social services in which the rural communities of the Third World have been neglected. While there has been undeniable progress in the eradication and control of tropical diseases, notably as a result of the impressive work of the World Health Organization, most of the new facilities for curing the sick and for hospital care in LDCs have been concentrated in urban centres. In a number of countries, undue emphasis has been placed on imported, high-cost, ultra-modern facilities and equipment at the expense of basic health care which remains pitifully inadequate. In Ethiopia, for instance, there is just one doctor for every 59,000 inhabitants (as compared with 760 in the USA). In Morocco and Kenya there is just over one hospital bed for every 1,000 inhabitants and one doctor for every 10,000. In Indonesia the doctor ratio is 1:35,000. It is significant to note that these figures are national averages, and as such they reveal national shortages of medical facilities. Clearly, the shortages are far worse in rural areas because of lower population densities and inadequate means of communication and transportation in these areas relative to urban centres. Table 3.5 provides some data about the disparities (in terms of medical doctors) between urban and rural areas for some LDCs. It will be seen that in the extreme case (viz. Kenya) the urban superiority is as high as 57 times. The urban ratio of 880 persons per medical doctor is almost as low as the American ratio of 1:760.[16]

No less significantly, access to available health services is highly inequitable, being largely a function of wealth, status and power. Most of the LDCs possess health services primarily designed to service the rich. Thus more public funds are spent on heart disease treatment, the care of individuals sick in hospitals, and on drugs, than on sanitation programmes, malnutrition and simple medical needs of rural communities. In the former French colony of Upper Volta, for example, about $25 million is spent annually for all public health services, including drugs; yet twice the amount is spent by the government for transporting relatively few well-connected sick persons to Paris for intensive hospital care in France.[17] In most Latin American countries, hospital care is so expensive that it is well beyond the reach of all except the wealthiest: 'In Venezuela, one day in a hospital costs ten times the average daily income; in Bolivia, about forty times the daily income.'[18] These socially unjust health priorities reflect the elite control of the decision-making process, but they also demonstrate the failure of the medical profession — itself a subset of

Table 3.5: Population per Medical Doctor in Urban and Rural Areas

Country	Year	Population per Medical Doctor Urban	Rural	Urban Superiority in Medical Doctors per Unit of Population
Honduras	1968	1,190	7,140	6:1
Jamaica[a]	1968	840	5,510	7:1
Philippines	1971	1,500	10,000	7:1
Senegal[a]	1968	4,270	44,300	10:1
Panama	1969	930	3,000	3:1
Colombia	1970	1,000	6,400	6:1
Ghana[a]	1968	4,340	41,360	10:1
Iran	1969/70	2,275	9,940	4:1
Haiti[a]	1968	1,350	33,300	25:1
Kenya	1969	880	50,000	57:1
Tunisia[a]	1968	2,912	10,056	4:1
Pakistan	1970	3,700	24,200	7:1
Thailand[a]	1968	800	25,000	31:1

a. Urban = capital city only.
   Rural = all other rural and urban areas

Source: *Rural Development,* Annex 6, p.83.

the elite class — to respond to basic needs and problems.

Landless Peasants

Modern forms of serfdom still exist in many LDCs. Indeed, conditions of near-slavery are not unheard of.[19] For many LDCs as much as a third of the total active rural population is made up of landless peasants. In the case of Algeria, Chile, Uruguay, Costa Rica and Argentina this proportion is over 50 per cent (Table 3.6). The economic welfare of these groups has hardly been improved by post-war planning and economic policy. The position of smallholders, too, has often deteriorated. For example, evidence from India, Pakistan, Ethiopia and elsewhere show that one of the most important socio-economic effects of the 'Green Revolution' has been the displacement of small-scale farmers and peasant families.[20] New seeds, tractors and fertilisers have encouraged land consolidation and speculation by large owners, local elites and moneyed classes. In the process, thousands of smallholders have been made landless, sometimes

Table 3.6: Landless Farm Workers in Selected Countries[a]

	Number of Landless Workers (thousands)	Landless Workers as a Percentage of Active Population in Agriculture	Active Agricultural Population as a Percentage of Total Active Population
Asia			
India[b]	47,300	32	68
Indonesia	5,673	20	70
Pakistan[c]	8,013	29	70
Total	60,986	30	68
Middle East and North Africa			
Algeria	1,099	60	56
Egypt, Arab Republic of	1,865	38	55
Iran	903	25	46
Morocco	484	19	61
Tunisia	210	20	46
Total	4,561	33	58
Latin America and Caribbean			
Costa Rica	122	53	45
Dominican Republic	179	25	61
Honduras	138	27	67
Jamaica	72	41	27
Mexico (1970)	2,499	49	39
Nicaragua (1971)	101	43	47
Argentina	694	51	15
Chile (1971)	378	66	28
Colombia	1,158	42	45
Ecuador	391	39	54
Peru	557	30	46
Uruguay	99	55	17
Brazil	3,237	26	44
Venezuela	287	33	26
Total	9,912	35	39
Grand Total	75,459		

a. Except for India, data presented here are estimated from the ILO *Yearbook of Labor Statistics* for 1971 (pp.43-294) and 1972 (pp.44-301). Unless otherwise indicated, the data refer to the latest year available in the 1960s and thus do not reflect recent reform actions, on the one hand, nor changes in the work-force, on the other.

b. Agricultural labourers as shown in *Indian Agriculture in Brief* (eleventh edition, 1971), published by the Ministry of Agriculture, Government of India.

c. Includes population now belonging to Bangladesh.

Source: *Rural Development,* Annex 4, p.81.

by direct eviction or by manipulative selling-out. We shall return to
this problem in Chapter 11.

The Urban Sprawl

It is small wonder that the post-war period has witnessed a dramatic
drift of population from rural areas to urban centres. Urbanisation is,
of course, an integral part of economic and social development. But
the unplanned and chaotic swelling of urban areas in the Third World
represents an unprecedented concentration of people in high-density
areas, causing many complex socio-economic problems. The ever-
increasing influx of rural persons, typically undereducated and
unskilled, has led to severe overcrowding in slums and 'squatter
villages' in the major cities and towns of LDCs, generating
unmanageable pressures on health and educational facilities, housing
and other social services.

There are many reasons for the unprecedented drift of population
into urban centres in the Third World. In an era of 'rising expectations',
fuelled by generous foreign aid and ambitious promises, many
persons, even though undereducated and unskilled, moved in response
to the flimsiest opportunity of wage employment. Young people,
unable to obtain employment in rural areas, moved to towns after
schooling, partly to further their education and partly to seek a job.
Many hoped to escape the dullness and idleness of traditional life in
isolated villages dominated by parents and elders guided by
old-fashioned customs and values.

For the vast majority of migrants, however, transition from a
rural to an urban environment proved to be an exercise in futility,
leading to frustration, poverty and joblessness in some urban ghetto.
Gradually, many migrants joined the ranks of a new urban subculture
based on crime and violence, but designed to make a living in a hostile
and strange environment of unfulfilled expectations.

The urban sprawl in the Third World represents a fundamental
'shock' to established urban-rural equilibrium. The anti-rural bias
of post-war economic planning and growth created a regional
imbalance of alarming proportions. Available evidence on urbanisation
in LDCs shows that the urban growth rate in Latin America and
Africa is typically twice as fast as the population increase, much faster
in some cases. The inevitable results are overcrowding in
substandard housing, inadequate medical care and education, and
malnutrition. It has been estimated that in Seoul, Korea, 43 per cent
of the households live in slum-type dwellings with inferior services. In

Pusan, the country's second-largest city, 50 per cent of the households are in a similar situation, three or more families often having to share one home.[21] In Turkey, no less than 22 per cent of the country's entire urban population live in *gecekondus* or squatter houses, which have mushroomed around major cities.[22] While it provides inexpensive and immediate housing for poor migrants, squatter housing is substandard and generally unfit for healthy human habitation. Despite repeated efforts in the Turkish development plans to restrict the growth of squatter villages, *gecekondus* are expected to continue to expand. This is a universal trend in the developing world. In Lusaka, Zambia, for example, in just three years (1967-70), the number of shanty towns increased from 9 to 32, accommodating over one-third of the city's population.[23] These shanty towns grew spontaneously, outside municipal zoning and housing regulations. They lack pure water supply, proper sanitation and sewerage, and the inhabitants are always subject to sudden eviction by the authorities. Yet the position of Lusaka must be considered enviable, compared to the plight of such cities as Calcutta, Jakarta and Rio de Janeiro, to name just a few.[24]

Urban Unemployment

The disturbance of the traditional rural-urban equilibrium in LDCs by industrialisation has led to the emergence of a new phenomenon of urban unemployment. In many countries, precarious rural poverty and underemployment have been traded for open unemployment, overcrowding and deprivation in urban slums. Urban unemployment has assumed alarming proportions for many LDCs, far in excess of levels reached in the Great Depression in industrialised countries (Table 3.7). The unemployment problem in the Third World is now so serious, especially among the younger age groups, and lies at the root of so many related social, political and economic problems, that it qualifies as the major challenge of contemporary development planning and policy. The next chapter will be devoted to a detailed investigation of this problem.

Table 3.7: Urban Unemployment in Some Developing Countries,
by Age and Sex (per cent of labour force)

Country	Year	Age 15-24			Age 15+		
		Males	Females	Total	Males	Females	Total
Ceylon	1968	36.1	48.4	39.0	12.9	25 9	15.0
Colombia[a]	1968	21.8	24.3	23.1	10.3	18.5	13.6
Korea (South)	1968	16.4	15.3	16.3	9.3	7.9	8.9
Malaya	1965	17.7	26.8	21.0	7.4	16.7	9.8
Philippines	1965	23.8	16.9	20.6	10.8	12.9	11.6
Singapore	1966	—	—	15.7	—	—	9.2
Taiwan	1966	5.8	8.1	6.9	2.1	6.8	2.6
Guyana	1965	36.5	49.0	40.4	18.4	27.7	21.0

a. Bogotá.

Source: David Turnham and Ingelies Jaeger, *The Employment Problem in Developed Countries* (OECD, Paris, 1971), pp.48, 49, and article with the same title in *OECD Observer,* 49 (December 1970), p.9.

Notes

1. For empirical studies dealing with the construction and application of poverty lines, see Peter Townsend (ed.), *The Concept of Poverty* (Heinemann, London, 1970).

2. On the problems of using official exchange rates for international comparisons and other related issues, see P.A. Samuelson, 'Analytical Notes on International Real-Income Measures', *Economic Journal,* Vol.84 (September 1974).

3. *Rural Development, Sector Policy Paper* (World Bank, February 1975, Washington, DC). Also, see H. Chennery *et al., Redistribution With Growth* (Oxford University Press, London, 1974), especially the paper by Ahluwalia.

4. Derek W. Blades, 'Subsistence Activities in the National Accounts of Developing Countries with Special Reference to Latin America', *The Review of Income and Wealth,* No.4 (December 1975) and the references cited.

5. *A System of National Accounts and Supporting Tables,* Series F, No.2, Rev.2 (New York, United Nations, 1964).

6. *A System of National Accounts,* Series F, No.2, Rev.3 (New York, United Nations, 1968).

7. *Agricultural Commodity Projections, 1970-1980* (FAO, Rome, 1971).

8. Ibid.

9. Additional data based on case-studies is given in H. Oshima, 'Food Consumption, Nutrition and Economic Development in Asian Countries', *Economic Development and Cultural Change* (July 1967); A. Berg, 'Malnutrition and National Development', *Foreign Affairs* (October 1967); FAO, *Calorie Requirements,* FAO Nutritional Studies No.15 (Rome, 1968): G.B. Rodgers, 'A Conceptualisation of Poverty in Rural India', *World Development,* Vol.4, No.4 (1976).

10. J.P. Grant, 'Marginal Men: The Global Unemployment Crisis', *Foreign Affairs,* Vol.50, No.1 (October 1971).

11. P. Belli, 'The Economics of Malnutrition: The Dismal Science Revisited', *Economic Development and Cultural Change* (October 1971); M. Selowsky and

L. Taylor, 'The Economics of Malnourished Children', *Economic Development and Cultural Change* (October 1973).

12. Thus pregnant women in some LDCs are prohibited by local custom from eating eggs, chicken, milk or fish, thereby minimising their protein intake. Religious requirements, too, often discourage meat consumption. It should also be noted that poverty itself may oblige undernourished farmers to sell high-value food produce in order to earn cash.

13. Michael Lipton, *Why Poor People Stay Poor: Urban Bias in World Development* (Maurice Temple Smith Ltd, London, 1977).

14. Robert Savy, *Social Security in Agriculture* (ILO, Geneva, 1972), pp.256-7.

15. Ibid., p.15.

16. The statistics in this paragraph are from Savy, *Social Security in Agriculture,* pp.14-15.

17. Ivan Illich, *Limits to Medicine Medical Nemesis: The Expropriation of Health* (McClelland and Stewart, Toronto, 1976), footnote on p.237.

18. Illich, *Limits to Medicine,* p.239.

19. In many Latin American countries there are peasants, variously known as *yanacones, huasapungueros, colonos* or *inquilinos,* who are permanently or semi-permanently attached to land on the *latifundia* estates; they have no legal protection and work under *ad hoc* agreements with the landlords, often in return for residential rights only. See R. Farley, *The Economics of Latin America* (Harper and Row, New York, 1972), pp.174-5. The case of near-slavery in Liberia will be discussed in Chapter 6. See also Doreen Warriner, *Land Reform in Theory and Practice* (Clarendon Press, Oxford, 1969).

20. For a vivid description of the social and human costs of large-scale agrarian change in Punjab, Java, Mesopotamia and elsewhere, see R. Critchfield, *The Golden Bowl Be Broken* (Indiana University Press, Bloomington, 1973).

21. Quoted in D.T. Healey, 'Development Policy; New Thinking About an Interpretation', *Journal of Economic Literature,* Vol.10 (September 1972), pp.770-1.

22. John M. Munroe, 'Migration in Turkey', *Economic Development and Cultural Change,* Vol.22, No.4 (July 1974).

23. A.J.F. Simmance, 'Urbanization in Zambia', *Journal of Administration Overseas,* Vol.XIII, No.4 (October 1974).

24. G.F. Papanek, 'The Poor of Jakarta', *Economic Development and Cultural Change,* Vol.24, No.1 (1975); H. Lubell, 'Urban Development and Employment in Calcutta', *International Labour Review* (July 1973); M.R. Redclift, 'Squatter Settlements in Latin American Cities: The Response from Government', *Journal of Development Studies,* Vol.10, No.1 (October 1973).

4 THE UNEMPLOYMENT PROBLEM OF THE LDCS

Perhaps the single most alarming consequence of faulty planning and industrialisation policies in LDCs is the problem of chronic unemployment. It is not only persistent, but it continues to increase at an alarming rate, with no end in sight over the next several decades. Chronic unemployment has now become the most pressing issue of development planning and policy, and unless effective and adequate solutions are urgently found, there may be ominous consequences for world peace and security, as well as social and political stability in the Third World. This chapter utilises available statistical data to document the extent of the unemployment problem. First, however, it is necessary to explore the historical evolution of the problem and its definition and measurement.

From Colonial Scarcity to Unlimited Abundance

Unemployment of labour was hardly a concern of governments in LDCs until very recently.[1] Indeed, in colonial areas and plantation economies, labour *scarcity,* rather than unemployment, was the major problem. In traditional Africa, for example, the concept of unemployment was both unknown and incompatible with the customs of tribal culture, according to which roles and economic functions, such as tending crops, herding cattle, and hunting and gathering food, were determined. Tribal warfare, cattle raids, disease and poverty were accepted as part of the natural order. During European colonial rule, and specifically in connection with the development of plantations and export-oriented enclave sectors, the colonial administrators designed policies to alleviate labour shortages. Managerial, supervisory and technical personnel were directly imported from Europe, but the native rural areas were regarded as 'reservoirs' of wage labour. Schemes were formulated to transfer peasant labour from its traditional habitat to estates and mines.[2] In those regions where the native rural population was reluctant, or disinterested in wage employment away from its homeland, the matter was rationalised in terms of the famous 'backward-sloping supply curve' argument.[3] The solution was large-scale importation of indentured labourers from India, China and elsewhere. We shall return to this subject in Chapter 5 in connection with the development of rubber plantations and tin-mining in colonial Malaya.

The conceptual origins of the contemporary unemployment problem of LDCs can be traced to the post-Keynesian doctrines which guided much of the economic planning and model-building in the post-war period. In industrialised countries of the West, where full employment of labour is a reasonably normal state of affairs, such fundamental concepts as labour force, employment and unemployment — whether frictional or involuntary — are identifiable and measurable within tolerable margins of statistical accuracy. Even the more elusive concept of 'disguised unemployment', discussed in Chapter 1, was originally coined for the industrial countries, where its practical measurement has been less than fully successful.

In the general enthusiasm for economic planning in the post-war period, Western analysts and Western-trained economists applied Keynesian principles to the LDCs in an almost uncritical fashion. It was as if the structure and institutional framework of developing nations differed from those of advanced countries only in stage or phase of development. In fact, however, no such assumption, explicit or implicit, can be justified. Most LDCs possess structural characteristics that cannot be analysed effectively within the context of Western models or formulae. This is especially true for the measurement and identification of employment, unemployment and underemployment. In the large traditional sectors, labour utilisation is generally subject to important seasonal fluctuations, partly determined by agronomic factors and partly by institutional values. In many LDCs, especially in Africa, there is an extensive nomadic pattern of life which is clearly inconsistent with permanent, paid employment.[4] Even in urban sectors, where the concept of stable employment is most feasible, work patterns and job functions often do not fit the neat Western occupational classifications, partly due to imperfect specialisation and division of labour and partly because of limited domestic markets.[5] Except in the largest (usually foreign) enterprises, workers may be engaged in a variety of functions that appear to be casual or informal. Thus, some observers in recent years have coined the term 'informal sector'[6] in an attempt to describe and analyse the emergence of small-scale entrepreneurs trading in local produce, vegetables and other staples — activities which require small levels of working and human capital. While useful as a descriptive idea, the concept of 'informal sector' cannot overcome the basic problems of identifying and measuring unemployment in LDCs. Not the least difficulty faced by statisticians and survey enumerators is the fact that most firms do not keep adequate records relating to hours of work, wages and the number of workers.[7] While sometimes this reflects the entrepreneur's desire to minimise his costs or avoid taxes, in many cities (such as Calcutta, Lagos and Singapore, to name just a few), economic transactions and employment patterns are intricately merged into a way of life which neither requires nor lends itself to statistical measurement.

Accordingly, some analysts have recently attempted to define the unemployment problem in terms of inadequacy of current income. This links poverty and unemployment in a way which tends to minimise the statistical difficulties of labour utilisation in LDCs. In the Kenya report of the International Labour Organization, the concept of *working poor* was proposed as an operational guide for anti-poverty and employment policy. It was argued that the 'problem of the working poor (defined as the proportion of population lacking the opportunity of earning a reasonable minimum income) should constitute the major part of the employment problem'.[8]

The Evidence on Unemployment

The first awareness of the unemployment problem in the LDCs began to be felt in the early 1960s. As might be expected, the first signs of the problem were picked up, not from statistics of unemployment, but rather by direct observation of (a) an increasing drift of rural folk, mostly young school-leavers, into urban areas in search of jobs,[9] and (b) the resulting mushrooming of shanty towns and slums filled with frustrated job-seekers.

According to the latest statistics available, open unemployment in urban centres alone has reached two-digit levels in most LDCs (Table 4.1). In such countries as Algeria, Morocco, Ivory Coast and Guyana it is in excess of 20 per cent of the active population. It must be remembered that in all probability these figures are under-reported due to the measurement and identification problems, as discussed above. When unemployment and underemployment in rural areas are included, the dimensions of the problem assume alarming proportions.

What makes the unemployment problem of LDCs especially explosive is that it affects the young (i.e. those in the 15 to 24 age bracket) more severely than those in other age groups (Table 3.7). Frustrated and without hopes, many young persons may be forced into crime and violence, threatening social and political stability. The related problem of 'school-leavers', unable to find employment after schooling, is doubly costly because it represents wasted public resources as well as personal misery for the idle educated.[10]

Table 4.1: Rates of Urban and Rural Unemployment (per cent of the active population)

Country	Year	Unemployment	
		Urban	Rural
Africa			
Algeria	1966	26.6	—
Burundi	1963[a]	18.7[b]	—
Cameroon	1966	15.0[c]	—
Ghana	1960	11.6	—
Ivory Coast[a]	1963	20.0	—
Morocco	1960	20.5	5.4
Nigeria	1963	12.6	—
Tanzania	1965	7.0	3.9
Zaire	1967	12.9[b]	—
America			
Argentina	1968	5.4[b]	—
Bolivia	1966	13.2[c]	—
Chile	1968	6.1	2.0
Colombia	1967	15.5[c]	—
Costa Rica	1966-7	5.6	—
El Salvador	1961	6.6[b]	—
Guatemala	1964	5.4[b]	—
Guyana	1965	20.5[b]	—
Honduras	1961	7.8[b]	—
Jamaica	1960	19.0[b]	12.4[d]
Netherlands Antilles	1966	16.0[c]	—
Panama	1967	9.3	2.8
Peru	1969	5.2[b]	—
Uruguay	1963	10.9	2.3
Venezuela	1968	6.5	3.1
Asia			
India[e]	1961-2	3.2	1.7[e]
Indonesia	1961	8.5	—
Iran	1966	5.5	11.3
Korea	1963-4	7.0	1.8
West Malaysia	1967	11.6	7.4
Philippines	1967	13.1	6.9
Singapore	1966	9.1	—
Sri Lanka	1959-60	14.3	10.0
Syrian Arab Republic	1967	7.3	—
Thailand	1966	2.8[c]	—

a. Men only.
b. Capital city only.
c. Average (weighted by size of population) for a certain number of main towns.
d. Excluding capital city.
e. Account taken of the adjustment suggested by Turnham for improving the comparability of the two rates.

Source: David Turnham (assisted by Ingellies Jaeger), *The Employment Problem in Less Developed Countries: A Review of Evidence* (Paris, OECD, Development Centre, 1971).

The need for drastic measures to deal with the unemployment problem of LDCs is perhaps best illustrated by the fact that, on the basis of present productivity trends and labour absorptive capacity of industrialisation, total unemployment in all LDCs in 1980 may rise to as high as 22 per cent of the labour force.[11] It is useful to consider the prospects for some individual countries. Nigeria is Africa's most populated country with an important oil industry. Assuming that the non-agricultural sector's output grows at up to 14 per cent annually, it is estimated that after 25 years less than 7.5 per cent of the labour force will be employed in the modern sector, and to achieve a 15 per cent employment share would take no less than 75 years.[12] In the case of Singapore, where industrial growth in the 1960s has been quite phenomenal, there is an increasing volume of unemployment; it is estimated that the rate of growth of output required to absorb the expansion of the labour force during 1967-77 is 17.2 per cent per annum[13] − an unlikely prospect. In Colombia, where the labour force is growing at 3.3 per cent per annum, the 'labour surplus' is projected to rise from an estimated 18.8 per cent of the labour force in 1963 to 27.3 per cent in 1980, despite the assumption of 2.8 per cent productivity gain per annum in the high productivity sector.[14] For Pakistan, a projection for the period 1961-86 implies that more than half of the 2.5 per cent annual increase of the labour force will not be absorbed in the industrial sector; the new job-seekers will join the ranks of the unemployed.[15]

Major Causes of the Unemployment Problem

According to Walter Galenson, 'of the factors that have contributed to the present crisis, none is more important than the sheer growth of population'.[16] The 'population explosion' in the Third World underscores the success of the modern public health schemes that were introduced to combat tropical disease and epidemics such as cholera, typhoid and smallpox. These measures have dramatically reduced crude death rates. Unfortunately, there has been no corresponding levelling in birth rates. As a result, the present century has witnessed an unprecedented population increase, and renewed neo-Malthusian fears.[17] Such fears are particularly reinforced by (a) increasing awareness that the world's energy and natural resources are not limitless,[18] and (b) the fact that there are no signs that the population explosion is likely to end during the foreseeable future, despite programmes designed to introduce birth control into densely populated LDCs. In fact, there is evidence indicating that the rate of increase of population itself may be growing: according to the projections of Ettore Denti of the ILO, the total African population, which grew at 2.18 per cent annually during 1950-60, will increase at 2.86 per cent per annum during the decade 1970-80.[19]

These projections of population growth (and also of labour force) imply trends that are unparalleled in the experience of industrialised countries. During the Industrial Revolution in European countries, the growth rate of active population was between 0.5 and 0.6 per cent, as compared with the 2.0 per cent or more in today's LDCs, and the 2.5 per cent expected rate over the next two decades.[20] These rates and projections demonstrate that the demographic trends are not the only alarming prospects; the unprecedented shifts in the age-sex structure of the population and labour forces of LDCs pose enormous global challenges — not just for these developing nations themselves, but for the rest of the world as well.

There are several other causes of the unemployment problem besides the fact of 'population explosion'. In the following pages we shall briefly survey three additional issues: (i) the preoccupation of post-war planners with capital shortage and their neglect of an employment policy; (ii) the choice of technique problem; and (iii) institutional obstacles, including discrimination in labour markets, elitist or irrelevant education systems, and restrictive wage and income policies. It is well to state at the outset that it is the combination of these factors, rather than any one of them alone, which provides the basic explanation for the unemployment problem. Its solution, therefore, requires concerted action on many fronts — educational restructuring, land reform, rural development and, above all, a political system dedicated to the ideals of social justice and fair distribution of the benefits of growth. We shall discuss some of these issues in Part Three.

Capital Constraint, Co-operant Resources and Employment Policy

A deliberate employment policy was not a leading objective of post-war planners, as we have seen in Chapter 1.[21] In retrospect, it is hard to understand this omission, especially in view of the emergence at about the same time of full-employment policy in Western countries in accordance with the ideas of John M. Keynes. Nevertheless, the dominant view of planners in the early post-war years was that development in LDCs was a function of capital accumulation.[22] Since these countries, by definition, were characterised by a low capital income ratio, and at the same time suffered from a paucity of savings, they were effectively caught in a vicious circle: GNP could only be increased through capital formation, which required additional savings. But a low national income, and a large subsistence sector, kept the aggregate savings and investment rates at minimal levels; and a minimal rate of investment meant a low rate of capital formation with correspondingly low rates of productivity gains in agriculture and manufacturing; and low productivity once again contributed to a low level of GNP. There were two ways of breaking out of the perceived vicious circle: first, mobilisation of domestic saving through such measures as inflationary financing, reduced consumption (forced saving) or additional taxation;[23] and, second, foreign inflows of aid and investment funds. Justification for foreign aid appeared to be readily available from the success story of the Marshall Plan in war-damaged Europe. Economists designed various models for estimating and projecting capital requirements of LDCs and for efficiently distributing scarce aid funds among competing LDCs.[24]

The capital constraint argument was essentially a misleading over-simplification of a complex problem. While the LDCs suffered from capital deficiency and a saving gap, they also lacked adequate co-operant factors of production, especially skilled manpower, a large enough domestic market for industrial output, and a host of other socio-economic institutions essential for rapid growth. Even in those LDCs which received large inflows of aid on concessional terms (e.g. Pakistan) the productivity of capital was well below normal standards. Often there were costly delays in the implementation and construction stages of projects; completed factories were forced to stay idle or operate below capacity for lack of co-operant resources; and, of course, in many countries political elites and leaders allocated scarce capital to unproductive, prestige projects (e.g. in Nkrumah's Ghana and Sukarno's Indonesia).

The capital constraint school had missed the single most important lesson of the Marshall Plan success in Europe: that economic reconstruction there was made possible by the infusion of external assistance only because of the existence of adequate stocks of highly educated and properly motivated human capital; and that full employment of labour was vigorously pursued by governments as an explicit policy objective and a vital part of economic planning.[25] For the LDCs, the prescriptions were based on contrary assumptions. We have already cited the views of Bettelheim.[26] Arthur Lewis explicitly downgraded the importance of manpower training in the early stages of development:

There may be at any time a shortage of skilled workers of any grade — ranging from masons, electricians or welders to engineers, biologists or administrators. Skilled labour may be the bottleneck in expansion, just like capital or land. Skilled labour, however, is only what Marshall might have called a 'quasi-bottleneck', if he had not had so nice a sense of elegant language. For it is a very temporary bottleneck, in the sense that if the capital is available for development, the capitalists or their government will soon provide the facilities for training more skilled people. The real bottlenecks to expansion are therefore capital and natural resources, and we can proceed on the assumption that so long as these are available the necessary skills will be provided as well, though perhaps with a time-lag.[27]

In fact, however, many LDCs simply relied on imports of expatriate personnel, at no small cost, often as an alternative to educational expansion at home, as we shall see in the case study of Liberia in Chapter 6.

The Choice of Technique Problem: Capital-Intensiveness of Manufacturing

The choice of appropriate techniques of production in LDCs has long been a subject of intense theoretical and empirical investigation.[28] We can only offer a brief discussion here. According to the classical theory of comparative advantage, countries which are capital-poor but labour-abundant should specialise in the production of commodities with high labour content per unit; and similarly, they should concentrate on the development of labour-intensive industries. Such a growth strategy would maximise productivity gains (i.e. output per unit of scarce inputs) and employment of labour.

During much of the post-war industrialisation drive, governments of LDCs pursued policies diametrically opposed to the prescriptions of the theory of comparative advantage, in many cases upon the advice of expatriate planners. Thus they deliberately over-valued their currencies in relation to other countries'; they gave preferential tariff rates to capital imports; and they encouraged highly capital-intensive industrial projects even in those LDCs which lacked mineral or natural resources to sustain such projects without expensive imports of raw materials. These illogical and wasteful policies were partly due to faulty advice by foreign planners, but also significantly due to what Nurske has called the international Demonstration Effect: the fact that inhabitants in an LDC may be tempted to imitate high consumption patterns of advanced countries, at the expense of savings and capital formation.[29] Richard Eckaus, in the formulation of his famous Factor Proportions Problem, has wisely argued that a similar demonstration effect operates in the case of investment: 'Indian businessmen, for example, may believe that the "American way" of producing is the best and only way and that this always involves high ratios of capital to labour.'[30]

It is, therefore, hardly surprising that industrialisation in LDCs has made only minimal contribution to employment generation. Evidence presented in Table 1.1 on p.23 demonstrates that, while manufacturing output grew impressively in many LDCs, employment in this sector grew at an average of 50 per cent of the output growth rate. In addition, the size of manufacturing is typically too small to absorb adequate numbers of job-seekers.

> The expansion of industrial manufacturing alone cannot be expected to solve the unemployment and underemployment problem in most developing countries. A manufacturing sector employing 20% of the labour force would need to increase employment by 15% per year merely to absorb the increment in a total work force growing at an annual rate of 3%. The required rate of increase of manufacturing output is even greater than 15% if increases in labour productivity are taken into account. In the light of these orders of magnitude, the contribution of the industrial sector to employment growth over the last decade has been disappointing in many developing economies. In a number of countries in Latin America and Africa, despite significant investments in manufacturing, employment in the sector grew less rapidly than population, and in some cases even declined in absolute terms.[31]

It should, perhaps, be stated that manufacturing in LDCs is not necessarily labour-saving. In many cases this is probably valid, but with proper policies and appropriate technology, manufacturing and processing industries can generate increasing volume of employment. Recent empirical studies from the Philippines, Argentina, Nigeria and elsewhere[32] indicate that the output elasticity of employment may be greater than unity, i.e. a 1 per cent growth of manufacturing output may be accompanied with increased employment of more than 1 per cent. The extreme example of 'intermediate technology' as a tool of employment creation is the case of the People's

Republic of China. Consistent with Mao's self-reliance doctrines, rural industries have been developed on the basis of simple (but not primitive) home-made techniques of production which deliberately save scarce capital equipment and use labour-intensive methods. These small-scale rural industries, not to be confused with cottage industries, represent one of the two 'legs' on which Chinese industrial policy stands; the other 'leg' being the modern, state-controlled complex industrial sector. The Chinese model is significant because it demonstrates the feasibility of an industrialisation strategy based on self-reliance and home-made techniques. Given the enormous transportation and geographic differences between China and most LDCs, it may be difficult to transplant the Chinese model in other countries, and its coercive labour allocation policies would be additionally objectionable.[33] Yet, the Chinese model proves that self-reliance methods can be made to work.

Institutional Obstacles for Employment Creation

It would be a serious error to think that the unemployment problems of LDCs stem directly from economic causes such as inappropriate production techniques, distorted factor pricing policies or misguided exchange rates and tariff structures. Also relevant are a number of institutional or cultural factors. Some of the more important ones are discussed briefly below.

Elitist Wage and Income Policies

In many LDCs, especially the newly independent ones, the lion's share of government budgets are allotted to salaries and fringe benefits of government personnel. Invariably these are set at lavish scales, far in excess of national average income levels. One year after independence, Dahomey spent 60 per cent of its total budget on the salaries of public servants. In neighbouring Nigeria, Ministers and managing directors, prior to the civil war, drew salaries between 3,500 and 10,000 Nigerian pounds, while unskilled workers in the state sector earned an average of 50 to 60 pounds a year. Yet, the latter were much better off than many rural peasants and agricultural workers. This wasn't all:

On top of their salaries Ministers were given houses specially built at a cost of £32,000 each. They also pay no electricity, telephone or water charges; they get a basic car allowance of £80 a month and when on an official trip they are also paid 1s 3d a mile. In addition they get cheap petrol from Public Works Department pumps . . .

Senior Civil Servants and officials of Corporations fare little worse.[34]

These kinds of lavish salaries and fringe benefits for the civil service and political elites in LDCs are all too common. More than any other factor, they explain the high demand for civil service jobs amongst school-leavers.

In the private sector, too, wage and income policies have tended to hold back the growth of employment opportunities. Stiff anti-firing provisions and high severance payments have sometimes forced employers not only to prefer capital over labour, but to deliberately minimise their work-forces simply because of fears that, in the event of uncertain sales opportunity, they may be unable to release their employees without substantial losses.[35] Similarly, the setting of minimum wages at artificially high levels has generated downward inflexibility of wage rates, thereby causing urban unemployment and rural-urban drift of job-seekers. Herein lies the explanation for the puzzling fact that, in spite of high unemployment in urban centres, great disparities between urban wages and rural earnings continue to exercise a strong pull effect on internal migration.

The appropriateness of such restrictive wage and income policies in labour-surplus countries is, to put it mildly, highly questionable. In some countries (e.g. Argentina, India) the political strength of trade unions appears to be the major cause of such policies; in others (e.g. Brazil, Chile) it is primarily because governments, for political survival reasons, periodically grant increases in minimum wage rates and/or in the pay of government employees. This, however, generates a general upward movement of the entire urban wage structure, and widens further urban-rural wage differentials. 'The growing discrepancy between the levels of social well-being typical of country and town life. . .provides the essential driving force for the rural exodus.'[36] Available evidence shows that the 'average real wage for workers outside agriculture of two to three times average family income in the traditional sector' is quite usual.[37] And so long as 'the gap between urban and rural incomes remains so high, one must expect the towns to be full of partially employed people, who hope to get by with an average of two or three days' work per week.'[38]

Non-Competitive Labour Markets

Another important cause of unemployment in LDCs is widespread discrimination in labour markets. Lack of equal opportunity for equally qualified job applicants is sometimes based on ethnic or tribal grounds, but often it may be based on family connections. Because of its elusive and politically delicate nature, discrimination in LDCs is little publicised, although its existence is generally recognised.[39] It lies behind such important problems as 'intellectual unemployment' and the international 'brain drain'. In addition to open unemployment, discrimination in labour markets may also cause underemployment. Frequently, qualified and competent persons, lacking suitable connections, may be obliged to take positions far below their technical capacities.

There is a second form of discrimination as well: preference for expatriate over local job applicants. The extent of expatriate employment in a group of eleven African LDCs is shown in Table 4.2, which indicates that the heaviest reliance on expatriate personnel is at the high-level manpower category, i.e. A. For example, in Zambia no less than 96 per cent of such jobs in 1965-6 were occupied by expatriates; in Swaziland the ratio in 1970 was 80 per cent; in the Ivory Coast, Malawi, Uganda, Tanzania, the ratio ranged from 66 per cent to over 80 per cent.

In some cases, reliance on expatriate workers is a reflection of acute manpower shortages, especially for technical and skilled categories. In several cases, however, it mirrors a form of discrimination against high- and middle-level manpower educated locally. Thus, an ILO study on Colombia reported that between 1955 and 1968 more than 20,000 college graduates (mostly physicians and engineers) and about 8,000 persons at an intermediate level emigrated to the USA (which took about half), Spain, France and Canada.[40] The Pearson Report estimated that in 1967 alone, 40,000 professionals emigrated from LDCs to advanced countries; yet in the same year, the LDCs were utilising the services of over 100,000 technical assistance personnel, including 16,000 short-term advisers.[41]

Discrimination is also extensively practised by multinational firms, especially at the senior ranks, often as a result of concessions provided by the host governments to attract foreign investment. Expatriate personnel working for multinational firms (as with technical advisory staff of foreign aid programmes) are paid salaries several times higher than even the top paid local employees — a fact which often leads to resentment between foreign and local communities.

Elitist and Irrelevant Education

Lack of equal opportunity in the employment market is, of course, closely linked to educational inequalities. Today, after several decades

Table 4.2: Expatriate Employment as a Percentage of Total
Employment in Selected African Countries by Level of Skill and
Education

Country	Year of Survey	Educational level[a]				
		A	B	C	D	Total
Botswana	1967		94	81	19	42
Ivory Coast	1962	79	61	n/a	n/a	n/a
Kenya	1964	77[b]	25[b]	54[b]	18[b]	48[b]
	1969	58	48	36	n/a	41
Malawi	1966	64	10	14	n/a	18
Nigeria	1964	39	5	n/a	n/a	13
Somalia	1970	7	2	20	2	2
Sudan	1967-8	12	6	2	0	3
Swaziland	1970	80	74	57	23	35
Tanzania	1965	82	23	31	9	31
	1969	66	20	12	6	18
Uganda	1967	66	32	16	11	21
Zambia	1965-6	96	92	88	41	62

a. A = university degree or equivalent; B = 'A' levels (higher secondary school
examination generally taken after six or even seven years of secondary
schooling) or 'O' levels (examination taken after four or sometimes five years
of secondary schooling) plus one to two years of formal training; C = 'O' levels
or secondary school, form II, or primary schooling plus one to four years of
formal training. For simplicity, the educational classifications used in all the
manpower plans analysed in this article have been converted into the above
four categories.
b. All non-Africans.

Source: R. Jolly and C. Colclough, 'African Manpower Plans: An Evaluation',
International Labour Review, Vol.106 (Aug.–Sept. 1972), p.210.

of political independence in Asia, Africa and Latin America, educational
opportunity is still beyond the reach of many school-age children,
especially in rural areas. In some countries, the illiteracy rate is over
70 per cent, sometimes exceeding 90 per cent in rural regions.
Furthermore, although many LDCs have, in recent years, experienced
rapid growth of enrolments, the quality of education has deteriorated
equally rapidly because of lagging or stationary education budgets.
This has been particularly true for basic, primary education programmes.

Basically, the problem of education in many LDCs is that the
political leaders are either not aware of, or deliberately choose to
ignore, the social benefits of universal education. Unlike the human
capital revolution in the advanced countries in the 1950s and 1960s,
many LDCs have yet to reach such a stage. In many oil-rich Middle

Eastern countries, for example, the windfall gains realised from the OPEC cartel revenues are mostly being used for military expenditure, manpower imports, various forms of conspicuous consumption and capital exports to industrialised countries, all of which are at the expense of educational and social investments at home; yet, these countries suffer from extremely high illiteracy, especially amongst women and rural populations.

In contrast with the general neglect of universal, primary education, many LDCs have accorded high priority for university-level expansion in the post-war period. Often, however, such expansion was unplanned and unco-ordinated with employment creation, and there was undue emphasis on a classical, general type of education. As a result, in many LDCs there has been an increasing phenomenon of 'intellectual unemployment', i.e. young university graduates unable to find employment. In Sri Lanka, for example, 90 per cent of the young job-seekers in 1969-70 were under 20 years of age and had advanced educational qualifications; two-thirds of this group were still unemployed when 20-24 years old.[42] In India, a similar study of the employment prospects of university graduates revealed that 26 per cent of the graduates had to wait for an average of one year before finding a job, 15 per cent had to wait for two years, 7 per cent for three years, and 3 per cent for four years.[43] The pattern of education-employment mismatch is widespread for several LDCs, including Iran, Argentina, Malaysia, Syria, Kenya, Egypt, Turkey and Venezuela.[44]

These conditions do not indicate (as some observers have concluded) that there is *general* over-investment in education in LDCs. Rather they indicate that there has been over-investment in *particular* types of education, especially university-level programmes. At the primary level, and in so far as rural areas are concerned, there remains an acute under-investment, as we shall see in Chapter 10. Educational reform is a critical requirement for many LDCs. It would be feasible to restructure the existing elitist educational system in such a way that a number of highly desirable social objectives may be achieved simultaneously, such as more efficient utilisation of rural manpower and increased food production. Of major importance is the fact that such an educational restructuring need not be unduly costly even in the least developed countries. In some cases, the costs of rural education could be financed as a result of a socially more efficient reallocation of the education budget; in others, there might be increased reliance on low-cost, non-formal types of education, as we shall see in Chapter 10. Realistically, however, as with all structural reforms with egalitarian objectives, educational restructuring suggested here can be expected to encounter stiff elite resistance.

Notes

1. There is a vast literature on the unemployment problem of the LDCs. For a recent and comprehensive study, see D. Turnham and I. Jaeger, *The Employment Problem in the Less Developed Countries* (OECD, Paris, 1971). Also see P. Bairoch, *Urban Unemployment in Developing Countries* (ILO, Geneva, 1973).

2. For the African case, see Guy Hunter, 'Employment Policy in Tropical Africa: The Need for Radical Revision' in P. Ndegwa and John P. Powelson (eds.), *Employment in Africa: Some Critical Issues* (ILO, Geneva, 1973).

3. A discussion of this topic is in Peter T. Bauer and Basil S. Yamey, *The Economics of Under-developed Countries* (University of Chicago Press, Chicago, 1963), pp.82-9.

4. For early attempts at classifying and defining various forms of employment situations in LDCs, see C. Hsiesh, 'Under-employment in Asia', Parts I and II, *International Labour Review,* Vol.LXVIII (June-July 1952); Nurul Islam, 'Concepts and Measurement of Unemployment and Underemployment in Developing Economies', *International Labour Review,* Vol.LXXXIX, No.3 (March 1964). A more recent discussion of this subject is given in Jean Mouly, 'Some Remarks on the Concepts of Employment, Underemployment and Unemployment', *International Labour Review,* Vol.105, No.2 (February 1972).

5. Bauer and Yamey, *The Economics of Under-developed Countries,* pp.33-42.

6. J. Weeks, 'Policies for Expanding Employment in the Informal Urban Sectors of Developing Economies', *International Labour Review,* Vol.91, No.1 (January 1975); Keith Hart, 'Informal Income Opportunities and Urban Employment in Ghana', *Journal of Modern African Studies,* Vol.II, No.1 (March 1973).

7. In some LDCs, even the total population is not reliably known, a population census never having been attempted.

8. ILO, *Employment, Incomes and Equality: A Strategy for Increasing Productive Employment in Kenya* (Geneva, 1972), p.63. See also Turnham and Jaeger, *The Employment Problem,* p.18.

9. Bairoch, *Urban Unemployment,* esp. Ch.2.

10. M. Blaug, *Education and the Employment Problem in Developing Countries* (ILO, Geneva, 1973); A. Gallaway, 'Unemployment Among African 'School Leavers', *Journal of Modern African Studies,* Vol.1, No.3 (1963); Turnham and Jaeger, *The Employment Problem;* Bairoch, *Urban Unemployment.*

11. Turnham and Jaeger, *The Employment Problem,* p.116.

12. C. Frank, as quoted in ibid., p.119.

13. H.T. Oshima, as quoted in ibid., p.119.

14. D. Zschock, as quoted in ibid., p.119.

15. S. Bose, 'Labour Force and Employment in Pakistan', *Pakistan Development Review,* Vol.II, No.3 (Autumn 1963).

16. ILO, *Essays on Employment,* selected and with an Introduction by Walter Galenson (Geneva, 1971), p.1.

17. Paul R. Erlich, *The Population Bomb* (Ballantine, New York, 1968); Anne H. Erlich, 'The World Food: No Room for Complacency', *Social Science Quarterly,* Vol.57, No.2 (September 1976); George Allen, 'Agricultural Policies in the Shadow of Malthus', *Lloyds Bank Review,* No.117 (July 1975).

18. Jagdish N. Bhagwati (ed.), *Economics and World Order from the 1970's to the 1990's* (Macmillan, New York, 1972); Dennis L. Meadows *et al.*, *The Limits of Growth, A Report for the Club of Rome* (Universe Books, New York, 1972).

19. Ettore Denti, 'Africa's Labour Force, 1960-1980' in Ndegwa and Powelson, *Employment in Africa,* p.4.

20. Bairoch, *Urban Unemployment,* p.10.

21. See pp.22-24.

22. Cf. W.A. Lewis, *The Theory of Economic Growth* (Unwin University Books, London, 1955), pp.225-44.

23. W.A. Lewis, 'Economic Development with Unlimited Supplies of Labour', *The Manchester School,* Vol.22 (May 1954). Reprinted in A.N. Agarwala and S.P. Singh (eds.), *The Economics of Underdevelopment* (Oxford University Press, New York, 1963), pp.400-49.

24. For a sample, see J. Bhagwati and R.S. Eckaus (eds.), *Foreign Aid* (Penguin, Harmondsworth, 1970).

25. T.W. Schultz, *Transforming Traditional Agriculture* (Yale University Press, New Haven, Conn., 1964).

26. Ch.1, p.24.

27. Lewis, 'Economic Development with Unlimited Supplies of Labour', p.406. However, there were notable exceptions to this point of view. For example, see Bauer and Yamey, *The Economics of Under-developed Countries,* p.129.

28. Amartya Sen, *Employment, Technology and Development* (Clarendon Press, Oxford, 1975).

29. R. Nurske, *Problems of Capital Formation in Under-developed Countries* (Blackwell, Oxford, 1953), pp.68-70.

30. R.S. Eckaus, 'Factor Proportions Problem in Underdeveloped Areas', *American Economic Review* (September 1955). Reprinted in Agarwala and Singh, *The Economics of Under-development,* p.353.

31. D. Morawetz, 'Employment Implications of Industrialization in Developing Countries: A Survey', *Economic Journal,* Vol.84 (September 1974), pp.491 and 496.

32. ILO, *Technology and Employment in Industry,* edited by A.S. Bhalla (Geneva, 1975).

33. Jan S. Prybyla, 'The Chinese Economic Model', *Current History* (September 1975); Thomas G. Rawski, 'Problems of Technology Absorption in Chinese Industry', *American Economic Review* (May 1975).

34. J. Bullock, quoted in I. Davis, *African Trade Unions* (Penguin, Harmondsworth, 1966), pp.127-8.

35. Morawetz, 'Employment Implications', p.517.

36. E.F. Fischlowitz, 'Manpower Problems in Brazil', *International Labour Review* (April 1969), pp.409-10.

37. H.A. Turner, as quoted in I. Little, T. Scitovsky and M. Scott, *Industry and Trade in Some Developing Countries: A Comparative Study* (Oxford University Press for the OECD Development Center, 1970), p.81.

38. W.A. Lewis, as quoted in Little, Scitovsky and Scott, *Industry and Trade,* p.82.

39. For example, see G. Myrdal, *Rich Land and Poor Land* (Harper, New York, 1965), Chapter 20; P.T. Bauer, *Dissent on Development* (Harvard University Press, Cambridge, Mass., 1972), pp.192-3.

40. *Toward Full Employment: A Programme for Colombia* (Geneva, 1970), p.223.

41. Lester B. Pearson *et al.*, *Partners in Development* (Praeger, New York, 1969), p.202.

42. E. Thorbecke, 'The Employment Problem: A Critical Evaluation of Four ILO Comprehensive Country Reports', *International Labour Review,* Vol.107 (May 1973), p.339.

43. A. Rahman, 'Scientists in India', *International Social Science Journal,* Vol.22, No.1 (1970), p.64.

44. M. Blaug, *Education and the Employment Problem in Developing Countries* (ILO, Geneva, 1973), p.9.

Part Two

SOME CASE-STUDIES OF THE INFLUENCE OF ELITES
ON ECONOMIC PLANNING AND POLICY

5 MALAYSIA: FROM COLONIAL TO BUMIPUTRA ELITISM

The Malaysian economy is one of the most 'open' in the world with an export/GDP ratio that has varied between 42 per cent and 51 per cent during 1954-67.[1] This reflects a strong colonial economic structure, dominated by a few primary products such as rubber, tin, oil palm and timber, that keeps Malaysia highly vulnerable to fluctuations in international terms of trade and generates cyclical instability in her domestic growth and development. The same fact mirrors the failure of post-independence economic policies to diversify the economy in order to transform it from a lopsided, dependent status to one manifesting balanced economic growth and equitable distribution of income.

The Malaysian case of lopsided growth is particularly significant inasmuch as it casts doubt on the traditional view of international trade as 'an engine of growth'.[2] Despite the fact that British Malaya was one of the earliest countries to receive large inflows of European investment capital prior to the First World War for the development of export-oriented plantations and tin-mining, the Malaysian enclave sector failed to act as a 'leading sector' generating linkages and spread effects[3] in the rest of the economy. Thus, the economy is still heavily dualistic with a large subsistence sector coexisting with the dynamic, small export-enclave sector. Analysis of the reasons for the failure of international trade to operate as an engine of balanced growth in Malaysia, therefore, makes a revealing case-study of persistent underdevelopment in the Third World countries, throwing light on the dependency controversy.[4]

The main theme of this chapter is that the fundamental explanation for the lopsided growth pattern in Malaysia is to be found in the elitist management of the economy, with economic planning calculated to benefit a small ruling class and foreign interests. In British Malaya, colonial policies, such as cheap labour imports, were designed to create a steadily rising trade balance for the benefit of the mother country and the expatriate ruling class and their commercial counterparts in the enclave sector. Likewise, colonial fiscal and financial policies were so regulated in order to produce a budget surplus which again benefited the foreign interests. After independence in 1957, the British

95

transferred political power to a small Malay aristocracy clustered around the hereditary Sultans. While there has been considerable government emphasis on economic planning since, it has been highly elitist, rather than egalitarian, and the economic structure has remained essentially unchanged since colonial days — this policy being rationalised on the basis of the classical comparative advantage argument. As a result, while the average national income *per capita* is the second highest in the region, there are sharp regional and racial disparities and income inequalities which pose a constant threat to the stability and prosperity of the country. As we shall presently see, the principal gainers of economic growth since independence have been the urban Malay (bureaucratic) elite along with foreign multinational firms.

Colonial Fiscal and Trade Policies

Economic policies in British Malaya were formulated first and foremost for the benefit of the mother country, the colonial ruling class and foreign investors and businessmen.[5] The welfare of the native population was not considered as a direct responsibility of the government; in fact, consistent with the *laissez-faire* philosophy of the time, the administrators deliberately followed a non-interference policy *vis-à-vis* the Malay community.[6]

The Problem of Revenue[7]

One of the earliest problems faced by the British colonial administrators in Malaya was that of raising adequate revenue to pay for the cost of maintaining law and order so that trade and commerce could be conducted in an orderly and profitable way. The problem was made all the more difficult in the early days of colonisation when the Strait Settlements were governed by the East India Company from Bombay, and the company insisted on a policy of free trade. While this assured a highly profitable trade for the company and its stockholders in Britain, it also forced the colonial administrators to impose on the native population highly unfair taxes to pay for the cost of government.[8] The two major sources of revenue in the late nineteenth century were the duty on tin production in Perak and Selangor, and the sale of licences under the tax farming system. During the decade 1885-95, these two sources accounted for about 80 per cent of the total revenue of Perak and Selangor.[9] The tax farming system capitalised on the vices of the Chinese, including opium smoking, gambling, prostitution and liquor.[10] Since the tax farmers were typically leaders of 'secret societies' who regarded their licences as investment, the tax collection was often accompanied with intimidation and violence.

In 1909 the Federated Malay States (FMS) came into being, consisting of Perak, Selangor, Negri Sembilan and Pahang. While the resident system, initiated under the Treaty of Pangkor of 1874, was preserved in theory, in practice the Federation ushered in greater British control of Malaya, with a Resident-General, based in Kuala Lumpur, heading the colonial administrative structure. Under the Federation, and especially as a result of the emergence of rubber as the corner-stone of the economy, the sources of revenue expanded. In 1900 the tin duty brought in nearly 46 per cent of the total revenue, but by 1920 this had declined to less than 17 per cent and to 14 per cent by 1930. In the same fashion, the opium revenue fell from 15 per cent in 1924 to under 10 per cent in 1932. During the first quarter of the twentieth century duty on rubber exports emerged as a major source of revenue, reaching a peak of $11 million in 1926, but dropping to an annual average of only half a million dollars during the depression years of 1931-3 and recovering thereafter (amounts in strait dollars). At the same time, new sources of revenue were realised, notably excise duties on imports of tobacco, petroleum and sugar, and receipts from railways, posts and communications. But as late as the mid-1930s there was no income tax or any form of direct taxation. Since all of the officials of the Malayan civil service were Europeans, receiving lavish salaries and allowances, lack of income tax was a boon to the colonial administrators, while the presence of excise duties, land taxes and other indirect taxes were unduly burdensome on the native population.[11]

The Expenditure Policies

Colonial budget and expenditure policies were not designed for the welfare of the native population, but rather for the promotion of the export-enclave sector. Only the barest minimum allocations were budgeted for public education, health and sanitation. In 1902 total education expenditures amounted to $223,000 or 1.4 per cent of the budget, and most of these funds were assigned to English-medium schools run by missions or directly by the government.[12] The vernacular schooling was ignored in line with the *laissez-faire* policy. The position changed little during the first three decades of the twentieth century; by 1929, educational expenditures by the FMS government represented 3.6 per cent of the budget,[13] although a modest expansion took place in subsequent years.

The provision of public health was somewhat better, but limited in scope. The early residents in Perak and Selangor recognised the relationship of productivity and good health in tin mining, and they earmarked small but steadily increasing amounts to improve health and hospital care for the mining communities. Epidemics of cholera, malaria and beri-beri and other tropical diseases were common occurrences in the tin mines and casualties among Chinese workers as well as European supervisory and technical staff were high. In 1897, the Institute for Medical Research in Kuala Lumpur was founded, largely as a result of the encouragement given to this project by the Secretary for Colonies, Chamberlain. The research done at this Institute in subsequent years was vital to the eventual success in controlling malaria and beri-beri and the development of Malaya's tin and rubber industries.[14] While the colonial administrators and medical officials deserve a lot of credit for these achievements, it must be remembered that the scope of public health programmes was limited to the enclave sector, and actually regarded as an investment in labour productivity on tin mines and plantations. In fact, even these limited health expenditures were liable to be cut in times of economic depression. Thus, during 1929-33, at a time when pensions and allowances to civil servants jumped from $4 million to $6.1 million, public health and medicine expenditures declined from $5.5 million to $4.4 million.[15]

The major component of the FMS expenditures was public works, especially railway construction in the enclave sector on the west coast. The first railway was the Port Weld-Taiping line of 8 miles. It was opened in 1885 and served the tin-mining interests in the Larut district of Perak. It was fully financed out of state revenues. While the Larut line was being constructed, the Selangor government decided to build a railway from its mining centre in Kuala Lumpur to the port of Klang, 22 miles away, through difficult and swampy country. It, too, was financed by state revenues raised locally, despite the fact that the principal beneficiaries were the tin-mining and commercial interests. This pattern of railway construction and financing was the model for subsequent railway development in Malaya.

One of the largest items of expenditures in British Malayan budgets was for personal emoluments, pensions and allowances of civil servants, who were all British and European expatriates. Many qualified and competent local personnel were excluded from public service.[16] Salaries and benefits to the expatriate personnel represented a substantial volume of *invisible* imports into the FMS that supplemented capital outflows during the inter-war years, rising from $8 million in 1916 to

$22 million in 1932.[17] In the Great Depression, when revenues sharply declined, causing many economy measures, pensions, allowances and gratuities more than doubled, increasing from 5 per cent of the budget in 1929 to over 11 per cent in just three years' time.[18]

It is worth quoting Emerson's highly critical view of the imperial rule in Malaya:

> The FMS has been run on a lavish scale by Europeans primarily on behalf of the Europeans and Chinese, and it has been financed, directly or indirectly, almost exclusively from the highly organized European and Chinese tin and rubber industries. The political and administrative structure must be brought down from the empyrean European heights to which it ascended during the boom years until it comes into some sort of organic relation to the whole society which it serves . . . If the economic base of the Federation can be broadened by an effective encouragement of food crops and of other export crops and industries, if the Malay and the Chinese and Indian coolie can be given a real and significant place, it will begin to take on some of the characteristics of an economically sound and socially healthy community; but even this program is more than can be expected within the framework of imperialism].[19]

It is small wonder that Emerson's book was severely criticised by the colonial administrators from the former High Commissioner Sir Frank Swettenham down. What Emerson was especially critical about was the imperial budget policies which he caricatured as *surplusomania*. This was the idea that the fiscal policy of the FMS should be so regulated that it relied on the momentum of prosperity to enable the Federation to get through the times of depression. It was recognised by the FMS government that the economy was vulnerable to fluctuations in the international prices of two commodities, rubber and tin,[20] and as a result, the revenues were apt to rise and ebb according to world trade cycles. In order to stabilise the finances, the FMS government's fiscal policy was aimed at building a budget surplus, and accumulating an increasing amount of reserves for use in depression years. These budget surpluses and reserves, in fact, became a regular phenomenon in both boom years as well as depression years as the data in Table 5.1 indicate. During the period 1875-96, there was only a modest budget surplus, amounting only to 1.2 per cent of average annual revenue. During 1898-1902, the average annual budget surplus increased substantially to represent 9.0 per cent of revenue. In the early 1920s there was a

Table 5.1: Revenues and Expenditures of Federated[a] Malay States, 1875-1935

Period		R	E	S	S/R per cent
		(in millions of strait dollars)			
1875-1896	(1)	3.27	3.23	0.04	1.2
1898-1902	(2)	15.10	13.74	1.36	9.0
1919-1923[b]	(3)	63.04	61.60	1.44	2.3
1927-1935	(3)	64.54	63.20	1.34	2.1

a. FMS was created in 1909.
b. In 1921-2 two long-term development loans (for railway and road construction) totalling $80.1 million were raised in London and a sinking fund was created for its repayment, i.e. out of future FMS revenues. These development expenditures have been excluded from the annual (recurrent) expenditure figures used in the table above. See Emerson, *Malaysia,* p.188.
R = average annual revenue.
E = average annual expenditure.
S = average annual budget surplus.

Sources: (1) E. Sadka, *The Protected Malay States 1874-1895* (Kuala Lumpur, University of Malaya Press, 1968), pp.410-13.
(2) K.G. Tregonning, *A History of Modern Malaya* (Singapore, Eastern University Press for University of London Press, London, 1964).
(3) R. Emerson, *Malaysia: A Study in Direct and Indirect Rule* (Kuala Lumpur, University of Malaya Press, 1964), pp.156, 187.

post-First World War recession which severely hit FMS. Total revenue dropped from $72.1 million in 1919 to $52.5 million. Previously accumulated budget reserves and surpluses of $100 million were largely utilised to pay for the cost of an excessively large bureaucracy and for pensions and allowances payable to colonial civil servants.[21] In addition, the practice of making official donations in substantial amounts to the imperial war effort, as an expression of loyalty of the Malay rulers to the British Empire, was a significant drain on the resource of the FMS. Accordingly, the FMS government felt obliged to borrow in London and accumulate a national debt. In 1921-2 two sterling loans, totalling $80.1 million, were raised; a sinking fund was set up for repayment. While these loans were justified for railway and highway development, the financing method selected in fact burdened the native population from whom future revenues were taxed.

The colonial passion for budget surpluses and reserves was pursued at the expense of the economic well-being of the vast majority of the native population. In the words of Emerson,

The Malays remain much as they were in earlier days although their land is more limited and their dependence on the world economy greater. Among the Chinese there are a few who have grown wealthy, as have the Malay rulers and the aristocracy, *but the bulk of the wealth has been drained away to Singapore and further afield to Europe, America and China.* To the Malay, Chinese, and Indian laborer the difference between prosperity and depression is the difference between a low or inadequate subsistence level on Oriental standards and a small margin above bare subsistence. Between the statistics and indices of progress and the improvement of the conditions of the people there is a vast gap which has scarcely begun to be bridged. It may be regarded as a splendid gesture of imperial loyalty that the Sultan (of Johore) should present £500,000 to the imperial government to speed the Singapore defenses on the occasion of the King's Silver Jubilee in 1935, but he need only have strolled through the back streets of his little capital to have found more significant uses for his generosity [emphasis added].[22]

The roots of poverty and inequality in modern Malaysia go back to the colonial history and traditions of the country.

The Creation of the Dual Economy

The formation of the export-enclave sector in Malaysia is the direct result of the colonial policies. Commercial profit was the|principal objective from the earliest days of British intervention in Malaya down to the rubber boom of the early twentieth century. Since the development of plantations and mines was based on foreign investment funds, profits and dividends were largely returned to Britain and expatriate investors. Table 5.2 contains statistics regarding the international trade of the FMS during 1875-1935. It will be noted that the volume of imports increased by more than ten times and exports by over fifteen times. The international trade of the FMS, conducted largely within a regime of free trade, reflected a steadily rising volume of trade balance. During 1875-96, the trade surplus averaged 10.4 per cent of the combined value of annual imports and exports. During 1899-1902, it was 21.1 per cent. With the onset of the rubber boom, it increased rapidly and reached almost 30 per cent by the early 1920s. Even during the Depression of the 1930s it registered only a minimal decline, dropping from 29.6 per cent to 27.8 per cent. Clearly, the social costs of economic depressions and trade slumps were not felt by foreign commercial interests, nor (as we have already shown) by the

Table 5.2: Imports, Exports and Trade Surpluses in Malay States,
1875-1935

Period	X	M	T B	TS
	(in millions of strait dollars)			per cent
1875-1896	13.2	10.7	2.5	10.4
1899-1902	62.2	40.6	21.6	21.1
1919-1923	208.4	113.3	95.1	29.6
1927-1935	200.5	113.4	87.1	27.8

X = average annual exports.
M = average annual imports.
TB = average annual trade balance = X − M.
$TS = \dfrac{TB.100}{M + X}$ = average annual trade surplus as a percentage of the average annual volume of trade.

Sources: As for Table 5.1.

colonial ruling class. They were passed on to the native population. The mechanics of this unfair process will be discussed shortly. It is first necessary to examine further the manner in which rubber became the corner-stone of the Malayan economy.

The 'Rubber Boom' of the first decade of the twentieth century was the immediate by-product of the new motor-car age. During the early years of the present century there was a shortage of rubber production. This reflected a general reluctance by Western investors to provide investment capital for rubber plantations. The early pioneer planters were private entrepreneurs and speculators operating small 100-acre estates. One of the earliest big London companies to start large-scale estate operations was the Pataling Rubber Company, formed in 1903 by Harrisons and Crosfields of London, which had long been trading in the East. Although investment funds to float the company were raised with difficulty, seven years later in 1910 when the rubber trees reached productive age, large profits were realised and three dividends were declared in that year, returning to the original investors in one year a sum equalling 200 per cent of their investment. From then on Harrison and Crosfield, as well as other similar companies, had no difficulty in floating rubber plantation companies. So profitable was rubber that by 1910, out of a total of 142 estates in Selangor, no less than 122 were owned by European companies, despite the fact that in 1885 there was not a single registered Western rubber company in that state.

The typical Western rubber companies consisted of either agency houses, such as Harrison and Crosfield, Guthries or Sime Darby &

Company, with head offices in London and managed from Singapore; or the rubber manufacturing concerns themselves, such as Dunlop; or other companies, mostly Chinese, floated locally.[23] The managing agents, all European, were paid handsomely for their services by a commission based on the acreage managed, or the profits earned, or both. They also received commissions on the purchases of supplies for the estate and on the sale of the product. In addition, the agency firms developed horizontal and vertical linkages within the export-enclave sector. Thus, shipping lines anxious to participate in the carrying trade appointed them as agents in Singapore and other ports. For similar reasons, they became agents for Western insurance companies. As well, they set up engineering and service departments in order to service estate machinery and equipment, and they became associated with the business of importing machinery and capital goods from Europe.[24]

The Financial Sector and the Currency Board System

The banking and financial sector was the linchpin of the enclave sector. It was dominated by British institutions. The commercial banks specialised in the provision of short-term financing for the export-import trade, with little direct participation in investment for long-term domestic growth.[25] The banks and credit institutions were controlled by the Currency Board System, based on 100 per cent sterling cover rule, i.e. that the currency liabilities be backed by 100 per cent sterling securities issued in London.

While the Currency Board System ensured a balance of payments equilibrium and internal price stability, it was subject to serious limitations. Reserves and surpluses were transmitted to England and the money supply in Malaya was quite unrelated to the long-term growth of the economy. In fact, since accumulation of a balance of payments surplus was impossible, export earnings in periods of trade booms (e.g. the Korean War in the early 1950s) were kept in London in the form of additional sterling reserves; as a result, income multiplier effects were minimised in Malaya, but realised in Britain. On the other hand, in trade slumps, the system generated an automatic 'deflationary bias' through falling prices and incomes in Malaya.[26]

The social costs of the 'deflationary bias' fell disproportionately on the native population, especially the tappers and mine labourers. One of the severest and most inequitable examples of this was the colonial rubber restriction scheme in the 1930s, introduced with a view to offsetting the effects of falling rubber earnings.[27] Under this scheme, many estate workers were thrown out of jobs, small rubber farmers subjected to production cuts, and during 1930-3, 243,000 Indian tappers were repatriated to India.[28] There was a deliberate attempt to restrict production on the small estates. Despite the fact that the Malayan smallholder was producing good rubber at a cost of 0.5 cents per pound in 1932 (as compared to 12 cents on large estates), the administration continued the myth that the small farms were inefficient.[29] This was, in fact, due to the discriminatory policy of identifying the rubber industry with the European-operated large estates. Thus, during the Depression years, thousands of small indigenous rubber farms were merged into one by the Controller of Rubber, who was a senior British officer in the Malayan civil service, and who was charged with the task of implementing the supply restriction scheme. The Controller of Rubber was assisted by a committee of eight, all of whom, except one Malay, were representatives of estates or the colonial administration. The Controller and his committee concentrated their efforts on reducing production on small farms, while favouring the large estates. For example, in 1934, the smallholding production of rubber was 217,000 tons compared with 260,000 tons on the estates. By 1940, the Controller and his committee had seen to it that this smallholding production had dropped to 213,000 tons while that of the estates had risen to 334,000.[30]

These figures tell an astonishing story of favouritism exercised by the colonial authorities in a flagrant violation of the means of livelihood of the native population. Bauer estimates that the rubber production restriction cost the smallholders of Malaya an amount equalling $360 million.[31] This scandalous treatment was not without consequence in the Japanese invasion during the Second World War.

The Creation of the Plural Society: 'Cheap Labour Policy'

Today, the major problem in LDCs is chronic unemployment. At the turn of the century, during the rubber boom, and during the growth of the tin mines before, the major concern of the authorities and European entrepreneurs in Malaya was the problem of persistent labour shortage. Given the reluctance of the native Malay population to accept wage employment on estates and mines, the colonial remedy was the 'Cheap Labour Policy' of organised large-scale imports of unskilled labourers from China (for tin mining) and from India and Ceylon (for rubber estates).[32]

There were three stages in Indian labour imports into Malaya.[33] During the early plantation development stage, the *indenture* system was used. This applied to the coffee and tea estates as well as the early rubber estates in the first decade of the twentieth century. Indentured labourers signed a certificate or contract before leaving Madras by which they pledged themselves to work for 3 to 5 years for a particular estate. It was an unjust system, open to serious abuse. For example, potential labourers were often misled by false promises into signing contracts that were subsequently enforced only by violence or threats of prison. Often, too, the indentured worker would be required to purchase his staples at the estate store, operated for profit by the planter, and he would be deliberately extended excessive credit so as to accumulate a debt forcing him to sign on for further periods of indenture. In 1910, the indenture system was abolished in British colonies and it was replaced in Malaya by the *kangany* system. Under this system, a foreman or senior labourer from the estate was sent back to India, empowered to recruit in his old village. The new recruits would be provided with free passage to Malaya and were employed on the estate on a 3-year contract which would be subject to cancellation on one month's notice by either party.

In 1907, the colonial government started the Indian Immigration Fund in order to cope with increased demand for tappers caused by the rubber boom. Under this scheme, a levy was collected from all estates for the purpose of financing labour migration from India. It operated until 1938, when it was banned by the Indian government.

While the history of the Chinese in Malaya goes back several centuries, especially in the tin-mining state of Perak, the creation of a plural Malaya Peninsula followed the British intervention and colonisation. During the 32 years between 1895 and 1927, some six million Chinese arrived in Singapore from the southern provinces of China such as Fukien, Kwangsi and Kwangtung. In 1877, the British appointed an official Protector of Chinese with the responsibility of overseeing the Chinese community and regulating their secret societies. Previously, Chinese migration occurred under the most appalling conditions, virtually as a slave trade controlled by Chinese labour contractors and coolie brokers.[34] There was public uproar in Britain in the 1860s over reports of inhuman conditions regarding Chinese immigration into the Strait Settlements and the plantations of the Dutch East Indies. Despite opposition to reform from the Singapore shipping and commercial interests, an Ordinance was finally passed in 1874 regulating the Chinese immigration trade. Within three years, an office of Protector of Chinese was created to control the activities of secret societies that actually tyrannised the Chinese communities of Singapore and Malaya. These two reforms introduced a direct line of communication between the colonial administration and the Chinese community who co-operated actively in the economic and commercial development of British Malaya in later years.

It must be noted, however, that ethnic relations in Malaya were compartmentalised and regulated by the authorities with one object in mind: to maintain peace and security for the pursuit of trade and commerce. Within the plural society of Malaya, each ethnic group occupied a definite and distinct status playing a specific economic role, defined, sanctioned and overseen by the British. In this ordered society the roles assigned to the Chinese were those of middlemen in domestic trade, facilitating the profitable import/export business controlled by the European entrepreneurs, as well as workers in the tin mines. The Indian was the rubber-tapper on the European estates. The Malay peasant was left very much on his own, while the British administrators ruled the country in the name of the Sultans.

Post-Independence Growth and *Bumiputra* Elitism

After *Merdeka* (independence) in 1957, political power was transferred to a ruling class of the *Bumiputra* ('Sons of the Soil') clustered around the hereditary Malay Sultans. With technical advice from foreign planners, this elite has strongly endorsed the dualistic growth of the economy on the presumption that Malaysia's comparative advantage lies in plantation and export crop development along traditional lines.[35] While the Malaysian gross domestic product has grown impressively,[36] the country remains dependent on her historic export products, rubber and tin, supplemented in recent years by oil palm and timber. Industrialisation, based on foreign investment, has created a number of branch plants in the small manufacturing sector, concentrated in the vicinity of Kuala Lumpur, but it has made only minimal contribution toward job creation. Open unemployment in urban areas has increased steadily and exceeds 10 per cent of the labour force, according to official figures which, almost certainly, are understated.[37] Migration into towns and cities has also resulted in the growth of urban *kampongs* for poor Malays.

In the rural areas, social and economic conditions have lagged far behind the overall growth performance of the economy. In the large Malay peasant sectors chronic poverty and socio-economic inequities, far from being checked, appear to have actually worsened, despite the official policies promising top priority to rural and community development. Rhetoric and political 'window-dressing' aside, expenditure policies have been utilised by the *Bumiputra* elite controlling the bureaucracy and government to one paramount end: to politicise economic planning and development policy to gain 'exclusive right of access to the rural population'.[38] The elite has devoted its utmost energies on how to get the votes of the large Malay peasant society without altering the basic economic structure of the country, in part because it has yet to fully realise the inherent causality between rural poverty on the one hand and dualism and dependency on the other. The principal beneficiaries of economic growth since *Merdeka* have been the urban Malay elite, and the foreign interests.

In May 1969, Malaysia was the scene of bloody race riots.[39] Although this violence was the immediate by-product of a hotly contested general election which went badly for the ruling Alliance Party, its causes were fundamentally socio-economic, reflecting a severe maldistribution of income and economic opportunity between the Malays, Chinese and Indian races, as well as between the rural and urban regions of the country. Following the riots, the Malaysian government launched a New Economic Policy (NEP) aimed at accelerating the pace of the so-called *Bumiputra* policy, i.e. improving the socio-economic status of the Malays *vis-à-vis* the Chinese and Indian races by direct policies providing for increased Malay ownership and control of the modern sectors of the economy. NEP is the basic philosophy behind the *Second Malaysia Plan, 1971-75 (SMP)*, the *Third Malaysia Plan, 1976-80 (ITMP)*, as well as the *Outline Perspective Plan, 1970-90 (OPP)*. The two fundamental objectives of these documents are eradication of poverty, especially in rural areas, and achievement of a 30 per cent Malay ownership of the manufacturing and commercial sectors by 1990. The feasibility of these objectives is highly doubtful primarily because the specific policies proposed in support of these objectives differ little, if any, from earlier policies, conceived and conducted within a colonial framework. For example, the TMP declares a new National Ideology *(Rukunegara)* designed to forge harmony and unity in the country so as to prevent any recurrence of the racial riots of May 1969.[40] Yet, the OPP and NEP are designed to bring about a drastic restructuring of the ethnic make-up of Malaysia in a way that is bound to generate racial tension and conflict.

This is especially true in the case of the employment policies proposed, which aim at redistributing jobs from the Chinese to the Malay community. As the data in Table 5.3 show, the OPP expects to reduce the Chinese share of employment in the secondary and tertiary sectors from 59.5 per cent and 48.3 per cent respectively, in 1970, to under 40 per cent by 1990, while increasing their share of primary-

Table 5.3: Employment Shares by Race and Sector in Peninsular
Malaysia, 1970-90

Year and Sector	Malay	Chinese	Indian	Others
1970				
P[a]	67.6	21.4	10.1	0.9
S[b]	30.8	59.5	9.2	0.5
T[c]	37.9	48.3	12.6	1.2
1975				
P	67.3	20.7	11.1	0.9
S	36.5	53.3	9.8	0.4
T	42.3	47.3	9.5	0.9
1990				
P	61.4	28.3	9.6	0.7
S	51.9	38.1	9.5	0.5
T	48.4	39.0	11.7	0.9
Population				
1970	52.7	35.8	10.7	0.8
1975	53.1	35.5	10.6	0.8
1990	54.1	34.6	10.6	0.7

a. Primary includes agriculture, fishing and hunting.
b. Secondary includes mining, manufacturing, construction, utilities and transport.
c. Tertiary includes wholesale and retail trade, banking, public administration,
   education, health and defence.
Source: *Third Malaysia Plan*, Table 4-14, p.71.

sector employment from 21.4 per cent to 28.3 per cent. This shift is
expected to work to the advantage of the Malays who, by 1990, are
projected to account for approximately half of the total employment
in the secondary and tertiary sectors and just over 60 per cent of the
primary sector.

Such a drastic transformation is bound to generate increased Chinese
resistance, since traditionally they have concentrated on urban-based
industries rather than agriculture. At any rate, land ownership and
tenure are largely under state jurisdiction rather than federal, and,
therefore, would present serious legal and constitutional obstacles since,
in the past, land alienation laws have often prevented Chinese
ownership.[41]

During 1970-5, there appear to have been considerable gains in
Malay employment in the secondary and tertiary sectors. However,
on closer inspection it is obvious that this gain was due to two factors:
(i) the regulations applied in pioneer firms to favour Malay employment,
and (ii) pro-Malay recruitment policies adopted in the public utilities
sector, which is included in the secondary sector rather than in the

public service. In any event, the number of jobs involved is too small in relation to total employment[42] and most of the Malay employees have been placed in relatively unskilled, low-paying jobs. Future relative gains, especially in magnitudes proposed under the OPP, are very likely to encounter increased resistance from the non-Malays.

Ownership of Industrial Capital

Another major instrument of socio-economic restructuring proposed under the OPP is the 30 per cent Malay ownership of industrial equity capital by 1990. As the data in Table 5.4 indicate, this is a tremendous challenge, since in 1970 the Malay share was no more than 2.4 per cent of equity capital and 2.3 per cent of fixed assets. Evidently, the Malay gains are expected to be at the expense of foreign investors, whose share of equity capital is projected to decline from 63.3 per cent to 30 per cent during 1970-90. The difficulty of this target can be gauged from the fact that recently the Malaysian authorities were obliged to relax restrictions on foreign investment introduced under the Industrial Coordination Act and the Petroleum Development (Amendment) Act of 1975, in order to arrest a serious decline in inflows of private investment funds.[43] The fact remains that the emerging Malaysian secondary sector is heavily dependent on foreign investment and, therefore, any restrictions can only have a negative effect on the existing economic structure.

The Problem of Poverty and Income Inequality

Eradication of poverty and the promotion of a more balanced income distribution are two of the stated objectives of NEP, SMP, TMP and OPP. It is recognised that poverty is especially severe for the Malay community, with two out of every three Malay households living below the official poverty line.[44] Most of these families live in rural areas outside the mainstream of economic and social development realised by the more prosperous sectors and groups.

Yet the Malaysian plans are conspicuous by the relatively small allocation of public expenditure earmarked for a direct attack on the poverty problem. For example, the recently published TMP provides a great deal of statistical and rhetorical information about poverty and income distribution in Malaysia, but, as the data in Table 5.5 demonstrate, the priority areas of public expenditure remain the traditional fields of plantation development, physical infrastructural projects and urban-based industries. Although about one-quarter of total TMP expenditures are allocated for agriculture and rural

Table 5.4: Ownership of Equity Capital and Fixed Assets in Secondary
Sector, by Race, 1970 and 1990 (target)

| Race | Equity Capital (per cent) | | Fixed Assets (per cent) |
	1970	1990 (Target)	1970
Malay and Malay interests	2.4	30.0	2.3
Chinese	27.2)		92.2
Indian	1.1)	40.0	2.3
Other	6.0)		0.8
Foreign	63.3	30.0	2.4

Source: *Third Malaysia Plan*, p.6, and Table 4-16, p.86.

Table 5.5: Allocation of TMP Expenditure, 1976-80, by Sector and
East/West Malaysia[a] ($ million)

Sector	Grand Total	West Malaysia	Per Cent	East Malaysia	Per Cent
Agriculture and rural development	4,735.5	3,901.8	82.4	883.7	17.6
Transport	2,819.0	2,071.3	73.5	747.7	26.5
Communications	1,192.0	1,051.2	88.2	140.8	11.8
Mineral development	5.0	2.0	40.0	3.0	60.0
Feasibility studies	36.0	25.0	69.4	11.0	30.6
Utilities	2,143.0	1,823.2	85.1	319.8	14.9
Commerce and industry	1,734.5	1,600.8	92.3	133.7	7.7
1. Economic sectors sub-total	12,665.2	10,475.6	82.7	2,189.6	17.3
Education and training	1,671.3	1,282.6	76.7	388.7	23.3
Health and family planning	377.2	327.2	86.7	50.0	13.3
Social and community services	1,043.7	901.5	86.4	142.2	13.6
2. Social sectors sub-total	3,092.2	2,511.2	81.2	581.0	18.8
3. General administration sub-total	597.7	418.9	70.0	178.8	30.0
Police	650.0	570.0	87.7	80.0	12.3
Defence	1,550.0	1,470.0	94.8	80.0	5.2
4. Security sub-total	2,200.0	2,040.0	92.7	160.0	6.3
Total	18,555.0	15,445.7	83.2	3,109.3	16.8

a. Includes Federal, state and statutory authority sources.

Source: *Third Malaysia Plan*, Appendix II.

development, the largest components are for plantation development rather than for improvements at the village level. In such sectors as housing, health and welfare, education and training, too, the largest shares of planned expenditures are for urban areas. On the surface the TMP allocation for social sectors combined adds up to no more than 16.3 per cent, which is hardly an adequate share in the light of the tremendous socio-economic inequalities in the country.

There is a second — and more fundamental — shortcoming of the Malaysian long-term plans, namely the official policy of stressing inter-racial income inequalities, while remaining totally silent on the growing economic disparities within the Malay community itself. The TMP and the NEP, drawn up in the aftermath of the 1969 riots, explicitly suggest that ethnic disparities lie at the root of Malaysia's poverty problem.[45] This actually tends to hide a second type of inequality, namely intra-Malay differences, which appear to have become bigger since *Merdeka.*

Trends in Income Shares since 1957

Available data on Malaysian income distribution[46] since *Merdeka* indicate that the aggregate share of the Malay community increased significantly over 1957-70 relative to the Chinese and Indian ethnic groups. Table 5.6 shows that the Malay share of aggregate income increased sharply from about 32 per cent in 1957 to almost 38 per cent in 1970, while the Chinese share declined from 55 per cent to 50 per cent and the Indian share dropped marginally from 13 per cent to 12 per cent. Despite these shifts in racial income shares, the 1970 income distribution was still below the Malay population share (just over 50 per cent) and above the Chinese share (of 35 per cent). To this extent, there is an important problem of inter-racial income disparity; but its magnitude is diminishing, and it is by no means the only form of disparity, as we shall shortly see.

The increased Malay income share was not achieved evenly during 1957-70; nor was it distributed evenly within the Malay community. There is evidence indicating that most of the improvement occurred during the first five years of *Merdeka,* and it was related to the sudden growth of Malay public service employment. Table 5.7, computed from the value-added shares of the Malay and non-Malay races in 1962 and 1967, shows that the Malay share of gross domestic product (at factor cost) remained virtually constant at between 36 and 37 per cent over this period. This is a highly significant result, implying that the policies followed prior to the 13 May 1969 riots were generally

Table 5.6: Malaysian Income Distribution, by Race, 1957 and 1970
(all amounts in Malaysian $ million)

	1957 (1)		1970 (2)	
Race	Total Individual Income	Per Cent Share	Total Individual Income	Per Cent Share
Malay	1,150	32.2	1,860	37.8
Chinese	1,950	54.5	2,483	50.5
Indian	475	13.3	578	11.7
Total[a]	3,575	100.0	4,921	100.0

a. Excludes Europeans and others.

Sources: (1) Household Budget-Survey, Report of Inland Revenue Department, 1958, and Census of Malaya, 1957, as tabulated in T.H. Silcock and E.K. Fisk (eds.), *The Political Economy of Independent Malaya* (University of California Press, Berkeley and Los Angeles, 1963), p.279. (2) *Third Malaysia Plan,* Tables 9-5 and 9-6.

Table 5.7: Racial Distribution of Gross Domestic Product (at Factor Cost) of West Malaysia, 1962-7

	1962	1967
Value Added/Person (Malaysian dollars)		
Malay	511	657
Non-Malay	886	1,128
Population (million)		
Malay	3.75	4.0
Non-Malay	3.74	3.9
Value Added (million Malaysian dollars)		
Malay	1,916	2,628
Non-Malay	3,314	4,399
Total GDP (million Malaysian dollars)	5,230	7,027
Malay share (per cent)	36.6	37.4
Non-Malay share (per cent)	63.4	62.6

Source: Computed from data in Lim Lin Lean, 'Racial Income Differentials in West Malaysia', *Kajian Ekonomic Malaysia,* Vol.VII, No.1 (June 1970). For further details see Ozay Mehmet, 'Racial and Rural-Urban Distribution of Income in Malaysia, 1962-67', *Proceedings of the Conference on Southeast Asia,* Canadian Council for Southeast Asian Studies (University of Guelph, 14-15 November 1975).

ineffective in their aim of increasing the Malay share of national income. On closer study, however, this is a plausible result, as a review of rural and industrial development policies will show.

Rural Development as a Political Tool

Consider first the rural and community development policies. Although development plans earmarked substantial amounts of public expenditure for these purposes, in practice only relatively small amounts were actually spent, partly because of rivalry and competition between various administrative agencies concerned with rural development (e.g. Ministry of National and Rural Development, FLDA and RIDA), but mainly because the *Bumiputra* elite regarded rural and community development as a political tool to be used for self-survival. Key politicians, such as Tun Razak, were accustomed to distributing public funds during political trips to rural communities as a means of winning popular support. The typical promise was to build a mosque, community hall or some small village project.[47]

Under the *First Five Year Malaya Plan (1956-60)*, prepared prior to *Merdeka*, 24 per cent of total planned expenditure was allocated to agriculture and rural development.[48] This allocation was dropped to 18 per cent under the *Second Five Year Malaya Plan (1961-65)* in line with the new emphasis on the development of urban-based infrastructure and social overhead capital. Although the next plan, i.e. *First Malaysia Plan (1966-70)*, contained a 31 per cent allocation for agricultural and rural development, much of the amount was for land-clearing and plantation development under the Federal Land Development Authority (FLDA), and it was largely unspent owing to delays.[49] The largest FLDA scheme was the Jengka Triangle project, financed with World Bank assistance, covering over 330,000 acres in the State of Pahang.[50]

At the community (i.e. *kampong*) level, only marginal efforts were initiated to improve the social and economic well-being of the inhabitants. Government schemes designed to break the unfair monopoly/monopsony activities of traditional money-lenders and middlemen generally proved inadequate.[51] For example, the Federal Agricultural Marketing Authority (FAMA), created in 1966 to provide marketing facilities and research assistance to rural smallholders, was virtually inoperative by the end of the 1960s.[52] The Federal Land Rehabilitation and Consolidation Authority (FELCRA) which was also established in 1966, was able to settle only 2,400 settlers by 1970. An attempt to introduce rural co-operatives was virtually a total failure owing to lack of supervision and political control. Political interference with the selection of settlers on FLDA schemes as well as in the management of these schemes was a regular practice, and it was generally counter-productive.[53]

Industrialisation Policies

Measures designed to increase Malay participation in the modern sectors, too, had limited success.[54] Thus, during the years following *Merdeka,* various schemes were launched to provide loans and credits to Malay businesses through Bank Bumiputra, MARA and other institutions. Due to managerial deficiencies, as well as political interference in the allocation of credits, there was considerable waste and inefficiency. While the MARA Institute in Petaling Jaya trained an increasing supply of Malay accountants, book-keepers and technicians, they could obtain few jobs in the private sector owing to the ethnic fragmentation of the labour market.[55] Prior to May 1969, there was a growing problem of unemployed Malay graduates, many of whom became politically active. Government regulations requiring increased Malay ownership of private industry were equally ineffective and could easily be evaded by the Malaysian tokenism known as the 'Ali Baba' practice.[56]

As with other LDCs, Malaysia began independence with a wide-ranging incentives scheme to attract foreign investment capital to develop import-substituting (and later) export-promoting domestic manufacturing and processing industries. Called the Pioneer Industries Programme, the scheme was administered by a new Federal Industrial Development Authority (FIDA). As a result of active world-wide search, FIDA was quite successful in attracting a large and rising volume of private investment funds into Malaysia (see Table 5.4). The Pioneer Industries Programme, however, had significant social costs. For one thing, the enterprises and firms created have generally been capital-intensive; thus by 1974, only 93,668 new jobs were created[57] — a mere 16 per cent of 588,000 additional jobs generated during 1970-5.[58] In addition, it is obvious from the ownership of equity capital that much of the benefits of industrial growth accrued to foreign interests rather than to Malaysians themselves. Outflows of dividends are not only reminiscent of colonial times, but also represent a serious balance of payments burden on the country.[59]

On balance, the growth pattern in the private sector since *Merdeka* was such that only marginal gains accrued to the Malay community as a whole. But there was a rapid expansion of Malay employment in the public service sector, reflecting the preferential recruitment policies of the Malaysian government.

Intra-Ethnic Income Inequality

While the overall income shares of the Malays and non-Malays appeared
to have stayed stationary during the 1960s, there were significant shifts
within each ethnic group leading to greater inequality. Rising intra-
ethnic inequality is a problem that is little discussed in Malaysia;
Malaysian plans are totally silent on the matter. Significantly, the
Malay community manifested the fastest growth of this type of
inequality during 1957-70, although both the Chinese and Indian races
registered widening disparities between the rich and poor. The most
recent and comprehensive data on this matter are found in the work
of D.R. Snodgrass, summarised in Table 5.8. The Gini coefficient of
inequality rose from .342 to .466 for the Malays; from .374 to .455 for
the Chinese; and from .347 to .463 for the Indians. The data clearly
imply that the type of economic planning and policy which have been
followed in Malaysia since independence have benefited the wealthy
and the upper classes within each of the three races, whereas the bottom
80 per cent lost ground.

Table 5.8: Distribution of Income Within Malay, Chinese and Indian
Ethnic Groups, 1957/8-1970

	Per Cent of Total Income					
Year	Top 5 per cent	Top 10 per cent	Top 20 per cent	Next 40 per cent	Bottom 40 per cent	Gini ratio
			Malays			
1957/8	18.1	27.6	42.5	38.0	19.5	.342
1967/8	22.2	32.7	48.2	34.8	17.0	.400
1970	24.6	36.2	52.5	34.8	12.7	.466
			Chinese			
1957/8	19.6	30.5	45.8	36.2	18.1	.374
1967/8	19.9	31.7	46.7	36.3	17.0	.391
1970	25.3	37.1	52.6	33.5	13.9	.455
			Indians			
1957/8	19.5	29.5	43.7	36.6	19.7	.347
1967/8	22.3	32.7	48.1	35.6	16.3	.403
1970	28.2	39.6	54.2	31.5	14.3	.463

Source: D.R. Snodgrass, 'Trends and Patterns in Malaysian Income Distribution,
1957-70' in D. Lim (ed.), *Readings on Malaysian Economic Development*
(Oxford University Press, Kuala Lumpur, 1975), p.264.

The intra-Malay inequality is of a special significance. It is not only politically embarrassing to the Malay ruling class, but it is heavily concentrated in the backward rural sector where subsistence farming and fishing predominate. According to the TMP, 74 per cent of all the official poor population in Peninsular Malaysia in 1970 were Malays, mostly in rural areas.[60] In urban areas, too, there are sharp differences in living standards between the aristocratic Malays and the underprivileged squatters in urban *kampongs,* who have drifted into towns in recent years in search of jobs and opportunities. But the really critical problem in the country continues to be the persistence of rural Malay poverty.

Malay Conservatism: The Root Causes of Rural Poverty

The Malaysian growth strategy and experience since 1957 represent a classic case of elite resistance to modernisation and progress. This is the fundamental explanation for the failure of the authorities to deal with the economic and social causes of rural poverty and backwardness. The elite resistance to change is, in turn, partly due to motives of political survival on the part of the existing ruling class, but even more fundamentally it stems from the traditional conservatism of Malay society itself. Social, economic and personal relations among the Malays are still based on feudal and archaic custom and tradition, untouched by post-independence planning or development. Thus, financial and economic transactions and land tenure, as well as family and kinship relationships, are rigidly regulated by customary values. Partly derived from Moslem religion, and partly from pre-Moslem Malay heritage, these traditional customs pose as the greatest obstacle for social and economic development. Ignorance, illiteracy and a fatalistic acceptance of poverty adversely affect personal initiative and desire for self-improvement.[61]

The traditional Malay conservatism is actively promoted, and utilised to good advantage, by the ruling elite and vested interests. As we have seen, the political leadership has a strong inclination to equate economic development with political control of the rural community, and is more interested in cultivating (if not actually exploiting) the religious customs of the Malay peasantry than in the elimination of their poverty. Thus, it tends to focus, in economic planning and policy statements, on inter-racial disparities in incomes while totally ignoring intra-Malay inequalities.

The present analysis leads to the conclusion that the remedy for Malaysian poverty may actually require *structural* changes in the economy, along with far-reaching political reform to secularise Malay politics and rural development. So far as the former are concerned, a central (long-run) objective would seem to be the reduction of the external dependency of the country on a handful of primary products[62] in favour of agrarian diversification focused on food production utilising the smallholder. This would necessarily include the relevant elements of the egalitarian development policy instruments discussed in Part Three. Industrial diversification, on the other hand, is a growth strategy that must remain dependent on foreign investment and export markets. As such, it would hardly be more satisfactory than the country's long experience with dualistic growth as a primary producer, especially in view of limited export opportunities for LDC manufactures in rich countries. Needless to say, agrarian diversification suggested above would tend to conflict with vested elite interests (both at the federal and state levels) whose wealth, status and power are derived from an externally dependent economy managed at home according to colonial formulae. And therein lies the crux of the Malaysian poverty problem.

Disparities between East and West Malaysia

Not the least economic and political challenge facing Malaysia stems from the geographic fact that the Federation is split into two parts: West Malaysia and East Malaysia, separated by 500 miles of the South China Sea. The latter, made up of Sabah and Sarawak, is rich in natural resources, especially timber, oil palm and petroleum. Yet it lags behind West Malaysia in every respect: retained income *per capita,* population density, physical infrastructure, social overhead facilities, etc.[63] The substantial export earnings realised from the exploitation and export of natural resources of Sabah and Sarawak benefit chiefly West Malaysia, along with the foreign interests involved in this exploitation. According to Table 5.5, TMP allocates a total of $3,109.3 million for public expenditure in East Malaysia during 1976-80, i.e. 16.8 per cent of total TMP expenditure. This sum is only a small fraction of the export earnings of East Malaysia during 1971-5. This pattern inevitably brings to mind the tragic fate of Pakistan, which will be examined in Chapter 7.

Notes

1. Douglas S. Paauw and John C. Fei, *The Transition in Open Dualistic Economies, Theory and Southeast Asian Experience* (Yale University Press, New Haven, Conn., and London, 1973), p.220.

2. This term was originally used by D.H. Robertson in 'The Future of International Trade', reprinted in American Economic Association, *Readings in the Theory of International Trade* (Blackiston, Philadelphia, 1949), p.501. For a recent reassessment of this classical view, see I.B. Kravis, 'Trade as a handmaiden of Growth: Similarities between the Nineteenth and Twentieth Centuries', *Economic Journal,* Vol.LXXX, No.320 (December 1970).

3. One of the earliest studies of linkages in development is A.O. Hirschman, *The Strategy of Economic Development* (Yale University Press, New Haven, Conn., 1958). A micro case-study of linkages in Malaysia is given in J.T. Thoburn, 'Exports and the Malaysian Engineering Industry: A Case Study of Backward Linkage', *Oxford Bulletin of Economics and Statistics,* Vol.35, No.2 (May 1973).

4. This controversy, with strong roots in Marxist ideology, is the dominant theme in the writings of such writers as Samir Amir, R. Prebisch, H.W. Singer, G. Frank, P. Baran and other neo-Marxists.

5. A classic study of British imperialism in Malaya is Rupert Emerson's book: *Malaysia, A Study in Direct and Indirect Rule* (University of Malaya Press, Kuala Lumpur, 1964). When it was first published in 1937 it was greeted with open hostility from former British members of the Malayan civil service, including Sir Frank Swettenham, who found the term 'Malaysia' in the title 'repellent'. A more favourable study is Lennox A. Mills, *British Rule in Eastern Asia, A Study of Contemporary Government and Economic Development in British Malaya and Hong Kong* (Oxford University Press, London, 1942). A recent study is Paauw and Fei, *The Transition in Open Dualistic Economies.*

6. A notable exception to this non-interference policy is the British initiative and influence with respect to the abolition of the Malay custom of 'debt slavery'. For details see B. Lasker, *Human Bondage in Southeast Asia* (University of North Carolina Press, North Carolina, 1950). For a detailed report of debt slavery in Perak at the turn of the century, with original documents, see E. Sadka, *The Protected Malay States 1874-1895* (University of Malaya Press, Kuala Lumpur, 1968).

7. A historical account of the problem of revenue is given in K.G. Tregonning, *The British in Malaya; the First Forty Years 1867-1926* (University of Arizona Press, Tucson, Arizona, 1965), esp. Ch.5.

8. Prior to the coming of the European powers, the local rulers in the Malay archipelago had a variety of taxes on trade and commerce — their main source of revenue — as well as taxes on local produce, land and poll taxes, varying in incidence and method of collection according to local custom. The abolition of import and export levies effectively cut off the primary source of funds of the local rulers and made them dependent upon the colonial powers. The British in Malaya had a system of paying salaries to *Pengulus* (local chiefs) which effectively placed them under British control and influence. See Sadka, *The Protected Malay States*, p.332 *et seq.* On the flourishing indigenous trade and commerce prior to the appearance of Europeans in the Malay archipelago, see Benjamin Higgins, *Economic Development, Principles, Problems and Policies* (Norton, New York, 1959), p.683 *et seq.*

9. Sadka, *The Protected Malay States,* p.332.

10. For details of early tax farming methods, see Tregonning, *The British in Malaya,* p.61 *et seq.*

11. Emerson, *Malaysia,* p.189.

12. Chai, Hon-Chan, *The Development of British Malaya 1896-1919* (Oxford University Press, Kuala Lumpur, 1964), p.252 *et seq.*

13. Emerson, *Malaysia,* p.191.

14. See Chai, *The Development of British Malaya,* Ch.9, for more details.

15. Emerson, *Malaysia,* p.191. Amounts in Malayan dollars.

16. See Chai for details of highly qualified native personnel who could not enter the elitist Malayan civil service, which was reserved for British and Europeans.

17. Emerson, *Malaysia,* p.190.

18. Ibid., p.191.

19. Ibid., pp.192-3.

20. 'The Chief Secretary of the FMS said in 1931: "Our administrative structure has been built on trade prices"' — Emerson, ibid., p.190.

21. Ibid., p.156.

22. Ibid., p.220.

23. Tregonning, *The British in Malaya,* pp.197-8.

24. G.C. Allen and Audrey C. Donnithrone, *Western Enterprise in Indonesia and Malaya* (Allen and Unwin, London, 1962), p.53.

25. Ibid., p.59.

26. P.J. Drake, *Financial Development in Malaya and Singapore* (Australian National University Press, Canberra, 1969), esp. pp.59-63. Also see W.M. Corden, 'The Malayan Balance of Payments Problem' in *The Political Economy of Independent Malaya,* edited by T.H. Silcock and E.K. Fisk (University of California Press, Berkeley and Los Angeles, 1963), esp. pp.123-7.

27. In 1932 the price of rubber had dropped to 5 cents per pound from $2 in 1925. Few European-managed estates could then cut costs to below 12 cents per pound, while the native family-owned farms had far more flexibility in cost-saving. For more details see P.T. Bauer, *The Rubber Industry* (Longmans, London, 1948); also see the pros and cons of the colonial rubber policies in the articles by Bauer and Silcock reprinted in Part III of *Readings in Malayan Economics,* edited by T.H. Silcock (Eastern Universities Press, Singapore, 1961).

28. While 127,000 Indians migrated during this period, 370,000 went back to India. See K.G. Tregonning, *A History of Modern Malaya* (Eastern Universities Press, Singapore, 1964), p.205, footnote 18.

29. Ibid., p.204, footnote 17.

30. Further details are given in Bauer, *The Rubber Industry,* and Norman Parmer, *Colonial Labor Policy and Administration, A History of Labor in the Rubber Plantation Industry of Malaya, c. 1910-1941* (J.J. Augustin, New York, 1960).

31. Bauer, *The Rubber Industry,* p.100.

32. A brief account of colonial cheap labour policies in the south-east Asian context is given in H. Hla Myint, *The Economics of Developing Countries* (Hutchinson, London, 1973). A historical discussion of labour utilisation in south-east Asia is given in G. Myrdal, *Asian Drama: An Inquiry into the Poverty of Nations* (Pantheon, New York, 1968), esp. Part V.

33. Parmer, *Colonial Labor Policy.* Also see J.C. Jackson, *Immigrant Labour and the Development of Malaya 1786-1920* (University of Malaya Press, Kuala Lumpur, Singapore, 1968).

34. The history of Chinese immigration is presented in V. Purcell, *The Chinese in Malaya* (London, 1948); *idem, The Chinese in South-east Asia* (London, 1951). A brief account is given in Tregonning, *A History of Modern Malaya,* pp.173-85.

35. For recent studies of Malaysian economic conditions, see David Lim, *Economic Growth and Development in West Malaysia, 1947-1970* (Oxford University Press, Kuala Lumpur, Singapore, 1973); David Lim (ed.), *Readings on*

Malaysian Economic Development (Oxford University Press, Kuala Lumpur, 1975).

36. During 1957-60, GDP (at factor cost) increased at over 6 per cent p.a.; at 7.4 per cent p.a. during the Second Malaysia Plan period 1971-5; and it is projected to grow at an average rate of 8.2 per cent p.a. over the period 1976-90. See Malaysia, *Third Malaysia Plan, 1976-1980* (Kuala Lumpur, 1976), p.3 and Table 4-4, p.58 (hereafter referred to as *TMP*).

37. See the article by D.J. Blake, 'Unemployment: The West Malaysian Example', reprinted in Lim, *Readings on Malaysian Economic Development.* Unemployment among the age group 15-19 is as high as 20 per cent, especially for the urban youth. See TMP, p.141. In addition to open unemployment, there is a significant volume of rural underemployment, with more than 10 per cent of the rural labour force working under 25 hours a week. See TMP, p.141.

38. Gayl D. Ness, *Bureaucracy and Rural Development in Malaysia* (University of California Press, Berkeley and Los Angeles, 1967), p.216.

39. See John Slimming, *Malaysia: Death of a Democracy* (John Murray, London and Southampton, 1969). For a more concise analysis of the May 1969 riots, see the author's 'Race Riots in Malaysia', *Queen's Quarterly,* Vol.LXXVIII, No.2, Summer 1971.

40. *TMP*, p.1.

41. For a detailed, but somewhat biased discussion of FLDA policies, see R. Wikkramatileke, 'Federal Land Development in West Malaysia 1957-1971' in Lim, *Readings on Malaysian Economic Development,* in which one finds the curious remark: 'the reduced number of Chinese and Indians now seeking placements on the [FLDA] schemes is likely to be in the interests of continued tranquillity in the long run' (p.120).

42. Total manufacturing employment in 1975 was 363,000, whereas the number of jobs created by the pioneer industries during 1971-4 was about 94,000 (i.e. about 25 per cent). However, the manufacturing industry represented only 11 per cent of total 1975 employment of 3,317,000. See *TMP,* Table 8-2, p.142.

43. R. Sutter, 'Malaysia: Tighter Control Over Foreign Capital', *Intereconomics,* No.3 (1976); see also the article on Malaysia, 'A Drive to Step Up Foreign Investment', *Business Week,* 25 October 1976, p.49.

44. *TMP,* p.5 *et seq.* For additional information on the problem of Malay poverty, see Ungku A. Aziz, 'Poverty and Rural Development in Malaysia', *Kajian Ekonomi Malaysia,* Vol.1, No.1 (1964); E.K. Fisk, *Studies in the Rural Economy of Southeast Asia* (Eastern Universities Press, Singapore, 1964); M. Rudner, 'The Malayan Quandary: Rural Development Policy Under the First and Second Five-Year Plans', reprinted in Lim, *Readings on Malaysian Economic Development,* as well as Ness, *Bureaucracy and Rural Development.*

45. The 'restructuring' policies on which the NEP and OPP are based focus attention on the income and wealth differentials between the Malays and non-Malay races, especially Chinese. See *TMP,* especially Chapter IX dealing with poverty and racial disparities.

46. Other studies of Malaysian income distribution patterns – all showing increased inequality – are by D.R. Snodgrass, 'Trends and Patterns in Malaysian Income Distribution, 1957-70' in Lim, *Readings on Malaysian Economic Development;* and L.L. Lim, 'Income Distribution in West Malaysia' in *Income Distribution, Employment and Economic Development in South East and East Asia* (The Japanese Economic Research Center, Tokyo, and the Council for Asian Manpower Studies, Manila, July 1975), Vol.I. Some of the data utilised in this chapter are from the author's own calculations, using sources indicated at the end of the relevant tables.

47. For additional and specific details, see Ness, *Bureaucracy and Rural Development,* esp. pp.214 *et. seq.*

48. The percentages in this sentence and the following two are based on data in the various plans as tabulated by Stephen Chee, *Rural Development and Development Administration in Malaysia,* SEADAG Papers, No.74-5 (New York), Table 5, p.12.

49. During 1961-5, FLDA was able to develop 119,000 acres of land and to settle about 8,000 families, or about 48,000 persons. Under the First Malaysia Plan period, viz. 1966-70, it developed about 179,000 acres (as compared with the Plan target of 400,000 to 450,000 acres) and settled 11,900 families (as compared with a target of 21,250 families). The achievements under the Second Malaysia Plan covering 1971-5 were significantly better. See *TMP,* p.302 *et seq.* and Table 16-2.

50. See Federal Land Development Authority, *Annual Report, 1969* (Kuala Lumpur).

51. P.F. Bell and J. Tai, 'Markets, Middlemen and Technology; Agricultural Response in the Dualistic Economies of Southeast Asia', *Malayan Economic Review* (April 1969); Clifton R. Wharton, Jr., 'Marketing, Merchandising and Moneylending: A Note on Middleman Monopsony in Malaya', *Malayan Economic Review,* Vol.VII, No.2 (1962).

52. For an assessment of the land and rural development policies up to 1970, see Lim, *Economic Growth,* esp. Ch.10.

53. The early settler selection procedures of FLDA are discussed in Ness, *Bureaucracy and Rural Development,* pp.136-9. For an interesting study of social rates of return on a specific land scheme, see I.M.D. Little and D.G. Tipping, *A Social Cost Benefit Analysis of the Kulai Oil Palm Estate* (OECD, Paris, 1972).

54. Lim, *Economic Growth,* Ch.12; Wolfgang Kasper, *Malaysia, A Study in Successful Economic Development* (American Enterprise Institute for Public Policy Research, Washington, DC, 1974); Lim, *Readings,* Part V.

55. See the author's study, 'Manpower Planning and Labour Markets in Developing Countries: A Case Study of West Malaysia', *Journal of Development Studies,* Vol.8, No.2 (January 1971).

56. See Oliver Popenoe, 'A Study of Malay Entrepreneurs', reprinted in Lim, *Readings.* This study, based on a survey of 140 leading Malay businessmen plus a stratified sample of 150 other Malays, concluded that: 'The preferential granting of licences and concessions in a great many instances has not produced new Malay businessmen but only Ali Baba businesses in which the Malay Ali provides the licence and the Chinese Baba runs the business' (p.350).

57. *TMP,* p.143.

58. *TMP,* p.140.

59. The Malaysian balance of payments, and the country's heavy dependence on export earnings, are discussed in G.R. Munro, 'The Malaysian Balance of Payments to 1980: Part I' and 'The Malaysian Balance of Payments to 1980: Part II' in Lim, *Readings.*

60. *TMP,* para.561, p.179. The absolute poverty line in this context is subject to the measurement problems discussed in Chapter 3.

61. Brien K. Parkinson, 'Non-Economic Factors in the Economic Retardation of the Rural Malays', *Modern Asian Studies,* Vol.1, Part 1 (January 1967), reprinted in Lim, *Readings;* Syed H. Alatas, 'Feudalism in Malaysian Society: A Study in Historical Continuity', *Civilisations,* Vol.18, No.4 (1964); *idem,* 'The Grading of Occupational Prestige Amongst the Malays in Malaysia', *Journal of the Malaysian Branch of the Royal Asiatic Society* (July 1968). On kinship and social customs amongst Malays, see Judith Djamour, *Malay Kinship and Marriage in Singapore* (London School of Economics, Monographs on Social Anthropology,

No.21, 1959).

62. In this connection it is interesting to note the conclusion of a recent study of plantation economies, including Malaysia, by George L. Beckford: 'To put the matter rather bluntly', he writes, 'the plantation system must be *destroyed* if the people of plantation society are to secure economic, social, political and psychological advancement' (emphasis added): *Persistent Poverty, Underdevelopment in Planatation Economies of the Third World* (Oxford University Press, New York, 1972), p.215. While this conclusion may be too drastic for Malaysia, our own study would support his finding that 'the sum of social costs (of colonial plantation development) always tends to outweigh the sum of social benefits by a significant margin' (p.213) and that this is causally linked to persistent underdevelopment and poverty. Beckford cites other studies of plantation economies that confirm this conclusion, including Guerra's study on Cuba, Nicholl's on Brazil, Snodgrass's on Ceylon, Geertz's on Indonesia, and Jacoby's on south-east Asia (p.214).

63. John C. Beyer, 'Regional Inequalities and Economic Growth in Malaysia', *Yorkshire Bulletin of Economic and Social Research,* Vol.21, No.1 (May 1969).

6 LIBERIA: THE AMERICO-LIBERIAN ELITE

Liberia, in West Africa, has one of the most compact and durable elites in the world. It is characterised by an unusually high degree of concentration of wealth and political power in a handful of families, known as the 'honourable' class of Americo-Liberians.[1] Even though this class represents less than 4 per cent of the total population of 1.5 million, it has dominated the economic, social and political life of the country since its founding in 1822 by freed slaves from the USA with moral and financial support from a number of American missionary organisations. The Americo-Liberian elite, made up of the descendants of the original settlers, received in 1970 over 60 per cent of the national income, whereas in the large subsistence sector the average income *per capita* was estimated at $70 per annum[2] — a mere 2 per cent of the average individual income for members of the elite (Table 6.1). The estimated Gini coefficient of income inequality (viz. 0.63) is among the highest in the world.

Table 6.1: Income Distribution in 1970, by Rural Urban Areas and Economic Status

Area and Economic Status	Population (thousand)	Per Cent	Income Per Capita (dollars)	Total Income (thousand dollars)	Per Cent
Rural	1,123	73.7	70	78,610	24.6
Urban					
Unskilled — no job[a]	52	3.4	75	3,900	1.2
Concession	109	7.2	100	10,900	3.4
Unskilled — job	52	3.4	150	7,800	2.4
Skilled	128	8.4	200	25,600	8.0
Top income-group[b]	59	3.9	3,272	193,020	60.4
Gini Coef. = 0.63					
Total	1,523	100.0	210	319,830	100.0

a. Defined as lack of formal employment.
b. The Americo-Liberian elite.

Source: MPEA, *Indicative Manpower Plan of Liberia for the Period 1972-1982* (Monrovia, June 1974), p.53 (based on the estimates of the International Bank for Reconstruction and Development).

A Synopsis of Liberian History

Liberia has the dubious distinction of being the original case of 'growth without development'.[3] A proper understanding of this phenomenon requires some knowledge of Liberian history. Only a brief sketch can be offered here.[4]

From 1822 to 1847 Liberia was a settler colony, administered and financed largely by the American Colonization Society and other missionary groups that hoped to create a beach-head for Christianity in dark Africa. The freed slaves, repatriated to Africa, were to take part in a bold, new experiment dedicated to the ideals of liberty and freedom from slavery. The name 'Liberia' and the national motto, 'The Love of Liberty Brought Us Here', were testimony to the lofty expectations of the philanthropists who launched the Liberia project. In recognition of the good offices of the then American President Monroe, the capital city of Monrovia was named.

From the very beginning, the originators of Liberia were imbued with two paramount ideals: (1) a self-proclaimed manifest destiny to bring 'civilisation' and Christianity to the African tribes; and (2) a strong emotional and cultural attachment to American norms and values. Hence arose the fundamental distinction, written into the constitution, between the 'civilised' Americo-Liberian group, descending from the settlers and the aboriginal population (Art.V, Secs.14,15). As with some European colonisers elsewhere in Africa, the Americo-Liberian settlers subdued the tribes with force, beginning with questionable land 'purchases' in 1821-2 in exchange for beads, muskets and tobacco given to local chiefs.[5] The relations between the Americo-Liberians and the native population since 1822 have been dominated by almost constant warfare, exploitation and mistrust.

In 1847, faced with the threat of British colonial expansion in West Africa, Liberia declared herself an independent republic and the first President, J.J. Roberts,[6] sought USA protection and financial assistance. Since then, Liberian dependence on American aid has been crucial to her survival, especially during the European 'scramble for Africa' prior to 1914. Interestingly, Liberian authorities have lamented the fact that Liberia was not a European colony and thus was denied the 'benefits of colonialism'.[7] In fact, however, American influence was so great that the country was effectively a USA colony. Its constitution is virtually an exact copy of the American model; the Liberian flag is identical to the American except that it has only one star; and the American dollar is the national currency.

Under American tutelage, Liberia evolved as a bastion of privilege; an exclusive monopoly of the Americo-Liberian ruling class. In 1877, the True Whig Party was established, and the country has been a virtual one-party state ever since — a prototype of the now common African one-party regimes. Over the years, the Americo-Liberian elite has developed a system of government and public service with one objective in mind: the preservation of its privileged position. This oligarchical state has been maintained partly through the exclusive True Whig Party, and partly through a 'caste-like' web of family-lodge-church cliques,[8] ultimately converging on the incumbent President of Liberia. The Americo-Liberian elite controls the political process and the bureaucracy, and makes all important decisions (usually secretly) affecting political matters, appointments, government contracts and concession agreements with foreign firms. Senior officials and Ministers are selected more on the basis of family connections than on personal merit.[9] All public officials serve at the pleasure of the President, and there are no uniform procedures for recruitment, promotion, salary scales or fringe benefits. As described by Elliot Berg:

> For more than 100 years the Liberian government operated like a kind of private club — without budgets, records, accounts, filing systems and procedures for making public decisions and executing them once made. It was a system in which expenditure control resided in the presidential power to sign all checks over $25, and in which formal budgeting was also unknown, it was something dealt with in conversation with the President. That things worked this way didn't matter much before the 1950's, since governments had only a few million dollars to spend anyway, most of it for salaries.[10]

Prior to 1950 Liberia was a small, virtually bankrupt West African state. Its international image had been badly damaged as a result of the slavery scandals of 1929-30 when the President and Vice-President were forced to resign following a damaging report by an International Commission of Inquiry appointed by the League of Nations.[11] The only major and viable enterprise in the country was the Firestone rubber plantation at Harbel started in 1926.

The Liberian Economic Take-Off

The assumption of the Presidency in 1944 by William Tubman[12] marks the turning-point in the history of Liberia. Under Tubman a programme of political integration was started, designed to bring the tribal population, long neglected and exploited, into the mainstream of Liberian economic and political life.[13] As a result, in the last two decades, a growing number of persons from the interior have been given access to education and public service, although key positions are still denied them. In the preceding decades, education for the tribal population was regarded as futile, except where provided through the 'ward system'. Under this system, members of the Americo-Liberian elite 'adopted' promising rural youths to be raised and educated for urban life. While sometimes abused, the 'ward system' has produced several important figures in Liberian history.[14]

Of more immediate concern than the political integration policy, President Tubman launched a far-reaching 'open door policy' of attracting foreign investment into Liberia. This proved so successful that during the 1950s and 1960s Liberian GNP growth rate was one of the highest in the world. With an annual average rate of over 12 per cent, the Liberian growth was preceded only by Japan and led external observers to refer to yet another instance of economic miracle.[15] By 1967, there were over 40 major foreign concerns and many smaller ones operating in Liberia with a total investment capital of $750 million. Whereas in 1950 Liberia lacked a mining sector, by 1970 she became Africa's leading producer and exporter of iron-ore, possessing the continent's largest single joint-venture project: Liberian American-Swedish Minerals Company (LAMCO).[16]

Table 6.2 provides some of the key indices of Liberia's sudden economic transformation since 1950. Gross domestic product increased from less than $36 million to over $450 million in 1972. Total government revenue rose from under $4 million to about $80 million, including $13.9 million gross capital formation. Up to 1950 Liberia produced no iron-ore, and was heavily dependent on rubber production and exports. By 1972, this mineral resource became the leading export item with an output of 22.6 million long tons worth $182.1 million, or 75 per cent of Liberia's entire export earnings. In addition to LAMCO (started in 1963), there were the Liberia Mining Company (1951), National Iron Ore Company (1961) and German Liberian Mining Company (1964-5) exploiting some of the world's richest iron-ore deposits. In 1950 Liberia had only 230 miles of roads; by 1972 the mileage increased to 2,718 and there were new harbours and railroads constructed to service the booming mining industry. Wage employment increased from about 30,000 in 1950 (practically all engaged in rubber estates, principally the Firestone plantation) to an estimated 125,000 in 1970 (with about 11,000 in the new mining

Table 6.2: Some Indices of Liberian Economic Growth, 1950-72

Item	1950	1960	1972
Gross domestic product[a] (US $ million)	35.8	154.7	450.6
Government revenue (US $ million)	3.9	32.4	78.1
Rubber exports (million lb.)	66.7	95.4	182.9
Iron-ore exports (million long tons)	—	2.9	22.6
All-weather roads (miles)	230	1,150	2,718
Monetary sector employment (man-year)	30,000	82,000	125,000[b]
Enrolment in primary school[c] (no.)	1,300	58,600	139,045

a. In current market prices; excluding subsistence sector.
b. 1970.
c. Includes pre-grade and 1-6 grades of elementary school.

Sources: Data for 1950 and 1960 are from R.W. Clower *et al., Growtn Without Development: An Economic Survey of Liberia* (Northwestern University Press, Evanston, Ill., 1966), p.4. Data for 1972 are from MPEA, *Economic Survey 1972*, except for (1) monetary sector employment which is from ILO, *Total Involvement: A Strategy for Development in Liberia,* a report prepared by an inter-agency team organised by the International Labour Office and financed by the United Nations Development Programme (Geneva, 1972), p.27; (2) enrolment data for 1950 and 1960 which are from ibid., p.62; and (3) enrolment data for 1972 which is from Ministry of Education, *Education Statistics for 1972.*

sector). School enrolment increased from a few hundred to over 139,000 during 1950-72, although the quality was generally poor and limited to the capital city of Monrovia and a few other coastal towns. The landscape of the capital changed dramatically, with new, high-rise government buildings and a huge Executive Mansion for the President of Liberia[17] amidst shanty-towns and urban slums housing impoverished migrants.

Foreign Concessions and the Open Door Policy

Thanks to President Tubman's open door policy, Liberia quickly joined the ranks of LDCs with a booming export sector and a lopsided economy. Using capital-intensive technology, multinational firms have been exploiting Liberia's iron-ore, timber and rubber, all intended for export markets. In his Second Inaugural Address in 1952, Tubman summarised his open door policy:

We shall encourage foreign investments and the granting of foreign concessions where Liberians have not reached the position where they are capable and competent to explore and exploit the potential resources of the country. We shall continue to guarantee protection to investors and concessionaries of all investments and concessions. All concessions, I stress again, must be on a basis of mutuality.[18]

In 1955, he justified the open door policy in terms of economic and social benefits for his people:

Seeing that we have been seriously handicapped by a closed door policy, and wishing to bring to fruition the dream of our fathers. . ., we have, since the beginning of this administration, enunciated and vigorously fostered an Open Door Policy. Because of this policy, thousands. . .have come. . .in search of a land where they can be helpful in securing themselves and our citizens against the curse of ignorance, poverty and disease; where. . .business of every kind and profitable investments on a basis of mutuality can be established.[19]

In fact, however, the concession agreements have greatly benefited the privileged Americo-Liberian elite on the basis of its highly profitable partnership with foreign interests. The early concession agreements stipulated tax and royalty payments into the Liberian treasury controlled by the elite. More recently, it has been customary to enter into profit-sharing arrangements, and to require that a certain proportion of stock be sold to Liberian citizens at reduced cost.[20] These arrangements have favoured the wealthy Americo-Liberians and not the tribal population in the subsistence sector. Indeed, there is evidence to indicate that the social costs of the open door policy have been excessively high.[21] The rural population has suffered in aggregate terms, partly because of limited job creation, partly because of the anti-rural bias of the Americo-Liberian elite, and partly because of being dispossessed of tribal lands.

The Liberian constitution restricts land ownership to its citizens (and philanthropic institutions such as missions). However, foreign individuals and corporations can obtain lease agreements from Liberian citizens for up to 21 years, with two additional option periods. In the case of foreign concessions, the Liberian government has provided for leases of up to 99 years. The classic Firestone concession covered 1 million acres, of which the company has developed only about one-tenth.[22] The lands granted to foreign enterprises were tribal lands, but the native population has not been compensated financially for the loss of its homelands. The rubber and mining companies have provided social services, including housing, education and health care, but these have been limited to their employees and their dependants. According to estimates of Clower *et al.,* the total acreage granted to foreign concessions amounted to 6.4 million acres or about 25 per cent of the total land area of Liberia. Thus, 6 rubber firms had 3.1 million acres; 4 iron-ore companies 0.5 million acres; 13 timber firms 2.1 million acres; and other concessions 0.7 million acres.[23]

Since Liberia uses the American dollar and has no exchange control, she is highly attractive for foreign investment. In addition, her peculiar political system and free enterprise make for an unusually 'liberal' climate for profit maximisation. Foreign firms are not only able to transfer profits, dividends and other remittances abroad freely; they are also assured of government help in keeping wages down[24] and trade unions in check.[25] Given the inefficient and corrupt administrative system of the country, foreign firms have taken maximum advantage of Liberia's official policy of free enterprise. In this atmosphere, foreign firms have joined hands with the Americo-Liberian elite to exploit the tribal workers as well as the natural resources of the country.

The Tribal Sector

The large African sector consists of two unequal subsets. In the monetary economy, there are an estimated 125,000 wage-employees[26] plus an unknown number in the urban 'informal sector' specialising in petty trading. These informal sectors, the largest located in Monrovia, have grown topsy-turvy during the course of the last two decades as a result of rapid urban migration of illiterate and unskilled rural job-seekers and youth seeking higher educational opportunities. The results, however, have been the swelling of tribal squatter villages and mining shanty-towns overcrowded with such marginal workers as 'shoe-shine boys' and women 'making market' in a grim struggle to earn a livelihood.[27]

The second, and by far the most important African sector, is the interior where some 20 tribes, with different languages and customs, live. Through decades of neglect and exploitation, the tribal population is characterised by their mistrust of the Americo-Liberian elite and the central government which it controls. Over the years since 1822, the Liberian tribes have been systematically dispossessed of their tribal homelands, and have been forced to work on rubber estates, owned by leading Americo-Liberians as well as by foreign companies, under conditions of near-slavery, which still exist today.[28] The tribal population, contrary to the provisions of the Liberian constitution, have begun to enjoy such services as education and health only in recent years, and these are provided more by foreign concession firms

and private missionary organisations than by the central government in
Monrovia. The rural population is heavily taxed, partly in the form of a
'hut tax' and partly through involuntary contributions imposed by the
Americo-Liberian leadership.[29]

Under these conditions, the rural economy has remained stagnant.
It is dominated by traditional subsistence farming, centred on rice.
The typical unit of cultivation is the family farm, based on the
participation of both men and women in agricultural tasks, determined
by customary rules of division of labour.[30] In some parts of the interior,
there is significant use of migrant labour, which is a characteristic of a
number of West African countries.[31] In keeping with collective, tribal
ownership of land, rice-growing is done largely on the basis of the
traditional 'slash-and-burn' or 'shifting' method, whereby the peasant
farmer moves to a different farm from year to year, repeating the cycle
of clearing and burning a piece of land from the forest for temporary
farming purposes. In some parts of Liberia, notably the Lofa County,
there have been experiments in recent years with 'swamp' rice grown in
rain-fed valleys.[32] These new initiatives, financed under bilateral and
United Nations aid programmes, have clearly demonstrated the great
potential for rice cultivation, using modern techniques, in Liberia.
However, the reluctance of the ruling Americo-Liberian elite to invest
in rural development makes the prospects of major success rather
unlikely. For example, agricultural extension programmes involving new
rice varieties have been going on since the 1940s thanks to US AID
assistance, but official indifference in Monrovia has effectively
precluded any significant progress.[33] Despite a great potential for
large-scale rice production in the country, Liberia remains dependent
on expensive imports of this national staple. The import trade is a
highly lucrative monopoly operated by influential members of the elite
in partnership with Lebanese merchants.

The economic interdependence between the enclave sector and the
large interior areas has been limited. In the last decade employment on
rubber plantations has been steadily decreasing owing to the
introduction of labour-saving tapping techniques. In the mining sector,
employment opportunities have reached a peak and, given its highly
capital-intensive nature, further expansion of the labour force in this
sector is unlikely. Indeed, there may be a significant reduction due to
the depletion of deposits at Bomi Hills, where a town of about 20,000
population is in danger of becoming a ghost town — a prospect likely
to be experienced elsewhere in Liberia in the future, barring effective
policies for regional development and diversification before revenues

from iron-ore disappear.

The Americo-Liberian Sector

Socially, politically and economically the Americo-Liberian elite occupies a distinct position in Liberian society. Thanks to its control of the political and governmental machinery, its members have acquired great wealth. Because of a traditional disdain for agriculture, trade and commerce, however, the elite has concentrated on political ends, using religion and classical education for this purpose. As Liebenow aptly puts it, in Liberia 'Politics is King'.[34] The elite has adroitly utilised its political supremacy not only to promote highly profitable joint ventures with multinational firms to exploit Liberia's natural resources, but virtually all senior officials and Ministers own — but do not manage — private firms, in addition to their official duties. These firms, often financed out of government subsidies (for example, through the Liberian Development and Investment Bank), operate as virtual monopolies; the largest such enterprise being the Mesurado group of companies of the late Stephen Tolbert, the brother of the President and the former Minister of Finance. In addition, foreign firms in the private sector, such as the German, Swiss, Swedish import/export agencies, include prominent Americo-Liberians on the boards of directors and retain lawyer-legislators to protect their interests.[35]

The same pattern exists in the plantation and agricultural sectors. Several years ago, Firestone, Goodrich and other major plantation firms initiated a scheme under which they provided leading Americo-Liberian figures with free rubber trees and technical advice to start production on private farms.[36] This resulted in a great scramble for tribal lands and involuntary recruitment of native labour contrary to international conventions. While there was expanded output of rubber — which could be sold only to major plantation firms at gate prices — the scheme generated more than economic gains for the foreign interests. It won considerable political goodwill from the Americo-Liberian elite, and it kept the wage rate on estates at a fixed rate of $0.08 per hour until 1973, when it was raised to $0.12 by President Tolbert, but even this increase was well below the rise in the cost of living.

The elite reluctance to divert investment funds for regional development in the interior stems from the long history of mistrust between the settlers and the tribal population. Aware of the potential threat of egalitarian reforms in Liberia's economic and social structure, the Americo-Liberian elite effectively vetoes measures to improve the well-being of the tribal population. For example, President Tubman was

opposed to the creation of farmer co-operatives in the interior because
he was well aware of the political roles of cocoa co-operatives in Ghana
and the nationalistic activities of coffee co-operatives in East Africa.[37]
Tubman's successor, President Tolbert — one of the largest private
rubber producers in the country — is carrying the long-established
Liberian tradition of rhetorical promises as substitute for action.[38]
With great emphasis on pomp and ceremony, the Liberian government
spends more funds on diplomatic and public relations activities than on
genuine rural development schemes, while the elite indulges in a major
(but unknown) volume of capital flight and an astonishing degree of
conspicuous consumption.

Dependence on Foreign Manpower *v.* Liberianisation

The economic transformation initiated by the open door policy was not
preceded by or accompanied with educational and training programmes
to develop Liberian human resources. The Americo-Liberian elite instead
relied on imports of foreign personnel, in line with the then fashionable
advisory opinion that such reliance would be only transitory. In fact,
however, increasing imports of high-cost expatriate manpower became
a central characteristic of Liberian growth without development.

By 1973, no less than 31 per cent of all high-level occupations in
Liberia were held by expatriate workers receiving up to 10 times the
average earnings of Liberian employees.[39] There is a work permit
programme operated by the Ministry of Labour and Social Security,
but it is administered inefficiently by corrupt officials. Virtually all of
the senior positions in the modern sector are held by expatriates. Such
essential public services as medical care, dental care and post-secondary
education rely heavily on foreign workers from Europe and the USA. The
trade and commerce sectors are dominated by Lebanese merchants,
wholesalers and retailers. The Lebanese control not only the internal
distribution of staples such as rice, sugar, cooking oil, etc., but also
handle the import of consumption goods required by the Americo-
Liberian and expatriate groups.

Reliance on expatriate manpower minimises the volume of jobs and
employment income of the Liberians themselves; it also adds to the
outflow of profits, interest and dividends payable to foreign interests.
Liberia's net factor payments abroad since 1964 have amounted to
about one-third of the country's GDP.[40] In recent years, the Americo-
Liberian elite has given increasing attention to Liberianisation, but its
readiness to undertake the necessary massive investments in education
and manpower development remains unproven.[41] In the meantime, a

glaring inequality of educational opportunity persists.

Educational Inequality

The Liberian education system is characterised by elite management, poor quality and shortage of funds. While there has been a rapid increase of enrolments, educational budgets have lagged severely, reflecting the fundamental fact that the Americo-Liberian ruling elite has preferred to rely on imported manpower rather than educational development at home.

Legally, education is both free and compulsory up to the age of high school,[42] but only a privileged fraction of the school-age children has access to schooling. In 1970, about 40 per cent of the age group 5-14, and only 1 per cent of those in the 20-24 bracket attended an educational institution. National illiteracy is over 80 per cent of the population aged 5 and over — much higher in the rural areas.[43] These official statistics invariably overstate educational accessibility and literacy.

Most of the young persons denied educational opportunity at the start of their lives reside in rural areas where tribal ways and norms have little changed since Liberia's emergence as a republic in 1847. Table 6.3 gives some interesting statistics regarding the area allocation of educational expenditure in 1973. Thus, there are more than twice as many schools in Monrovia and Montserrado County, which is essentially the metropolitan area of the capital, than in the rest of the country per 1,000 population. The superiority of the schools in and around Monrovia is evident from the fact that they have about four times as many teachers and absorb over four times as much funds for elementary and secondary education per 1,000 population as do the rest of Liberia. Furthermore, the quality of instruction in the rural schools is greatly inferior owing to a severe lack of supplies and teaching aids, and because over 75 per cent of the teachers are under-qualified, possessing less than high-school education.[44] There are no financial incentives to encourage qualified teachers to work in rural regions and often the scanty pay of less than $50 per month remains in arrears for several months.

The position of private schools, operated and financed by foreign companies and missionary organisations in Liberia, is altogether different. Unlike government schools, many private educational institutions are properly staffed and funded and as a result offer superior instruction. On the other hand, government schools suffer from a poor public image. Especially in rural areas, the respect accorded to the public-school

Table 6.3: Area Allocation of 1973 Education Expenditure

	Monrovia and Montserrado County	Rest of Liberia	Total
Elementary/secondary schools (no.)	290	831	1,121
Teachers (no.)	1,644	2,672	4,316
Elementary/secondary budget (thousand dollars)	1,925	1,878	3,803
Population (million)	0.2	1.3	1.5
Per 1,000 population			
Schools	1.45	0.64	0.75
Teachers	8.22	2.06	2.87
Elementary/secondary expenditure ($)	$9,625	$1,445	$2,535

Sources: School and teacher statistics are taken from the publication *Statistics of Education in Liberia 1971* (Division of Statistics, Ministry of Education, Monrovia, Liberia, April 1972) (mimeo.). Expenditure data is from *The Budget of the Government of Liberia* for 1973 (Executive Mansion, Bureau of the Budget, Monrovia, Liberia) (mimeo.). Population figures are estimates, since Monrovia's population is not reliably known.

teacher is very low and it leads to a reluctance on the part of the parents to send their children to school. This reluctance is strongly reinforced by a number of economic and institutional factors such as the high cost of uniforms, textbooks and school supplies imported from the USA and sold through a monopoly distributor,[45] various forms of education taxes and involuntary cash contributions,[46] as well as the pressure of traditional chores demanded by tribal elders around the house and on the farms.

Apart from glaring lack of educational opportunity, the schooling actually provided in Liberia is irrelevant to the needs of the majority of schoolchildren. Although about 80 per cent of the population live in rural areas, there is no rural education designed to equip students for rural living. The concept of primary school as terminal is unknown in Liberia. Instead, the curriculum, with a heavy bias in favour of classical liberal arts content, is patterned after the United States system and it is entirely oriented towards an industrially advanced, urbanised society. For example, history and geography of Europe and the USA are taught at great length, while African and Liberian content are virtually ignored. In home economics, girls are taught cooking and sewing using American supplies and equipment, which are not available or used in Liberia, where the vast majority of housewives use traditional methods.

In short, the Liberian education system 'is designed to produce failures'.[47] Only 29 per cent of total entrants into grade one successfully complete grade six and graduate with an elementary school diploma. English rather than one or more of the 20-odd tribal languages is the official medium of instruction in all public schools. Not surprisingly, many students face a 'culture shock' from having to learn an alien language and all about an abstract society in far-away lands. Pressed with the high cost of textbooks, school uniforms, tribal demands for labour, the reasons for dropping out become compelling for the majority of students. In the high school, the drop-out rate over the six-year period is 52 per cent. On a standard progression basis, out of every 1,000 entrants into grade one, 290 manage to graduate from elementary school and 141 complete high school.[48] The Liberian educational pyramid is a steep one indeed.

While the country lacks a nation-wide, basic education system, over 20 per cent of the educational budget is allocated to support a costly, wasteful university programme, and a further 10 per cent to subsidise a foreign scholarship fund for the benefit of the children of the Americo-Liberian elite. The University of Liberia, located in Monrovia, has about 1,500 students, but produces about 100 graduates a year, virtually all in liberal arts. Despite this high-cost university, plans are already under way to relocate it in a new site, closer to President Tolbert's country estate, some 20 miles from the capital. Relocation costs in 1973 were in the range of $80-90 million, a sum equivalent to the entire 1973 government budget (Table 6.4).

Table 6.4: Liberian Educational Priorities as Reflected in the 1973 Education Budget

	Amount (thousands US dollars)	Per Cent
Elementary and secondary education	3,803	38.6
Teacher training	739	7.5
Vocational training	520	5.3
University of Liberia	2,126	21.6
Foreign Scholarship Scheme	920	9.3
Local Scholarship Scheme	94	0.9
Other	1,657	16.8
Total education budget	9,859	100.0
Total public expenditure	83,000	

Source: *The Budget of the Government of Liberia for 1973.*

Of critical importance is the virtual neglect of technical, vocational and agricultural education in a country so heavily dependent on manpower imports from abroad. In recent years, there has been considerable talk of Liberianisation; but there has been no significant investment of public funds for technical and vocational training.[49] There is just one public technical institute, the Booker Washington Technical and Agricultural Institute at Kakata, which was established in 1926 by a group of American missionaries. It was taken over by the Liberian government in 1965 and has since been declining and abandoning its technical/vocational character in favour of an academic high school. In addition to this Institute, there is a small vocational school in Yekapa which was started with technical and financial assistance from Sweden. The best vocational schools in the country are run by foreign mining companies to meet their own junior and mid-level technical manpower requirements, although some graduates ultimately move to other firms. These private training programmes are insufficient to meet national needs. There is no agricultural education at all, although the vast majority of the population lives in rural areas depending on farming. A few years ago, a rural basic craft training centre was started in Kle, with assistance from the United Nations, but the project never took off owing to lack of official support.

Conclusion: Part and Future Prospects

It is difficult not to be pessimistic about the prospects of egalitarian development in Liberia. Her experience of growth without development demonstrates that poverty and persistent underdevelopment, especially amongst the rural masses, stem essentially from political rather than economic factors: i.e. from elite resistance to egalitarian reform. Under the open door policy, the Americo-Liberian leadership collaborated with foreign syndicates and investors searching for maximum profits in a more or less organised system of exploiting both the tribal labourers as well as the country's land, mineral and timber resources. The tribal communities have been dispossessed of their homelands in order to make room for foreign concessions; they have been forced into involuntary or low-wage employment; and they have received only minimal advantages in education and social services. In the meantime, the wealth generated by iron-ore, rubber and timber enrich the foreign interests and the Americo-Liberian 'honourables'. This mutually profitable partnership may well remain in effect until the depletion of non-renewable resources. In the final analysis, one can only concur that: 'Roads that bring good government to backward areas are clearly a blessing; roads that bring bad government may be a curse.'[50]

In recent years some signs of hope have emerged under the Tolbert Administration. For example, in 1976, a 4-year *National Socio-Economic Development Plan* was officially approved; and in October 1973 Liberia and Sierra Leone set up the Mano River Union establishing a custom union between the two countries and agreed to co-operate in trade promotion and regional development. Potentially, this Union could become an instrument of economic expansion in a more efficient way than would be feasible within a national framework. Finally, in 1977, Bishop Bennie Warner, a man of tribal origin, was chosen as the Vice-President of Liberia, despite strong Americo-Liberian opposition. Whether, however, these hopeful signs will actually lead to greater social and political participation at the grass-roots level — and a corresponding reduction in the Americo-Liberian monopoly over the decision-making process — remains to be seen.

Notes

1. For a perceptive account, see J. Gus Liebenow, *Liberia: The Evolution of Privilege* (Cornell University Press, Ithaca and London, 1969). A more concise study by the same author is the chapter on Liberia in James S. Coleman and Carl G. Rosberg (eds.), *Political Parties and National Integration in Tropical Africa* (University of California Press, Berkeley, 1964).

2. The American dollar is legal tender in Liberia.

3. Robert W. Clower *et al., Growth Without Development: An Economic Survey of Liberia* (Northwestern University Press, Evanston, 1966). An alternative interpretation is Elliot J. Berg, 'Growth, Development and All That' (Center for Research on Economic Development, University of Michigan, 1969) (mimeographed).

4. A brief historical account of Liberia is given in Lawrence A. Marinelli, *The New Liberia: A Historical and Political Survey* (Praeger, New York and London, 1964). Another useful source, with many original documents, is Nathaniel R. Richardson, *Liberia's Past and Present* (The Diplomatic Press, London, 1959).

5. Richardson, *Liberia's Past and Present,* p.17.

6. A. Doris Banks Henries, *The Life of Joseph Jenkins Roberts (1809-1876) and His Inaugural Addresses* (Macmillan, London, 1964).

7. Thus the Liberian Ambassador to the United Nations, C.T.O. King, in a speech in 1957 attempted to justify the economic underdevelopment of his country with the remark: 'Liberia did not have the advantages of colonial rule' which other African countries did. See Liebenow's article in Coleman and Rosberg, *Political Parties,* p.448.

8. Merran Fraenkel, *Tribe and Class in Monrovia* (Oxford University Press, London, 1964), p.v.

9. On influence-peddling and bribery — known as 'dashing' — see Clower, *Growth Without Development,* pp.15-22. Liebenow, *Liberia,* Ch.7, entitled 'A "Family Affair"', is highly revealing.

10. Quoted on p.6 in *Report on the Second Conference on Development Objectives and Strategy* (Monrovia, 19-23 April 1971), prepared by C. Campaigne, Resident Representative, United Nations Development Programme, Liberia. An extended discussion of the inefficiency of the Liberian civil service is given in the author's article, 'Administrative Machinery for Development Planning in Liberia', *Journal of Modern African Studies,* Vol.13, No.3 (1975).

11. This is the infamous Fernando Po Scandal involving forced recruitment of tribal labourers by the Liberian Frontier Force for shipment to the sugar plantations in the Spanish colony of Fernando Po. As a result of international indignation, a Commission of Inquiry was appointed by the League of Nations. The President and Vice-President of Liberia were implicated and forced to resign. Cf. Marinelli, *The New Liberia,* pp.47-8 and Appendix 3, pp.158-62 containing the original Labour Agreement of 1928. Also, Richardson, *Liberia's Past and Present,* Ch.XVII.

12. A. Doris Banks Henries, *President William V.S. Tubman* (Macmillan, London, 1967).

13. Known as the Unification Policy, Tubman's programme was essentially a political strategy. Thus, although the programme promised to upgrade the tribal population 'into good and useful citizens, capable of knowing their duty, status and rights as citizens, and competent of exerting, enjoying and asserting them', little effect was given to these promises, especially in education. For details of the Unification Policy, see Marinelli, *The New Liberia,* pp.61-72.

14. Fraenkel, *Tribe and Class.*

15. During 1954-60, the growth of income averaged about 15 per cent per annum. See Clower, *Growth Without Development,* especially Tables 1 and 2, p.24. An early and optimistic study of Liberian growth is Russell U. McLaughlin, *Foreign Investment and Development in Liberia* (Praeger, New York, 1966). Marinelli, *The New Liberia,* is even more optimistic.

16. A detailed study of this project, with emphasis on social overhead expenditures incurred by LAMCO, is Ronald F. Storette, *The Politics of Integrated Social Investment* (Bonniers, Stockholm, 1971). 'Fully 50%. . .of the entire financial investment of $275 million was devoted to social investment. 40% hereof was put into an economic infrastructure in the form of roads, harbor facilities and railways. The remaining 10% became part of a social infrastructure in the form of hospitals, dwellings, educational facilities, etc.' (p.17).

17. This mansion was estimated in 1963 at $12-15 million (i.e. over 40% of total government revenue), mostly financed through foreign borrowing. For details of this, and other wasteful and superfluous payroll and administration costs, see Clower, *Growth Without Development,* p.69 *et seq.*

18. Quoted in Marinelli, *The New Liberia,* p.75.

19. Ibid., p.72.

20. For the specific details of individual concession agreements with iron-ore, rubber and timber firms, see Clower, *Growth Without Development,* Tables 33-37, pp.125-33.

21. Robert E. Miller and Peter R. Carter, 'The Modern Dual Economy – A Cost-Benefit Analysis of Liberia', *Journal of Modern African Studies,* Vol.10, No.1 (May 1972). With reference to the iron-ore mining, Miller and Carter calculate the net total loss resulting from outflows of payments to foreign investors during 1964-8 at a figure 'ranging from $130 million to $300 million for the period' (p.120). As a comparison, it may be pointed out that the 1964 GDP (excluding subsistence economy) was $248.3 million, and in 1968 it was $321.8 million.

22. W.C. Taylor, *The Firestone Operations in Liberia* (National Planning Association, Washington, DC, 1956). Also see Clower, *Growth Without Development,* Ch.7.

23. Clower, *Growth Without Development,* p.128.

24. The minimum hourly wage rate on rubber plantations was established at $0.08 in 1963, and 15 cents in the industrial sector. International Labour Office, *Total Involvement: A strategy for Development in Liberia,* a report prepared by an inter-agency team organised by the International Labour Office and financed by the United Nations Development Programme (Geneva, 1972), para.195, p.31.

25. The Liberian trade unions are 'tame', i.e. they are controlled by the elite, partly owing to the fact that trade union leaders are members of the 'honourable' class. See Liebenow, *Liberia,* esp. pp.87-90.

Despite the fact that the Liberian government has ratified international conventions on Freedom of Association (No.87, 1948) and The Right to Organize and Collective Bargaining (No.97, 1949), there have been official complaints of comprehensive government violations of these conventions. For example, during the 1966 LAMCO strike, President Tubman sent in the army to break the miners' strike and arrest union leaders. Also, the government prevented the unionisation of plantation workers. In 1967, the International Confederation of Free Trade Unions, the International Federation of Plantation, Agricultural and Allied Workers, and the Miners' International Federation brought five official complaints against the Liberian government before the International Labour Organization in Geneva. For details, see ILO *Official Gazette,* Case No.506, Vol.L, No.3 (July 1967).

26. ILO, *Total Involvement,* Table 2, p.27. These figures relate to 1970. The government of Liberia, with about 20,000 employees, is the largest single employer in the country, with a further 15,000 in the public utilities sector.

27. ILO, *Total Involvement,* esp. pp.24-6.

28. Under the Aborigines Law, the Liberian central government and its district officers are empowered to recruit tribal inhabitants for 'public work' projects. In fact, however, this is liable to be abused by unscrupulous officials who would employ tribal workers on private farms for little or no pay. The existence of these conditions is confirmed by the ILO Report, *Total Involvement,* para.295, p.49. As well, forced recruitment of tribal labour was extensively utilised by Firestone and other rubber firms in collaboration with the Liberian government. See Clower, *Growth Without Development,* p.309 *et seq.*

In 1961, Portugal lodged an official complaint with the ILO charging the Liberian government with extensive violations of the Forced Labour Convention, 1930. For details of this case, see ILO *Official Bulletin,* Vol.XLVI, No.2, Supplement II (April 1963).

29. For example, in 1973 a nation-wide Rally Time fund-raising was organised and a sum of $4.5 million collected for development purposes. As part of this fund, every schoolchild was required to 'donate' $2 - by no means a small amount for the tribal population.

30. Gerald E. Currens, 'Women, Men and Rice: Agricultural Innovation in Northwestern Liberia', *Human Organization,* Vol.35, No.4 (Winter 1976).

31. Elliot Berg, 'The Economics of the Migrant Labor System' in Hilda Kuper (ed.), *Urbanization and Migration in West Africa* (University of California Press, Berkeley, 1965).

32. Currens, 'Women, Men and Rice'.

33. This is the Suakoko experimental station. For details, see Clower, *Growth Without Development,* p.239 *et seq.*

34. Liebenow, *Liberia,* Ch.5.

35. In theory, the Liberian Code of Laws prohibits conflict of interest in the public service, but in practice this is almost universally abused. Liebenow, *Liberia,* p.94.

36. Clower, *Growth Without Development,* p.167 *et seq.*

37. Liebenow, *Liberia,* p.87.

38. Some of the key slogans of the Tolbert administration are 'Total Involvement for Higher Heights', 'Wholesome Functioning Society', intended primarily for impressing Liberia's potential donors and investors.

39. The Ministry of Planning and Economic Affairs, *Indicative Manpower Plan of Liberia for the Period 1972-1982* (Monrovia, 1974).

40. Miller and Carter, 'The Modern Dual Economy'.

41. The ILO Report, *Total Involvement,* prepared at the request of the

Liberian government, offers a comprehensive programme of action for balanced and equitable economic development in the country, with special emphasis on rural reform and educational planning. The report, however, has had little impact on Liberian policy and public expenditure.

42. Liberian Code of Laws, Vol.1, Sec.1, p.453.

43. These figures are computed from statistics in the *Annual Reports* of the Ministries of Education and of Planning and Economic Affairs for 1971.

44. Ministry of Education, *Statistics of Education in Liberia, 1971* (Monrovia, April 1972).

45. The 1973 price-list of the government textbook agency gives the total cost of grade I books at $11.91 and grade XII at $35.96 — an excessive burden for the rural families where the estimated average *per capita* income is about $70.

46. During 1973, the Minister of Education imposed a $2 per student 'contribution' to the National Rally Time; as a result school attendance in many rural areas fell drastically.

47. The ILO Report, *Total Involvement,* para.365, p.63.

48. These figures are from the Statistics Division of the Ministry of Education, Monrovia.

49. Since 1972, the World Bank has been providing Liberia with a multi-million education credit for the construction of schools and vocational centres. While this is a commendable project, it is doubtful that the new institutions can be operated efficiently without adequate recurrent expenditure and (equally importantly) without a complete revision of the elitist educational priorities.

50. Clower, *Growth Without Development*, p.33.

7 REVOLUTION OR REFORM: THE EXPERIENCE OF PAKISTAN, BRAZIL AND UGANDA

One of the most difficult questions in the LDCs today is the precise form of the means to be used for promoting egalitarian development — one that is beneficial to the masses *as well as* the ruling elites. The three countries selected for brief study in this chapter — Pakistan, Brazil and Uganda — can shed useful light on the many issues involved in the trade-off dilemma between peaceful reform and violent revolution.

Brazil (as with Malaysia discussed in Chapter 5) represents an important contrary to the classical doctrines of comparative advantage and international trade as 'an engine of growth'. For despite her 400-year-long trade and specialisation consistent with these doctrines, she has only managed a boom-bust pattern of growth, acquiring external dependency, coupled with a lopsided and dualistic economy. Even after achieving independence in 1822, she continued, under elite control, to rely on colonial economic models, perpetuating external dependency, lopsided and dualistic growth that only benefited the ruling elites and their foreign collaborators.

The Pakistan experience since 1947 suggests that self-reliance *per se* is not a sufficient condition for balanced, sustained economic and social development. Unless political and institutional reforms along egalitarian lines are effectively introduced, rapid growth may be expected to accentuate economic and political power concentration in the hands of ruling elites, ultimately leading to catastrophic results.

While the Brazil and Pakistan experiences may suggest drastic revolutionary change as the only hopeful method of promoting egalitarian development, Amin's Uganda offers an important warning against any hasty prescriptions, especially if the means to be utilised entail violence and loss of human lives.

PAKISTAN: PLANNING FOR INEQUALITY

Pakistan's experience illustrates the tremendous political and institutional obstacles besetting economic planning and policy in a country, newly independent, but one with a long history of feudalism, ethnicity and regional divisions. The partition of 1947 created not only

141

an artificial marriage between East Pakistan (now Bangladesh) and West Pakistan, but it also endeavoured to unify the Punjabis, Pathans, Sindhis, Baluchis, Bengalis and an influx of refugees known as Muhajirs, under the banner of Islam.[1] The experience since — both in terms of the eventual break-up of the country in 1971 as well as in terms of the ongoing secessionist movements in Baluchistan and the North West Frontier Province — amply demonstrate the relative insignificance of a common religion as a unifying force and, conversely, the relative importance of social and economic inequalities within an ethnically plural society.

Contrary to official declarations by virtually every major Pakistani leader since 1947, as well as the lofty promises announced in the Five Year Development Plans, economic planning and policy since independence have failed miserably to foster national unity and to narrow down socio-economic disparities between individuals and regions. Indeed, the types of policies adopted and implemented have tended to widen those disparities and to intensify conflict and division. The Punjabi elites, traditionally the landed aristocracy and effectively in control of the political system, the armed forces as well as the bureaucracy, have relied more on military means[2] than egalitarian development policies in order to promote the paramount objective of nation-building.[3] In particular, industrial development policies helped to create a small class of 'Robber Barons'[4] clustered around '24 families'; while the politically powerful rural and land-owning elites have not only frustrated any major land reform,[5] but emerged as the principal beneficiary of the so-called Green Revolution, in many cases by evicting and displacing small-scale farmers and peasants. Thus, industrialisation and economic growth in the post-war period have worked to polarise the population of Pakistan between the affluent elites and the large underprivileged poor masses. This economic polarisation, in turn, is generating ethnic and geographic division, which even a common religion is unable to contain.[6]

Industrial Growth and Concentration

Industrialisation in Pakistan conformed to the post-war planners' blueprint. The dynamic sector was the industrial and manufacturing industry, and its development was built on neo-Calvinist doctrines and free-enterprise capitalism. Official policies were intentionally formulated to increase the income share of the capitalists and industrialists; social and welfare programmes were avoided; and the rural and agricultural sectors were directly and indirectly taxed in favour of industrialisation.

It was argued that functional inequality was essential in the early stages of capitalist development in order to stimulate savings and investment and encourage dynamic entrepreneurship. The Second Five Year Plan declared:

> Direct taxes cannot be made more progressive without affecting the incentives to work and save. The tax system should take full account of the needs of capital formation. It will be necessary to tolerate some initial growth in income inequalities to reach high levels of saving and investment.[7]

The Third Five Year Plan emphasised the same theme: 'the distribution of the national product should be such as to favour the saving sectors.'[8]

Industrialisation in Pakistan was carried out almost entirely by indigenous Muslim entrepreneurs. While there had been relatively few Muslim industrialists and major businessmen prior to 1947, a new industrialist class was created by direct government favouritism and incentive programmes within the relatively short period of a few years. Members of this class were well connected families capable of joining in profitable combinations and alliances with the political, military and bureaucratic elites ruling Pakistan. As a result, industrial growth in Pakistan has been a story of concentrated ownership and monopolistic collusion. As Papanek noted:

> While there were over 3,000 individual firms in Pakistan in 1959, only 7 individuals, families or foreign corporations controlled one-quarter of all private industrial assets and one-fifth of all industrial assets. Twenty-four units controlled nearly half of all private industrial assets.[9]

These leading families, 'Robber Barons' as Papanek labelled them, were able, through influence-peddling and corruption, to secure government credits and subsidies; whenever the government sold some publicly owned enterprises to the private sector, these leading families usually bought them, further increasing industrial concentration.[10] In addition, the industrial barons of Pakistan quickly developed horizontal integration. For example, according to Papanek's survey, 'approximately 15 families owned about three-quarters of all the shares in banks and insurance companies. This control of large pools of capital gave the leading families a clear advantage in financing new industrial ventures.'[11]

Large profits and fortunes were realised by the new capitalist classes, not only from industrial ventures, but from the sale and resale of export and import licences, tax evasion and avoidance. Corruption and bribery in the government and private sectors became so rampant that these practices were openly and publicly discussed, sometimes justified with the argument that, unlike India, Pakistan was a free-enterprise economy.[12]

In statistical terms, however, the Robber Barons achieved results to delight the diehard capitalist free-enterprisers. In 1949, the British pound and the Indian rupee were devalued, but Pakistan did not follow suit, despite the historical flows of trade and commerce. As a result, Pakistan's trade with India suddenly was deadlocked. The government then embarked on a far-reaching programme of import substitution, i.e. developing home industries designed to reduce import dependency. Initial stimulus was given to textiles and clothing industries. The Korean War brought a welcome economic boom with a tremendous rise in exports of jute and other products, creating an expansion of export earnings. During 1950-2, there was a policy of liberalised imports with unrestricted freedom available to registered firms under the Open General Licence scheme. At the end of 1952, following a reversal in export trade and declining export earnings, a policy of direct import controls was introduced and it remained in effect until 1959. This import control programme, placing quantitative limits on imports, created a highly protected home market for indigenous industry, which developed rapidly. During 1949-50 to 1954-5, the manufacturing sector grew annually at 29.6 per cent,[13] one of the highest growth rates anywhere in the world, although it reflected the low industrial base at the time of independence. Intermediate and producer-goods industries also expanded rapidly owing to the deliberate policy of maintaining an over-valued exchange rate and preferential, low tariff on capital goods imports.

'With high prices for consumer goods and low prices for capital goods needed to produce them, annual profits of 50-100% on investment were possible.'[14] These incredible rates of profit encouraged dynamic entrepreneurship, but they also encouraged waste and inefficiency. Expansion of investment, plant capacity and production were undertaken with little heed for efficient management and operations. Capital utilisation, at the expense of labour, became the fashionable practice.

In the second half of the 1950s the growth rate of the manufacturing sector declined to 11.8 per cent, as a result of changed political and economic circumstances. Incentives offered by the government to industrialists were less favourable, and continued political and social unrest finally resulted in the military take-over by General Ayub in October 1958. During 1956-8, the rate of return of the industrialists declined to 12.8 per cent.[15] The domestic investment rate fell significantly, and there was an extensive flight of capital out of the country. After the imposition of martial law some $16 million worth of illegal foreign exchange holdings were returned to the government,[16] and a further sum of $25 million was similarly reported in the Pakistan Budget for 1960/1[17] — yet, these sums represented only a fraction of amounts secretly taken out of the country in preceding years.

During the 1960s the manufacturing sector recovered somewhat, achieving a 14.7 per cent annual growth rate during 1959-60 to 1964-5.[18] There was also a reversal of policy from import substitution towards export promotion based on an export bonus scheme.[19] Under the Second and Third Plans, much greater emphasis than before was placed on food production with heavy concentration in West Pakistan. However, the oligopolistic foundations in the industrial sector laid in the 1950s have remained intact.[20]

The creation of highly protected, monopolistic industries in Pakistan was actively aided by foreign donors. Foreign aid funds were channelled into private industry through a number of semi-autonomous financial intermediaries, such as the Pakistan Industrial Credit and Investment Corporation (PICIC) and the Industrial Development Bank of Pakistan (IDBP).[21] These institutions showed open favouritism toward the large, established firms owned and operated by the leading families. Thus, despite the fact that IDBP was established in order to promote small and medium-sized enterprises through allocations of foreign loans and credits, by 1969, 71.5 per cent of its outstanding advances were in amounts exceeding Rs.1 million; 58.1 per cent were in loans of more than Rs.2.5 million. Conversely, a mere 10 per cent of IDBP loans were in amounts under Rs.200,000. Similarly, only 3 per cent of the total loans issued by PICIC during 1957-69 were in amounts of less than Rs.500,000.[22]

It is evident that the neo-Calvinistic doctrines behind Pakistan's industrialisation drive were misguided. Although the growth policies followed did increase income inequalities between the capitalists and the rest, the private saving and investment rates failed to generate sustained expansion and growth. While the top 30 per cent of the total income recipients accounted for 57.5 per cent of total personal income in the early 1960s,[23] and the bulk of the population lived at subsistence

level in abject poverty, the private saving rate actually declined from
2.9 per cent of GNP in 1959-60 to 2.7 per cent in 1967-8, although it
had risen somewhat in the early 1960s. Yet, the rates of return in the
private sector were as high as 25 per cent or better. Even the public
saving rate declined from 1.9 per cent of GNP under the Second Plan
to 1.1 per cent under the Third.[24] This last fact stemmed from the
substantial increase in defence and military allocations connected with
the war with India in 1965.[25] However, it also reflects the elitist control
of the public expenditure. Prior to 1959, Pakistan was ruled by an
alliance of civilian elites comprised of land-owning aristocrats,
professionals, bureaucrats and the new industrialists. From 1959 to
1971, it was ruled by military elites. During this period, large public
expenditure was voted, ostensibly for development projects, but
actually benefiting the elite members and the financial backers of the
ruling classes. Large investments were made in high-cost residential
housing which were subsequently allotted to upper-class families in the
bureaucracy, the military, the new industrialists, and foreign advisers.[26]
The elites also indulged in luxury consumption, causing a rapid increase
in the sale of consumer durables and luxuries, despite declining *per
capita* availability, especially in East Pakistan, of such staples as food
grains, edible oils, cotton cloth and tea.[27] And we have already noted
the illegal practice of capital flight, especially in times of political unrest.

All in all, post-war industrialisation in Pakistan must be described as
a false start in development for the important reason that it was based
on a deliberate policy of creating income inequality.

Agriculture, Food Production and Rural Economy

Consistent with the official objective of the government to favour the
industrial sector, agriculture and food production were deliberately
downgraded in the hastily compiled Six Year Development Plan (1951-7)
and the more serious First Five Year Plan (1955-60) which was not
approved until the late spring of 1956. While the Plan's target of 15
per cent income growth during 1955-60 was expected to be financed
mostly out of savings and surpluses to be squeezed from the agricultural
sector, only 7 per cent of the Plan allocations were earmarked for this
sector, intended primarily for resettlement, irrigation and drainage
works. As a result of this neglect, food production increased only at
0.8 per cent per annum against the Plan target of 4 per cent; and given
a 2.4 per cent population increase, Pakistan was compelled to import
food grains to feed itself. While some food aid was obtained under
US PL 480 (which provided further disincentive to local farmers)

valuable foreign exchange reserves had to be used up to pay for food imports.[28]

Available evidence[29] indicates that the daily *per capita* calorie consumption actually declined during 1949-56. Although the GNP increased by an impressive 12 per cent during the First Plan period, the population growth and shortfalls in food production more than wiped out the income gain; in real terms, Pakistan was actually worse off at the end of the First Plan than she had been at its start.[30]

East Pakistan, predominantly an agricultural economy, was particularly harmed during the 1950s as a result of deliberate taxation and exchange rate policies which transferred resources from the East (principally out of the jute export trade) for industrialisation in the West.[31] *Per capita* incomes in East Pakistan, expressed as a percentage of *per capita* urban incomes, fell from 44.4 per cent in 1949-54 to 40.8 per cent in 1954-9 and to 39 per cent in 1959-64.[32] Since the vast majority of the inhabitants in East Pakistan were poor peasant farmers, the transfer of resources to West Pakistan represented a highly regressive income redistribution from the poor to the rich. This inequality was further accentuated by the fact that in urban areas, where even larger income disparities between the rich and the poor prevailed,[33] real wages probably declined during 1954-67, with money wage rates lagging behind the cost of living.[34] These increasing inequalities were instrumental in the break-up of the country in 1971.

In the Second Five Year Plan (1960-5), prepared under the martial law government of President Ayub, who took power in 1958, planning priorities and strategies were changed significantly.[35] With increased foreign aid and expanded American technical assistance, agriculture and food production were given much greater priority; although, of course, the elitist control of the economy and the political system remained intact.

During the 1960s Pakistan appeared well on her way to self-sufficiency in food production. Despite an accelerated 3.5 per cent population growth in the period 1961-71,[36] there were major improvements in the agricultural sector. Expansion of water and irrigation programmes,[37] desalinisation projects, and land reclamation schemes resulted in increased land cultivation. Total land under cultivation increased from 32.1 million acres in 1960-1 to 35.8 million acres in 1967-8.[38] Most importantly, Pakistan began to reap the benefits of new technology ushered in by the 'Green Revolution' based on the seed-tubewell-fertiliser-tractor combination.[39] Food production increased dramatically, and (as always) foreign observers began to hail a new agricultural 'breakthrough'.[40] With the adoption of the high-yielding Mexi-Pak wheat, the yield per acre rose by 40 per cent between 1958-9 and 1970-1. Total wheat production increased from 3.6 million tons to 6.6 million tons, enabling Pakistan to become a net exporter of food grains in the last years of the sixties, and allowing increased domestic *per capita* consumption.[41] As a result of the dislocation caused by the 1971 war, as well as drought conditions, production of grains fell in the early 1970s and Pakistan, once again, was obliged to rely on food imports.

The agricultural achievements in Pakistan during the 1960s were indeed remarkable. But these achievements must be measured in terms of their social, institutional and regional consequences.

The principal thrust of agricultural policy under the Second and Third Five Year Plans was the mechanisation of farming, based on the introduction of new seeds, fertilisers and a large tubewell water programme. These new farming techniques were heavily concentrated in the fertile Indus Basin of the Punjab in West Pakistan. Mechanisation and modernisation of farming were deliberately encouraged by a variety of tax, credit and pricing policies designed to act as incentives to private farmers. All of these policies, however, were implemented in such a way that they benefited the big landowners and rural elites whose political support for the central government was crucial.[42] For example, the Agricultural Development Bank, which heavily subsidised tractor purchases through long-term loans at the concessional interest rates of 7 or 8 per cent (instead of the 12 to 15 per cent charged by commercial banks on medium-term credit), was effectively limited to wealthy large-scale owners who could supply the necessary collateral to secure the loan.[43] In addition, the foreign exchange supplied to finance the import of tractors was made available at the official rate, which was roughly 50 per cent of the free market rate. As late as 1969/70, there were no import duties on tractors when a nominal 5 per cent import levy and a further 15 per cent sales tax and a defence surcharge amounting to 25 per cent of the sales tax were introduced. These taxes, however, could not prevent the windfall profits resulting from the huge discrepancy between the market price of tractors in 1971 of Rs.25,000-30,000 and the Rs.16,000-18,000 paid for by the licence recipient.[44]

Tractor ownership was heavily concentrated on large farms. In 1969, 8 per cent of all farms in Pakistan (accounting for 35 per cent of total farm land) owned 88 per cent of the tractors.[45] Furthermore, evidence from the Pakistan Punjab, where most of the irrigated, tractor farms are located, indicate that, following the acquisition of tractors, the owner's farm size was increased through land purchases, at the expense of smaller neighbouring farmers; and previous tenants were evicted in order to make room for more intensive farming techniques. Thus, as many as 82 per cent of tenants on farms, whose owners purchased tractors, were directly evicted and several more were similarly displaced indirectly when the tractor farms acquired or rented land for consolidation.[46]

Mechanisation of Pakistan agriculture was actively encouraged by foreign donors, especially the US AID and the Ford Foundation, as well as the World Bank. The latter institution, for example, provided a $30 million loan as late as 1970 for the purpose of financing Agricultural Bank subsidies for tractor imports.[47] The US AID's pro-mechanisation aid policy 'was influenced by a desire to show that the environment of the Indus Basin was quite capable of producing the same crops and yields that have been achieved in comparable areas in the south-western part of the United States'.[48] While technically and diplomatically successful, seed-fertiliser-water-tractor technology, concentrated heavily in the fertile Pakistan Punjab, tended to aggravate, rather than reduce, the socio-economic disparities and inequalities in the country.

As a mild palliative to East Pakistan, in 1962 the foreign aid donors and the Pakistani leadership launched the Rural Works programme, financed by food and material aid under US PL 480. In addition, there was the Village AID programme patterned as a multi-purpose rural development project involving extension, cottage industry, health and social projects, and requiring voluntary local participation. Notwithstanding inadequate funding and poor management, these programmes were too small in relation to the needs of the rural population of East Pakistan to compensate for the official bias accorded to West Pakistan.[49]

Almost certainly the clearest case of the decisive role of rural elites on economic policy is the matter of land reform. In West Pakistan, after partition, political power was concentrated in the hands of the land-owning aristocracy and the emergent elites of industrialists and professionals.[50] These two groups dominated the political and economic scene from 1948 to 1971, the governing elites always coming from their ranks. Operating on a more or less tacit alliance aimed at the preservation and enhancement of group interests, the landlord-businessmen combination effectively blocked any significant land redistribution legislation in the West. In East Pakistan, however, the traditional landowners, including the biggest *Zamindari* holdings, were the Hindu *rajas* without much political power. Consequently, the Muslim League dominating the Assembly passed the East Pakistan Estate Acquisition and Tenancy Bill in 1950, over strong opposition from the Hindu Congress Party, limiting land to 33 acres per head. Although the enforcement of this legislation was delayed, by 1956-7 East Pakistan was virtually freed from feudalistic landlordism.[51]

In West Pakistan it was a different story. In the Assembly, the powerful landlords blocked any land reform. Indeed, they even expanded their feudal powers by influencing legislation to secure much of the evacuee property left by departing Hindus at the expense of the poorly organised Muhajir groups seeking refuge in Pakistan. However, following the take-over in October 1958 by General Ayub, some of this property was recovered under Martial Law Regulation 64 and redistributed to the refugee claimants. Ayub's land reform also imposed liberal ceilings of 500 acres in the case of irrigated, and 1,000 in the case of dry-lands. Since these ceilings were per person, rather than per family, most of the land-owning families merely transferred ownership amongst their family members; overall, this reform did not materially affect the landed elites, and it did not alter the pattern of land distribution in West Pakistan.

In March 1972, following A.Z. Bhutto's assumption of the presidency of Pakistan, a new land reform legislation was introduced under Martial Law Regulation 115. It placed ceilings on individual holdings of 150 acres in the case of irrigated, and 300 for unirrigated, land.[52] Any land owned in excess of the proclaimed ceilings was to be resumed by the government without any compensation to the owner. Also, and in contrast to the 1959 law, no exemptions for orchards, stud farms, hunting reserves, etc., were to be allowed; nor were the charitable, religious and educational institutions (with the sole exception of universities established by law) exempted.

While these reforms appear to be far-reaching, their enforcement and implementation remain very much in doubt. For example, the Provincial Assemblies of Sind, the North West Frontier Province, and the Punjab, controlled by the provincial and land-owning elites, passed amending acts soon after the enactment of Martial Law Regulation 115 aimed at undermining the scope and effect of the land reform.[53]

Conclusion

It is evident that industrialisation policies in Pakistan enriched the urban elites, while the agricultural policies enriched the rural elites.

The bulk of the population did not benefit, and many suffered reduction in their real incomes. Rejecting a type of internal colonialism, East Pakistan finally broke away in 1971 to become Bangladesh. These tragic results were achieved through economic and planning priorities determined within a highly elitist political system controlled by feudal landlords, military and civilian elites who, while building private fortunes on state subsidies, grants and loans, and large inflows of foreign aid, strongly believed that a common religion and a large army would provide adequate guarantees for continued national unity and survival. So long as these, rather than the kind of egalitarian principles outlined in Part Three, remain the fundamental premises of policy and planning in Pakistan, the future prospects can hardly be rated as promising.

BRAZIL: THE FUNCTIONAL POVERTY MODEL

Brazil is one of the oldest cases of profitable collaboration between domestic elites and foreign interests to the detriment of the welfare of the bulk of the local inhabitants. Remarkably, Brazil's participation in European trade and investment is even older than Malaysia's discussed in Chapter 5, and, furthermore, she has been politically independent since 1822. Therefore, the failure of a country with such a long record of independence and undoubted potential for development as Brazil to achieve sustained and balanced growth is, at first sight, highly surprising and quite paradoxical.

In fact, however, Brazil is a leading case of the Latin American model of *external* and *internal* dependency reflecting the fundamental fact that foreign trade and investment have acted as instruments of lopsided growth creating great regional imbalances and deep socio-economic inequalities.[54] Paralleling the dependency of Brazil's economy on the markets and demand conditions in industrialised countries, there is a second, internal dependency tying the underdeveloped rural regions to the high-density, dynamic urban sectors dominated by elite and foreign interests. Just as Brazil participates as the weaker party in international trade with industrialised countries which drain away huge profits, dividends and royalties, so in a similar pattern rural surpluses and resources are squeezed out and transferred to the more powerful urban sectors where they are unequally distributed in favour of urban elites. 'The countryside is poor not because it is feudal or traditional but because it has enriched

the cities. Latin America is underdeveloped because it has supported
the development of Western Europe and the United States.'[55]

The Boom-Bust Economy: The Origins of Functional Poverty

The economic and social structure of Brazil has been shaped by her
400-year-old boom-bust cycle of growth and stagnation.[56]

First there was the dye-wood trade in the sixteenth century,
developed by the Portuguese to satisfy the European demand for
natural dyes required by the expanding textile industries in Western
Europe. The seventeenth century witnessed the sugar boom, based in
the north-east, which peaked in 1651. Faced with increased competition
from the sugar plantations of the Antilles, Brazilian sugar prices and exports
began an irreversible downward decline, permanently dislocating the
economy of the north-east. Then in the eighteenth century there was a
mining boom, centred on gold and diamond discoveries in Mato Grasso
and Goias in the south and centre-south. New mining towns sprang in
formerly empty regions, and the port of Rio de Janeiro was created to
act as the chief outlet of the booming gold export trade. At the same
time, there was an expansion of cattle-breeding and ranching in the
south-east and south and some parts of the north-east. Then the greatest
boom, based on coffee, began, lasting from 1850 to 1930. Huge coffee
plantations were developed in the state of Sao Paulo, and millions of
immigrants from all over Europe settled in Brazil. In 1820 the Brazilian
coffee exports represented only 20 per cent of total exports, but just
before the Great Wall Street Crash of 1929, they accounted for 70 per
cent.[57]

The economy, based on one major export crop at a time, was
structured on a plantation basis along rigid feudal lines, with large
numbers of slaves, and, later on, illiterate estate workers, supporting
tiny groups of landowners and planters who supplied the unprocessed
raw products, through urban middlemen and traders, to the markets
of Europe and the USA. Whenever foreign demand for the export product
declined or became exhausted, the entire regional economy would
collapse and enter into permanent stagnation. The centre of new
economic activity would shift to another region, where more favourable
climate and soils for the new export crop existed. This pattern of
economic growth was not only dependent upon foreign markets and
demand conditions, but it also resulted in a shifting, lopsided and
exploitative type of economic growth.

The boom-bust pattern left Brazil with a permanent legacy of diverse
and distinct regional and socio-economic interest groups competing for

dominance of the decision-making process and a share of the national wealth. As one observer put it: 'The major miracle of Brazil is its existence as a single nation.'[58] These regional and group conflicts have generally played a retardative role in Brazilian economic, social and political development, presenting a virtually constant threat to her stability and requiring a large and costly military superstructure ready to intervene in national affairs.[59]

But the most fundamental legacy of the boom-bust cycle is that Brazil's political and economic decision-making has always been controlled by elite groups promoting their own interests at the expense of the masses. Since normally these elites have depended on foreign trade and investment, there has been a tradition for these 'associate bourgeoisie' to collaborate with foreign interests for mutual advantage and profit. As a result, the benefits of economic growth have been monopolised by these groups, while the masses have remained largely illiterate, unskilled and subordinate, befitting an essentially plantation, cheap-labour economy. This is the basic explanation for functional poverty, i.e. the affluence and survival of the ruling elites is made possible by the existence of a large pool of cheap labour.

The Brazilian Elites and Their Control Strategies

While functional poverty of the masses is a necessary condition for the convergence of political and economic power in the hands of the ruling elites and their foreign partners, it does not follow that the composition of the ruling elites and their strategy of manipulating economic and political decision-making have been static. Both have necessarily changed over time, in response to changing economic, social and political circumstances, often taking a highly complex and sophisticated form.[60]

During the Old Republic (1889-1930), the dominant elite was composed of the Minas-Sao Paulo alliance of coffee-planters and exporters. Beginning in 1907, they introduced the practice of engineered currency devaluations and price-support schemes designed to protect their incomes against fluctuations in international coffee prices and revenues. Paradoxically, these subsidy programmes, shifting income from the poor to the rich, were not regarded in violation of the prevailing doctrine of *laissez-faire.*[61]

Under the long Vargas regime, lasting from 1930 to 1954 (excepting the Dutra interregnum from 1945-51), there was a programme of managed populism, controlled and directed from above. With the end of the coffee oligarchy, a process of industrial diversification and

urbanisation was started, and an urban-based populist political
movement emerged. However, educational and human resource
development lagged behind and the elite control of the decision-making
process remained intact. Under Vargas' new Ministry of Labour,
pelegos (or agents managing trade unions and worker groups for the
state) mobilised popular support for the regime in return for some
important gains such as minimum wages, statutory holidays, etc.[62]
However, the constitution of 1934 disenfranchised the illiterates (the
vast majority of the population) and the rural and interior regions
remained stagnant. Vargas, himself a cattle-rancher from Rio Grande
do Sul, derived his political power from a compromise between the
rural *latifundist* oligarchy and the urban proletariat managed by the
pelegos. Under this system, known as *Getulism*, Vargas concentrated
his economic policy on the industrialisation of the relatively small
triangle of Rio-Sao Paulo-Belo Horizonte, with priority on the
development of a Brazilian steel industry and public infrastructure.[63]
There was relatively limited reliance on foreign investment. Instead,
there was a form of economic nationalism, based on exchange controls
and tariff protection for import-replacing industries. These policies
helped to create a new indigenous industrialist class, quite distinct from
the traditional 'associate bourgeoisie' dependent on foreign interests.
Vargas, however, was unable or unwilling to tear apart the old socio-
economic order of Brazil, and the elitist political system survived his
suicide in 1954 in the face of a military *coup.*[64]

Under Kubitschek (1955-61), Brazil, while maintaining a rapid pace
of industrialisation, became increasingly reliant on imports of foreign
investment, especially American. Multinational firms, utilising highly
capital-intensive technology, were established, occupying dominant
positions in the automobile, machinery, mining and manufacturing
industries, sometimes in joint ventures with the state. During 1955-61,
industrial output rose by 80 per cent, by far the largest growth rate in
Latin America. Infra-structural projects, including the construction of
the new federal capital Brasilia, were started. By 1961, the country
had developed huge external debts; and inflationary financing designed
in line with the structuralist theories[65] began to cause spiralling inflation.
In 1963 there was a major balance of payments crisis, and finally in
March 1964 the military intervened, ushering in military rule that has
remained in force ever since. Under this military-bureaucratic regime,
there has been disinflation and 'labour discipline' (declining real wages)
with political stability, achieved at the cost of repression and
dictatorship, and a major economic growth over 1968-72 leading foreign

observers to hail a new 'Brazilian Miracle'.

A 'Miracle' Based on Functional Poverty

The recent economic growth in Brazil is essentially another phase of the traditional model of functional poverty. Evidence shows that the principal gainers of the latest industrial boom have been the foreign investors and multinational firms, together with their associated Brazilian elites.

Brazilian growth since 1964 has closely followed the post-war capitalist model, relying on private investment, but with a major activist role by the state itself. Industrialisation, at the expense of agriculture, has been given the top priority, and direct foreign investment capital has been vigorously sought by a variety of direct and indirect incentives, including tariff protection, export subsidies and tax and credit facilities. The structuralist inflationary financing model of growth has been replaced by the orthodox monetarist stabilisation programme emphasising deflation, controlled wages and trade unions, and a strong balance of payments position.

In terms of aggregate macro data (Table 7.1) the results are highly impressive. The growth rate of GDP increased from 2.9 per cent in 1964 to 9.3 per cent in 1968 and 10.4 per cent in 1972. Industrial output, which was stagnant in 1964, expanded at more than 13 per cent annually during 1968-72. The dollar value of Brazilian exports more than doubled during this period, and despite a similar rise in imports, there was a surplus trade balance. The official foreign exchange reserves registered a healthy growth from US $257 million in 1968 to US $3.8 billion in 1972. Domestically, the rate of inflation, which was 87.3 per cent during 1964, was reduced drastically, and was a tolerable 17 per cent in 1972. The only major lagging sector in the Brazilian economy remained agriculture. But this, of course, reflected the official policy of concentrating on industrial expansion.[66]

Growth of the manufacturing sector was by no means even. The booming industries were the automobile plants, consumer durables (especially electric/electronic appliances) and capital goods such as machinery, metal and chemicals. On the other hand, such industries as textiles, footwear and clothing remained stagnant, while food production lagged behind total manufacturing output.[67] Thus inflation began to emerge as a new threat after 1972; in 1974, it was 28.7 per cent, and imports exceeded exports by US $4.6 billion (see Table 7.1).

The industrial boom of 1968-72 was the result of deliberate government policies which influenced both the investment pattern of

Table 7.1: Some Key Indicators of Brazil's Economic Performance
Since 1964

	1964	1968	1972	1974[a]
1. Growth rates (per cent)				
GDP	2.9	9.3	10.4	9.8
GDP *per capita*	0.0	6.3	7.3	6.9
Industry	5.2	13.2	13.8	8.2
Agriculture	1.3	1.5	4.5	8.5
2. Total exports (US $ million)	1,429	1,881	3,991	7,951
Manufacturing (US $ million)	229		1,048	2,599
3. Total imports (US $ million)	1,263	2,132	4,224	12,635
4. Total foreign reserves (US $ million)		257	3,800	
5. Total foreign indebted reserves (US $ million)		3,917	10,170	22,000
6. Interest, profits and dividends (US $ million)		228	510	
7. Real minimum wages (1970 Cr. $)	234.64	190.31	186.45[b]	
8. Rate of inflation (per cent)	87.3	27.8	17.0	28.7

a. = preliminary.
b. = 1971.

Source: Items 1, 2, 3 and 8 are taken from William G. Tyler, 'Brazilian
Industrialization and Industrial Policies: A Survey', *World Development*,
Vol.4, Nos.10/11 (1976). Items 4, 5, 6 and 7 are taken from Marcos Arruda,
Herbert de Souza, Carlos Afonso, *The Multinational Corporations and Brazil,
The Impact of Multinational Corporations in Contemporary Brazil* (Brazilian
Studies, Latin America Research Unit, Toronto, 1975).

private firms and the consumption habits of buyers. For example, the
boom in the consumer durables sector was significantly caused by the
expansion of consumer credit (available to middle and higher income
groups in urban centres) through the banking and financial sector, while,
at the same time, duty-free imports of equipment and capital goods and
high tariff protection, encouraged both foreign and domestic
industrialists to concentrate on the production of automobiles,
television sets and home appliances for the large urban markets of the
industrial triangle of Rio-Sao Paulo-Belo Horizonte. While some
incentives were also offered for regional diversification of industry,
especially under Law 34/18 of SUDENE designed to attract firms into
the north-east, the horizontal and vertical integration in the Brazilian
manufacturing sector resulted in very limited spread and diffusion
effects.[68] Thus, it has been estimated that the industries set up in the
north-east under 34/18 utilised less than 50 per cent local value-added,

relying instead on inter-regional imports of inputs, almost entirely from the south-east.[69]

Direct participation in the economy by the state itself was a major factor in the pattern of growth and industrial expansion since 1964. Of course, the Brazilian government's activist role extends back to the Vargas regime, but this role has grown at a fast pace, especially in the post-war period. For example, in 1947, government expenditure amounted to only 17.1 per cent of GNP, whereas by the early 1970s the ratio had risen to 32.2 per cent. Such a large volume of public spending is bound to have a major impact on the allocation of resources and the overall economic performance. Since 1964, the economic role of the state has undergone a radical transformation. While the traditional function of building the physical infra-structure has continued, especially in the construction of inter-regional highways, there has been an increased government role in the banking and financial sector, where in 1972, government banking accounted for 55 per cent of total deposits and 58 per cent of loans.[70] Additionally, there is a state dominance in such important sectors as steel, mining, petroleum and petrochemicals, energy and certain fields of transportation. State enterprises are not only some of the largest firms in terms of volume of sales, but also in terms of employment and assets as well.[71] This degree of direct government role has given rise to the Brazilian version of 'state capitalism'.[72] Much of this state capitalist expansion was financed by external public borrowing, through floating of bond issues in European and American money markets.[73] Thus, the external debt of Brazil rose from US $3.9 billion in 1968 to US $10.2 billion in 1972 and to an estimated US $22.0 billion in 1974 (Table 7.1).

Who Benefited from the 'Economic Miracle'?

The urban elites were the principal beneficiaries of the Brazilian 'economic miracle'. While there was a general rise in absolute income levels, the majority of Brazil's almost 100 million citizens experienced a shrinking income share — a trend which had been under way since 1960. According to available, but imperfect, data, the richest 5 per cent of the population appears to have increased its share from 27.4 per cent to 36.3 per cent during 1960-70, while the bottom 80 per cent suffered a reduction from 45.5 per cent to 37.8 per cent; the upper-income group of 15 per cent maintained a constant income share of 27 per cent.[74] The distributive gains by socio-economic groups during 1967-70 are summarised in Table 7.2. The bourgeoisie and upper classes (A and B_1 groups), making up 5 per cent of the total population were the chief

Table 7.2: Income Concentration in Brazil, 1967-70

Class	Population Share (per cent)	Income Share (per cent)	
		1967	1970
A	1	28	30
B_1	4	16	20
B_2	15	21	22.5
C	30	20	15
D	50	15	12.5

A = Upper class, bourgeoisie (property owners, managers).
B_1 = Upper-middle class (some liberal professions, executives, administrators).
B_2 = Urban middle class (public and private bureaucrats, small merchants).
C = Base wage-earners.
D = Rural workers, independent marginal urban workers.
Source: M.C. Tavares and J. Serra, 'Beyond Stagnation: A Discussion on the
   Nature of Recent Development in Brazil' in *Latin America: From Dependence
   to Revolution,* edited by James Petras (John Wiley, New York, 1973), pp.94-6.

gainers, while the working classes in urban and rural areas (C and D
groups) evidently lost during these 'miracle' years.

In addition to Brazilian elites, the 'economic miracle' benefited
foreign interests in two important ways. First, there was a substantial
increase in the volume of outflows of remittances payable to foreign
investors. Furthermore, multinational firms gained in a variety of
indirect ways, such as export subsidies, which amounted to as much as
50 per cent of domestic prices,[75] transfer pricing linked to the exports
of components and parts,[76] and administered wages and curbs on trade
unions and, most important of all, a government strongly dedicated to
the capitalist ideology and fully co-operating with foreign investors.

The majority of the population, especially in urban areas,[77] was
harmed by the post-1964 growth policies. For one thing, the type of
industrialisation, concentrated in the south-east and major cities,
stimulated the pace of urbanisation (which exceeded the population
growth rate of 3.5 per cent — one of the highest in the world). However,
the stabilisation policy of the government actually reduced the level of
real minimum wages. For example, during 1964-8, they dropped by
about 20 per cent, and continued declining (though at a slower rate)
through to 1971 (see Table 7.1). It is important to note that according
to the 1970 census, no less than 42 per cent of all urban workers had a
monthly salary equal to or less than the minimum wage.[78]

Constant or declining real wages would, under certain circumstances, be expected to result in employment creation. However, this failed to occur in Brazil owing to the high capital-intensity of industrialisation encouraged by the government. Both the choice of products and the choice of techniques by the private and state enterprises relied more on capital than on labour inputs.[79] Accordingly, open unemployment as well as underemployment increased significantly, despite the wage restraint policies. The expanding pool of low-wage labour had the dual role of generating functional poverty at minimal (subsistence-level) wages and increasing income inequality between the workers and the capitalists.

Increased income inequality was also significantly promoted by fiscal and credit policies of the government. Interest on personal loans were made tax-deductible up to 50 per cent of gross income; purchases of stocks in private and public enterprises were made tax-deductible up to 12 per cent of the purchase value of stocks; and there was a further 50 per cent tax deduction off bond purchases from state banks; finally, undistributed corporate profits were exempt from tax.[80] All these measures greatly assisted those already in high income brackets, while the overall regressive tax system further boosted the income share of the rich at the expense of the poor.[81]

The provision of public services, too, favoured the elites rather than the masses. In a country characterised by an illiteracy rate that is among the world's highest,[82] no less than 51 per cent of total federal expenditure for education was spent on university level, 12 per cent for secondary level and only 14 per cent for primary-level schooling in 1975.[83] The 1975 budget allocation for defence and security (i.e. 11.1 per cent) exceeded the combined allocations for education and R & D (5.5 per cent), health and sanitation (2.0 per cent) and agriculture (3.2 per cent). On the other hand, 28.3 per cent of the budget was earmarked for the transportation sector to create complementary infrastructure for industrial enterprises, and a further 15 per cent was budgeted for administration.

Conclusion

The Brazilian industrialisation boom following the military take-over in 1964 was designed without regard to equity or social justice. The economic growth policies, patterned after the conventional neoclassical model, were formulated to generate functional inequality. With active state participation, industrialisation relied on large inflows of direct foreign investment attracted by a variety of incentives. Administered wages, choice of technique and product as well as rapid urbanisation combined to minimise employment creation. As a result of these factors, industrialisation has been accompanied not only by widening income inequality, but also by functional poverty at subsistence level for the great mass of the Brazilian population.

The latest industrial boom must be seen in the context of Brazil's 400-year-old boom-bust pattern of growth. As with previous booms, the latest one has every appearance of benefiting merely the ruling elites and their associated foreign partners. In this sense, the real obstacle to egalitarian development in Brazil remains structural reform to replace its elitist political and institutional system with a new one in which decisions, including planning priorities and public expenditure allocations, are based on the choices of all its citizens rather than merely on sectional or elite interests. Such a structural transformation would clearly constitute a watershed in Brazil's long history of external and internal dependency. This fact alone casts the gravest doubt about the prospects of a peaceful or automatic introduction of the egalitarian development strategy to be discussed in the following chapters.

UGANDA: THE SOCIAL COSTS OF MILITARY TYRANNY

Amin's Uganda is one of the clearest and most tragic examples of the enormous social costs of violent transformations, especially those engineered by military elites.[84] Uganda represents not only a classic case of a lopsided, dual economy,[85] but also a plural society, with many tribal divisions and inter-regional inequalities; in addition, and until 1972, it manifested a visible colonial legacy in the form of a small, but prosperous, Asian community. In August 1972, General Amin, who had staged a successful *coup* against President Obote in January 1971,[86] suddenly announced the mass expulsion of 55,000 Asians living in Uganda within 90 days. This was Amin's 'War for Economic Independence', launched in order to improve the welfare of the African population by getting rid of the hated Asians and foreign exploiters of the country: 'those who milked the cow which they did not feed'. The 'War' began with great jubilation amidst the Africans, naturally in expectation of windfall gains at the expense of the departing Asians. In fact, however, the Ugandan military elite — and not the African masses — has been the beneficiary who acquired the assets and property left behind. As the post-expulsion economic and political chaos deepened, the tyranny of the military intensified, turning against the African tribes, destroying the social and economic life of the country and causing thousands of casualties.[87]

'Economic War for Independence': Destruction of Uganda's Economy

The damage done by Amin's reign of terror may well require many decades to be undone. This fact can only be appreciated in terms of the modern history of the country.

When Uganda became independent on 9 October 1962, she possessed a number of important advantages, such as a relatively well-developed system of government, a transportation network thanks to the colonial Development and Welfare loans,[88] and a promising regional economic market arrangement with neighbouring Kenya and Tanzania in the form of an East African Community.[89] The country's economy, however, suffered badly from a north-south dualism: the northern region was poor, stagnant and dominated by subsistence African farming; the south contained the large coffee and sugar plantations, owned by foreign interests, and the modern, urban sector concentrated in the fertile crescent stretching from Jinja to the capital city of Kampala and Masaka on the north-western shores of Lake Victoria.[90] This dualism represented far more than geographic inequalities: it had significant tribal implications as well. The south was the homeland of the Baganda elites, with a long history of political government,[91] whereas the northern regions were populated by a diversity of relatively backward tribes, including Obote's Ankole and Langi, and Amin's Nilo-Hamitic tribes.[92] One of Obote's central objectives had been to bring about a fairer regional distribution of incomes and economic opportunities, and his 'Move to the Left'[93] and economic plans were designed with this objective in mind.[94]

In addition to regional and tribal inequalities, Uganda was characterised by another type of racial division, owing to the presence of the Asian community. This was the direct result of British colonialism in East Africa. For, although trade contacts between East Africa and India go back many centuries,[95] it was during the construction of the Kenya-Uganda railway, started in 1895, that large numbers of Indians were imported by the British. This explains the general, but somewhat incorrect, view, that the ancestors of the present Asian community were railway workers. In fact, the occupational background of the Asian immigrants was highly diverse and included, besides railway employees, book-keepers, accountants, clerks, soldiers, and a wide range of artisans and labouring classes. Nevertheless, they were all drawn from just two regions of India, Gujarat and Punjab, and they all belonged to the lower castes of the merchants and artisans. This fact is crucial for two reasons:

first, it provides the original motivation (i.e. financial gain) which stimulated the Indian influx and subsequent emergence of the Indian community as the dominant commercial class in East Africa. Second, it explains
the cultural exclusiveness of the Asians built around the caste system,
imported from India with all its intricacies and sub-divisions. These two
factors were further cultivated and solidified during the colonial rule.
De facto racial segregation, if not *de jure,* was the principal rule of
colonial race relations. The Asians, however objectionable their image
as indentured coolies or as people of low caste, nevertheless rendered
an essential service in the colonial economy as shopkeepers, artisans
and traders. The Africans, on the other hand, were regarded as lazy,
unintelligent and untrustworthy, best left undisturbed in the subsistence
sector to serve as a reservoir of cheap labour. Such stereotyped racial
categorisation was bound, in due course, to result in bitter racial
conflict.

By Uganda's independence, the Asian community had emerged as
the dynamic entity in the manufacturing sector as well as in the
distributive and export/import sectors. A few Asian families, principally
the Madhavanis, controlled large enterprises in Jinja and Kampala,
while the British and foreign firms owned and operated the banking
and financial sector, and the large coffee and sugar plantations.[96]

The rise of African nationalism in the post-war period, and the
eventual achievement of 'Uhuru' (independence) in East Africa in the
early 1960s represent the turning point in race relations between Asians
and Africans. Thanks largely to their cultural exclusiveness, the Asians
themselves had helped to create an image amongst the African majority
that they were 'exploiters' with loyalties only to India or Pakistan. In
fact, during the 'Uhuru' years, Indian government officials sometimes
referred to the Asian community of East Africa as 'the guests of the
Africans',[97] clearly implying their transitory status. The extra-territorial
loyalties of the Asians in Uganda were strongly manifested immediately
following independence in 1962, when large numbers of Asians declined
to take out Uganda citizenship, but instead opted for British citizenship
under the British Immigration Act of 1962.[98] As the 'Africanisation'
movement during post-independence gathered momentum and the flow
of Asian immigration to Britain began to accelerate, the British
government passed the 1968 Immigration Act, putting a strict quota
limit on the number of Asians to be admitted into Britain. This British
action had the effect of hardening the anti-Asian stance of the East
African governments, as was demonstrated by the hard-line position
taken by Kenya, which had enacted legislation in 1967 designed to

remove the trading licences of non-citizens in the country.

In Uganda, the Kenya crisis of 1968 had generated a dramatic impact on race relations. It caused a panic among the British Asians (i.e. those holding British passports but nevertheless required to validate them at the British High Commission in Kampala in order to enter Britain) as well as Ugandan Asians who had previously opted for Ugandan citizenship. An exodus of Asians began, and an increasing number of wealthy Asians started a capital flight, often through illegal means such as over-invoicing imports and under-invoicing exports. In 1969-70 private capital outflows registered no less than a 60 per cent increase over the previous year. This was also, in part, due to the declared intention of the Obote government to nationalise key foreign enterprises in the country. As a result, the Uganda government was obliged in 1970 to use, for the first time, her Special Drawing Rights with the International Monetary Fund to offset a serious deterioration in her foreign exchange reserves.

The balance of payments crisis, especially news of the Asians' illegal monetary transfers abroad, generated an emotional African demand for 'Ugandanisation'. While largely based on xenophobia, 'Ugandanisation' was also a natural consequence of political independence. Available evidence indicates that while the size of public service employment remained almost constant during 1957-65, there was a substantial increase in the amount of the public wage bill, and by 1965 civil servant salaries and wages represented no less than 33 per cent of total government tax revenues.[99] On the other hand, there was a strict minimum wage legislation in effect which restrained private sector earnings,[100] while the rate of job creation was well below the rate of urbanisation and labour force expansion. Accordingly, rising migration into towns was beginning to create serious problem of open urban unemployment, especially amongst young school-leavers.[101]

Clearly, Ugandan independence well fitted the usual elitist model, with a new indigenous elite replacing the departing expatriate administrators, and utilising its powers for self-aggrandisement first and foremost. As a result, income inequality widened following independence. Ugandanisation policies of the Obote government were conceived against this contradictory record.

Ugandanisation

These policies were spelled out in the *Third Five Year Plan, 1971/2-1975/6*,[102] the last major statement of policy of the Obote regime. Plan III, as it was known, was subsequently endorsed by Amin, despite the fact that it was prepared in conformity with Obote's African Socialism and the *Common Man's Charter.*[103] It defined Ugandanisation as a long-term objective to provide greater employment opportunities for Ugandans themselves. However, its achievement was perceived as a gradual, orderly process of replacing skilled expatriate personnel by qualified Ugandans, at a rate commensurate with increased availability of Ugandan manpower. 'The ultimate weapon for speeding up Ugandanisation. . .is the planned expansion of educational and training facilities.'[104] No specific target date for manpower self-sufficiency was declared. It was merely stated: 'We have set ourselves the very ambitious goal of attaining virtual self-sufficiency in manpower in the early 1980's.'[105] Furthermore, the Plan recognised the equal right to employment of all Ugandan citizens whether of African, Asian or European origin. It declared that the provision of employment opportunities 'to all citizens who seek it. . .is indeed a fundamental right of the Uganda community'.[106]

The achievement of 'virtual self-sufficiency in manpower in the early 1980's' was by no means an unrealistic target. Employment data computed from the *Enumeration of Employees* Survey of the Ministry of Planning and Economic Development clearly demonstrated that Ugandanisation was largely an accomplished fact as early as 1964, when 94.5 per cent of total enumerated employment was held by Africans. By 1970, the African share of this employment had reached 95.7 per cent – a gain of 1.3 percentage points in 6 years. Even at this gradual pace, 100 per cent Africanisation of enumerated employment in Uganda would have been completed by the mid-1980s.[107] Of course, enumerated employment represented only a fraction of Uganda's total labour force, and, more significantly, its complete Africanisation by a gradual, orderly process might have failed to remove the foreign domination of the country's economy. On the other hand, the mass expulsion ordered by Idi Amin in 1972 has been an economic as well as a social disaster for the country.

The immediate economic consequence of the expulsion of Asians was a sudden and severe manpower gap. The departing Asians were predominantly in skilled and professional occupations. In addition, the saving, investment and tax revenues were largely provided by the Asian community; their removal created an immediate economic strangulation of the economy. But the main contributing factor for the economic strangulation was the military tyranny which followed the expulsion of Asians. Within a few months of the expulsion of the Asians, the military took over the businesses, factories and private property left behind.

Under 'Phase I' of his 'Economic War', Amin forced some 55,000 Asians out of Uganda within 90 days. Under 'Phase II', he set up Allocation Committees, made up of military officers, to transfer Asian properties and assets to Ugandans. The latter were subsequently distributed amongst senior military officers and those from Amin's own Kakwa and West Bank tribes. Abandoned cars were similarly taken over by the military, and the remainder were auctioned off to the general public, the proceeds going directly to the Army Paymaster.

The economic and social position of the bulk of inhabitants has gone from bad to worse. The urban consumer could not any more complain against 'profiteering' or 'exploiting' Asian traders, while staples, such as cooking oil, sugar and salt, began to disappear from the shops as the flow of trade trickled down towards a halt. While Amin was priding himself on a sudden rise in Uganda's foreign exchange reserves soon after November 1972, the cessation of import trade and domestic distribution began to generate an inflationary spiral, which was also caused by an increasing money supply. During the 1960s inflation was practically unknown, but consumer prices doubled during 1972-4, in no small way due to an unprecedented expansion of military expenditure.[108] This military expenditure was at the expense of development projects. In the private sector, commerce and industry stagnated or regressed owing to uncertainty and lack of managerial control and investment. In rural areas, farming and food production dwindled to the barest minimum as a reign of military tyranny evolved into tribal and religious warfare.

But the economic hardships of the masses are small indeed, compared with the consequences of military tyranny and reign of terror that have emerged in the wake of Amin's 'Economic War'. There is a complete breakdown of law and order, with frequent kidnappings, mysterious murders and illegal acquisition of private property all over Uganda, planned and implemented by the army. The civil service, once amongst the best in East Africa, has been reduced to an inferior and subordinate status by fear and punishment; civil servants are afraid to attend meetings, or prepare routine reports for fear of attracting the wrath of the dreaded military and secret service agents. Uganda's relations with Kenya and Tanzania have on several occasions reached breaking point, while the East African Economic Community has been largely paralysed and its future put into jeopardy.

Conclusion

It is ironic that such tragic results have followed policies (e.g. Ugandanisation) originally declared to promote the general well-being of the population. In a real sense, the tragedy of Amin in Uganda was an almost predictable, if not inevitable, culmination of deep socio-economic and regional inequalities of the country. Despite his declared intentions for African Socialism and egalitarian reforms, Obote had already started policies in the 1960s destined to create major upheavals in Uganda. Amin's emergence could be regarded as the next stage in a process that was started well before 1971.

There is little doubt that the social costs of Amin's reign of terror and his destruction of the country's economy will require several years, even decades, to be eradicated. The major 'lesson' which emerges from this tragedy — which has validity beyond Uganda's borders — is that glaring socio-economic disparities and inequalities between individuals, classes and regions are bound to lead to a catastrophe sooner or later, and that their elimination constitutes the surest preventative strategy. This is the basic theme of egalitarian development which is a strategy long overdue in the Third World. The next chapter is devoted to a discussion of the general outlines of an egalitarian development strategy, followed by detailed analysis of some major egalitarian policies in subsequent chapters.

Notes

1. Asaf Hussain and John P. Hutchison, 'The Impact of Religion and Ethnicity on Political Conflicts in Pakistan', *Asian Profile*, Vol.4, No.4 (August 1976). An up-to-date analysis of the recent situation in Pakistan is in the Special Issue of *Journal of Asian and African Studies*, Vol.VIII, Nos.3-4 (July and October 1973).

2. Thus, for the fiscal year 1972/3, no less than 60 per cent of the total budget of 7.43 billion rupees was allocated for defence expenditures. See *New York Times*, 18 June 1972.

3. The most tragic failure of this illogical policy was, of course, the use of the military to suppress the political demands of East Pakistan by Gen. Yahya Khan, leading to the creation of Bangladesh. See Raunag Jahan, *Pakistan: Failure in National Integration* (Columbia University Press, New York, 1972). The increased military budget allocations, noted in the preceding footnote, too, are connected with secessionist movements in West Pakistan. See Government of Pakistan, *White Paper on Baluchistan* (Printing Corporation of Pakistan Press, Islamabad, 19 October 1974).

4. Gustav F. Papanek, *Pakistan's Development — Social Goals and Private Incentives* (Harvard University Press, Cambridge, Mass., 1967).

5. See p.149 below. Also. see S.J. Burki. *Agricultural Growth and Local Government in Punjab Pakistan* (Cornell University Press, Ithaca, New York, 1974).

6. Indeed, religion may play a divisive role. Thus, in early 1974, in the wake of violent clashes between the Ahmadiya sect and other Muslims, President Bhutto was obliged to amend the Constitution to declare the former sect as 'not a Muslim for purposes of the Constitution or Law'. *Pakistan Times*, Lahore,

8 September 1974. For a detailed analysis of Islam and the Constitution, see Fazlur Rahman, 'Islam and the New Constitution of Pakistan', *Journal of Asian and African Studies* (see note 1).

7. Pakistan, Planning Commission, *The Second Five Year Plan (1960-65)* (Manager of Publications, Karachi, June 1960), p.49.

8. Pakistan, Planning Commission, *The Third Five Year Plan (1965-70)* (Manager of Publications, Karachi, May 1965), p.33.

9. Papanek, *Pakistan's Development*, p.67.

10. Ibid., pp.67-70.

11. Ibid., p.68.

12. G. Myrdal, *Asian Drama* (Pantheon, New York, 1968), p.323.

13. Papanek, *Pakistan's Development*, Table I, p.7. For similar, but slightly different figures, see Stephen R. Lewis Jr., *Pakistan, Industrialization and Trade Policies* (Oxford University Press, London, 1970), Table I.1, p.8.

14. Papanek, *Pakistan's Development*, p.33.

15. Ibid., p.36. However, this figure was seriously understated.

16. Ibid., p.35.

17. Ibid., p.109.

18. Lewis, *Pakistan*, especially Chapter 2. The growth rate is from Papanek, *Pakistan's Development*, Table I, p.7.

19. Syed Nawak Haider Naqvi, 'On Optimizing Pakistan's Export Bonus Scheme', *Journal of Political Economy*, Vol.79, No.1 (January/February 1971); H.J. Bruton and S.R. Bose, *The Pakistan Export Bonus Scheme* (Karachi, 1963).

20. Lawrence J. White, *Industrial Concentration and Economic Power in Pakistan* (Princeton University Press, Princeton, 1974).

21. Papanek, *Pakistan's Development*, p.87; Nural Islam, 'Foreign Assistance and Economic Development: The Case of Pakistan', *Economic Journal*, Vol.82, No.325a (March 1972) (Supplement).

22. Islam, 'Foreign Assistance', p.518.

23. Computed from A. Bergan, 'Personal Income Distribution and Personal Savings in Pakistan, 1963-4', *The Pakistan Development Review* (Summer 1967).

24. Islam, 'Foreign Assistance', p.514.

25. There was, also, cessation of foreign aid from the USA.

26. Myrdal, *Asian Drama*, p.323; Angus Maddison, *Class Structure and Economic Growth, India and Pakistan Since the Moghuls* (George Allen and Unwin, London, 1971), p.144, footnote 1.

27. Islam, 'Foreign Assistance', p.519, Table IV.

28. The Second Plan, p.2.

29. F. Kahnert *et al.*, *Agricultural and Related Industries in Pakistan* (Development Center Studies, OECD, Paris, 1970), p.71.

30. I. Little, T. Scitovsky and M. Scott, *Industry and Trade in Some Developing Countries* (Oxford University Press, London, 1970), p.43.

31. Lewis, *Pakistan*, p.148.

32. S.R. Bose, 'Trend of Real Income of the Rural Poor in East Pakistan, 1949-66', *Pakistan Development Review* (Autumn 1968), Table 1.

33. According to Bergan, in 'Personal Income Distribution', the ratio of the income share of the top 10 per cent wealthiest to the bottom 10 per cent in 1963 was 16.8 for urban, and 11.0 for rural areas. The ratios for the top 20 per cent to the bottom 20 per cent were, respectively, 8.7 and 6.5. It is significant to remember that 1963 was a good harvest year; as a result the extent of disparities implied by these figures are most likely understated.

34. A.R. Khan, 'What Has Been Happening to Real Wages in Pakistan', *Pakistan Development Review* (Autumn 1967).

35. Ayub's slogan was 'Islamic Socialism', although the Third Plan declared: 'What is basic to Islamic Socialism is the creation of equal opportunities for all

rather than equal distribution of wealth.' In the *Socio-economic Objectives of the Fourth Five Year Plan (1970-75)*, issued in November 1968, it was emphasised that 'We cannot distribute poverty. Growth is vital before income distribution can improve.' Quoted in A. Maddison, *Class Structure and Economic Growth*, p.136.

36. Lee L. Bean and A.D. Bhatti, 'Pakistan's Population in the 1970's: Problems and Prospects', *Journal of Asian and African Studies*, p.263 (see note 1).

37. Ghulam Mohammed, 'Private tubewell development and Cropping Patterns in West Pakistan', *Pakistan Development Review* (Spring 1965); S.R. Bose and E.H. Clark II, 'Some Basic Considerations on Agricultural Mechanization in West Pakistan', *Pakistan Development Review* (Autumn 1969); Chapter 6 by W.P. Falcon and C.H. Gotsch in *Development Policy II – The Pakistan Experience*, edited by Walter P. Falcon and Gustav F. Papanek (Harvard University Press, Cambridge, Mass., 1971).

38. Pakistan Central Statistical Office, *25 Years of Pakistan in Statistics, 1947-72* (Manager of Publications, Karachi, July 1972), p.82.

39. I. Ahmed, 'The Green Revolution and Tractorisation', *International Labour Review*, Vol.114, No.1 (July-August 1976); Carl H. Gotsch, 'Tractor Mechanisation and Rural Development in Pakistan', *International Labour Review*, Vol.107, No.2 (February 1973).

40. Walter P. Falcon and Joseph J. Stern in Falcon and Papanek, *Development Policy II*, p.4.

41. Pakistan, Government Finance Division (Economic Adviser's Wing), *Pakistan Economic Survey 1971-72* (Islamabad, June 1972), p.21.

42. S.J. Burki, *Agricultural Growth;* Craig Baxter, 'The People's Party Vs. The Punjab "Feudalists"', *Journal of Asian and African Studies* (see note 1); K.B. Sayeed, *The Political System of Pakistan* (Houghton, Mifflin, Boston, 1967).

43. Carl H. Gotsch, 'Tractor Mechanisation', p.138.

44. Ibid., p.139.

45. Ahmed, 'The Green Revolution', p.90.

46. Ibid., p.91.

47. Ibid., p.90.

48. Gotsch, 'Tractor Mechanisation', p.140.

49. R.V. Gilbert, 'The Works Programme in East Pakistan', *International Labour Review*, Vol.89 (March 1964): E.E. Hagen, *The Economics of Development* (Richard D. Irwin, Homewood, Ill., 1968), pp.76-7.

50. Maddison, *Class Structure and Economic Growth*, Chapter VII, provides a useful discussion of the various elite groups, including the bureaucrats, armed forces, other professional groups, agricultural and industrial entities.

51. Talukder Maniruzzaman, 'Group Interests in Pakistan Politics 1947-58', *Pacific Affairs* (Summer 1966), reprinted in Norman T. Uphoff and Warren F. Ilchman (eds.), *The Political Economy of Development, Theoretical and Empirical Contributions* (University of California Press, 1972).

52. Ronald Herring and M. Ghaffar Chaudry, 'The 1972 Land Reforms in Pakistan and Their Economic Implications: A Preliminary Analysis', *Pakistan Development Review*, Vol.13, No.3 (Autumn 1974).

53. Ibid., pp.248-9. For a more general study of the political aspects of agricultural change in Pakistan and elsewhere, see Keith Griffin, *The Political Economy of Agrarian Change: An Essay on the Green Revolution* (Macmillan, London, 1974).

54. There is a great volume of literature on Latin American external dependency, perhaps the extreme theoretician being Andre G. Frank, *Latin America: Underdevelopment or Revolution* (Monthly Review Press, New York, 1969). See also James Petras (ed.), *Latin America: From Dependence to Revolution* (John Wiley, New York, 1973); Ronald H. Chilcote and Joel C.

Edelstein (eds.), *Latin America: The Struggle with Dependency and Beyond* (John Wiley, New York, 1974).

55. Chilcote and Edelstein, *Latin America,* p.27.

56. For a concise economic history of Brazil, see Celso Furtado, *The Economic Growth of Brazil, A Survey from Colonial to Modern Times* (University of California Press, Berkeley, 1971).

57. Raouf Kahil, *Inflation and Economic Development in Brazil 1946-1963* (Clarendon Press, Oxford, 1973), p.13.

58. Rollie E. Poppino, *Brazil, The Land and People,* second ed. (Oxford University Press, New York, 1973), p.16.

59. Alfred Stepan, *The Military in Politics, Changing Patterns in Brazil* (Princeton University Press, Princeton, 1971).

60. Cf. Celso Furtado, 'Political Obstacles to the Economic Development of Brazil' in Claudio Veliz (ed.), *Obstacles to Change in Latin America* (Oxford University Press, New York, 1970); Joao Quartim, *Dictatorship and Armed Struggle in Brazil* (translated from the French by David Fernbach) (New Left Books, London, 1971).

61. A brief historical account of the changing role of the Brazilian government since the 1900s is given in Werner Baer, Isaac Kerstenetzky and Annibal V. Villela, 'The Changing Role of the State in the Brazilian Economy', *World Development,* Vol.1, No.11 (November 1973).

62. Quartim, *Dictatorship and Armed Struggle,* pp.28ff.

63. Werner Baer, *The Development of the Brazilian Steel Industry* (Vanderbilt University Press, Nashville, 1969). A fuller description of Brazilian industrialisation is given in W. Baer, *Industrialization and Economic Development in Brazil* (Richard D. Irwin, Homewood, Ill., 1965). See also H.S. Ellis (ed.), *The Economy of Brazil* (University of California Press, Berkeley, 1969).

64. For an analysis of the Vargas regime, see Quartim, *Dictatorship and Armed Struggle,* esp. pp.19-51.

65. For a good survey of this debate see Dudley Seers, 'Inflation and Growth: A Summary of Experience in Latin America', *Economic Bulletin for Latin America,* Vol.VII, No.1 (February 1962). See also D. Felix, 'An Alternative View of the "Monetarist"-"Structuralist" Controversy' in A.O. Hirschman (ed.), *Latin American Issues — Essays and Comments* (Twentieth Century Fund, New York, 1961).

66. For recent surveys of the post-1964 industrialisation in Brazil see William G. Tyler, 'Brazilian Industrialization and Industrial Policies: A Survey', *World Development,* Vol.4, Nos. 10/11 (1976); W. Baer, 'The Brazilian Boom 1968-72: An Explanation and Interpretation', *World Development,* Vol.1, No.8 (August 1973).

67. The significant increase in agricultural output in 1972 reflected the unusually good coffee harvest in 1971 relative to the previous year.

68. SUDENE is the Superintendency for the Development of the North-east. The basic features of the 34/18 incentives are described in A.O. Hirschman, 'Industrial Development in the Brazilian Northeast and the Tax Credit Scheme of Article 34/18', *Journal of Development Studies,* Vol.5 (October 1968); and in D.E. Goodman, 'Industrial Development in the Brazilian Northeast. An Interim Assessment of the Tax Credit Scheme of Article 34/18' in R. Roett (ed.), *Brazil in the Sixties* (Vanderbilt University Press, Nashville, 1972).

69. Cf. Tyler, 'Brazilian Industrialization', p.875, and D.E. Goodman, 'The Brazilian Economic "Miracle" and Regional Policy: Some Evidence from the Urban Northeast', *Journal of Latin American Studies,* Vol.8, Part 1 (May 1976), p.6.

70. W. Baer, 'The Brazilian Boom', p.7.

71. Ibid.

72. W. Baer, I. Kerstenetsky and A.V. Villela, 'The Changing Role of the State', esp. pp.28-34.

73. During the 1960s Brazil received substantial loans from the World Bank and US AID for transportation and electrification projects. In the second half of the decade, there was increasing government reliance on the Eurodollar and bond markets.

74. These figures are from Marcos Arruda, 'Notes on the Situation of Labour in Contemporary Brazil' in Marcos Arruda, Herbert de Souza and Carlos Afonso, *Multinationals and Brazil: The Impact of Multinational Corporations in Contemporary Brazil* (Brazilian Studies Latin American Research Unit, Toronto, 1975), p.53. Although this topic is a highly controversial one, the empirical data reported here are supported by several other studies, including those by Fishlow, Hoffman and Duarte, Langoni, and Wells — all referred to in Tyler, 'Brazilian Industrialization', p.874.

75. Arruda, 'Notes', p.74; Tyler, 'Brazilian Industrialization', p.871.

76. Tyler, 'Brazilian Industrialization', pp.868-73.

77. A. Fishlow, 'Brazilian Size Distribution by Income', *American Economic Review, Papers and Proceedings*, Vol.62, No.2 (May 1971). A recent re-examination of this subject is in G.S. Fields, 'Who Benefits from Development?', *American Economic Review*, Vol.67, No.4 (September 1977).

78. Petras, *Latin America*, p.116.

79. Samuel A. Morley and Gordon W. Smith, 'The Choice of Technology: Multinational Firms in Brazil,' *Economic Development and Cultural Change*, Vol.25, No.2 (January 1977).

80. J. Serra in Petras, *Latin America*, p.121.

81. Fishlow, 'Brazilian Size Distribution', p.400; J. Serra in Petras, *Latin America*, pp.121-5.

82. According to the 1970 census, 64.2 per cent of the population possessed 'incomplete elementary education' — up from 41.7 per cent in 1960. There is evidence to suggest that actual illiteracy data of this census are overstated. See J. Serra in Petras, *Latin America*, p.122.

83. These figures are taken from Herbert Souza and Carlos A. Afonso, *The Role of the State in the Capitalist Development of Brazil, The Fiscal Crisis of the Brazilian State* (Brazilian Studies, York University, Faculty of Graduate Studies, July/October 1975) (first draft, mimeo.), Table 19, p.76.

84. S. Decalo, *Coups and Army Rule in Africa* (Yale University Press, Yale, 1976); Michael F. Lofchie, 'The Uganda Coup — Class Action by the Military', *Journal of Modern African Studies*, Vol.10, No.1 (1972).

85. General studies of Uganda are presented in W. Elkan, *The Economic Development of Uganda* (Oxford University Press, London, 1961); International Bank for Reconstruction and Development, *The Economic Development of Uganda* (Johns Hopkins Press, Baltimore, 1962). A comparative study of land tenure in Uganda, Kenya and Tanzania is given in A. Segal, 'The Politics of Land in East Africa', *Economic Development and Cultural Change*, Vol.16, No.2 (January 1968).

86. James H. Mittelman, 'The Anatomy of a Coup: Uganda, 1971', *Africa Quarterly*, Vol.X, No.3 (October-December 1971); Michael Twaddle, 'The Amin Coup', *Journal of Commonwealth Political Studies*, Vol.X, No.2 (July 1972). The latter study, in contrast with the Lofchie article cited above, maintains that Amin's *coup* was the action of a deeply divided military lacking in political cohesiveness or aims.

87. There is a profusion of reports, especially in newspapers and popular magazines, detailing the social and human suffering of the Ugandans. For a perceptive analysis of tribal conflicts see Nelson Kasfir, 'Cultural Sub-

Nationalism in Uganda' in Victor A. Olorunsola (ed.), *The Politics of Cultural Sub-Nationalism in Africa* (Doubleday, New York, 1972). On the vital Baganda, Uganda's largest, best educated, and richest ethnic group, see David E. Apter, *The Political Kingdom in Uganda: A Study in Bureaucratic Nationalism* (Princeton University Press, Princeton, 1961).

88. The British government in 1929 enacted the first Colonial Development and Welfare Act enabling funding of development loans to the colonies, providing that these funds were used to purchase goods produced in Britain — probably the earliest example of 'tied aid'. In Uganda (as in other East African colonies) the CD & W loans were utilised for infrastructural investments to facilitate colonial trade and commerce. For example, during 1929-36 a mere 6 per cent of these funds were used for agricultural projects. See R.M.A. van Zwanenberg with Anne King, *An Economic History of Kenya and Uganda 1800-1970* (Macmillan, London, 1975), p.xxi.

89. Arthur Hazlewood, *Economic Integration: The East African Experience* (Heinemann, London, 1975).

90. An excellent account of regional economic conditions is given in Chapter Seven of *Uganda's Plan III: Third Five-Year Development Plan 1971/2-1975/6* (Government Printer, Uganda, 1972).

91. Apter, *The Political Kingdom in Uganda*.

92. Colin Leys, *Politicians and Policies: An Essay on Politics in Acholi, Uganda, 1962-65* (East African Publishing House, Nairobi, 1967); Ali A. Mazrui, 'Leadership in Africa: Obote of Uganda', *International Journal*, Vol.25, No.3 (Summer 1970); Jonathan Rollow, 'Uganda's Amin's Economic Revolution', *African Report* (May-June 1974).

93. A. Milton Obote, *Proposals for New Methods of Elections of Representatives of the People to Parliament* (Kampala, 1970), Document No.5 on 'The Move to The Left'.

94. This is clearly true of *Plan III*, which was prepared under Obote's Presidency, but subsequently endorsed by Amin, who ultimately made it utterly inoperative.

95. D.P. Ghai and Y.P. Ghai (eds.), *Portrait of a Minority, Asians in East Africa* (rev. ed.) (Oxford University Press, Nairobi, 1970); A Bharati, *The Asians in East Africa: Janhind and Uhuru* (Nelson-Hall, Chicago, 1972).

96. A critical analysis of foreign banking in Uganda is given in I. Gershenberg, 'Banking in Uganda Since Independence', *Economic Development and Cultural Change*, Vol.20 (August 1972).

97. Quoted by A. Gupta in 'Ugandan Asians, Britain, India and Commonwealth', *African Affairs*, Vol.73, No.292 (July 1974), p.316.

98. For a discussion of British attitudes and policies in the sixties leading to the Uganda crisis of 1972, see Justin O'Brien, *Brown Britons: The Crisis of the Ugandan Asians* (Runnymede Trust Publications, London, 1972).

99. J.B. Knight, 'Earnings, Employment, Education and Income Distribution in Uganda', *Bulletin of the Oxford University Institute of Economics and Statistics*, Vol.30, No.4 (November 1968).

100. J.B. Knight, 'The Determination of Wages and Salaries in Uganda', *Bulletin of the Oxford University Institute of Economics and Statistics* (October 1967).

101. W. Elkan, *Migrants and Proletarians, Urban Labour in Economic Development of Uganda* (Oxford University Press, London, 1960).

102. Section C of the 'Development Manifesto' (Chapter 1) of *Plan III*, and Chapter 6, 'Manpower and Employment'.

103. A. Milton Obote, *The Common Man's Charter with Appendices* (Government Printer, Uganda, 1970).

104. *Plan III,* p.11.
105. Ibid., p.12.
106. Ibid., p.5.
107. These calculations are based on data from *The Enumeration of Employees* (annual) 1964-1970 (Ministry of Planning and Economic Development, Entebbe, Uganda).
108. The Economist Intelligence Unit, *QER: Uganda, Ethiopia, Somalia Annual Supplement 1975* (London, 1975).

Part Three

EGALITARIAN PLANNING AND REFORM IN LDCS

8 TOWARDS MORE EGALITARIAN
DEVELOPMENT PLANNING

This chapter has a pragmatic rather than a philosophical or a doctrinaire purpose. We do not intend to propose any ideological or Utopian blue-prints for socio-economic restructuring in the Third World, and we not assume that a radical or violent revolution is a necessary precondition for a new order in LDCs.[1]

Central to our pragmatic approach is the assumption that the price-market system, reinforced by reformist and progressive intervention in the economic and planning process, is quite compatible with egalitarian objectives. What we wish to do is to formulate the broad outlines of a feasible economic and social development strategy which, unlike the 'Big Push' industrialisation drive of the post-war period, would be capable of delivering substantially greater income security and other benefits to the bulk of the population in Third World countries. In a word, we wish to make development planning an egalitarian tool so that planning promotes not income concentration but social justice,[2] serving the needs of all groups of citizens. Instead of what Hugo A. Bedeau has termed *radical egalitarianism,*[3] we shall be guided by a more limited concept of equality.

Distinguishing Between Economic Growth and Development

We start with the important distinction between the concepts of 'growth' and 'development'. The former is a narrower idea and refers to the expansion of national income or production, most typically measured as GNP or GDP *per capita,* as a result of increased capital formation and input utilisation. On the other hand, the idea of 'development' is much broader in scope and refers to a general improvement in the material and social well-being of the society as a whole. While this general improvement incorporates high income *per capita,* it also requires reforms in the institutional or quasi-economic framework such as wider accessibility to educational, health and welfare facilities, greater political participation in the national decision-making process, and a more equitable distribution of the benefits of progress, achieved through economic planning.[4]

This line of reasoning is essentially based on a fundamental difference between the *rate* and *pattern* of economic change.

Statistically, an LDC may achieve an impressive GNP growth; yet this growth may reflect a lopsided, uneven pattern with the mass of the population receiving marginal benefits or even being harmed, while a tiny privileged elite at the top increases its wealth and power. The case-studies of Malaysia, Liberia and other countries discussed in Part Two present evidence of the unjust effects of post-war industrialisation strategies and planning.

The idea that the poverty and underdevelopment of LDCS are intrinsically linked to their institutional and socio-economic framework has recently begun to gain international recognition. For example, the International Labour Organization, in its World Employment Programme,[5] is promoting the argument that it is futile to talk about unemployment without discussing the more basic problem of 'the huge, widening abyss between the rich and the poor [in LDCs]. . .the fault lies in the actual structure of the economy, which [supports] a tiny minority in great comfort and a very large majority in poverty.'[6] The clear implication is that development requires sweeping reforms designed to bring about an open society[7] based on equality of opportunity in the labour markets, equal access to quality education and training, balanced regional and rural growth, and generally a more equitable distribution of incomes and wealth.

Egalitarian Development: Some General Guidelines

Our concept of egalitarian development in LDCs does not call for perfect equality for everyone in consumption or living standards. Given the ambiguities surrounding the concept of 'equality'[8] and the fact that LDCs are anything but homogeneous, it would be too idealistic to do so. We rather focus attention on the elimination of *excessively large disparities* between different individuals, groups and regions which now characterise a great number of LDCs and which have often been worsened as a result of post-war industrialisation. In short, our concept of egalitarian development is a plea to make economic planning and policy an anti-poverty tool. That is to say, we are proposing a planning strategy that would *tend* to equalise living standards without necessarily leading to perfect equality as the final result.

For budgetary and administrative reasons, excessive disparities in income and living standards between individuals cannot be eliminated overnight; the task must begin urgently but proceed in an orderly fashion within a hierarchy of targets. The first and most urgent target is the equalisation of consumption of basic needs, such as food, shelter and clothing. Equally important is the equalisation of opportunity or access *vis-à-vis* the supply of public goods and services, such as education, health and welfare. Of critical importance is the necessity of institutional and administrative reforms in the governmental and political framework in order to execute an equitable distribution pattern.

The following three guidelines constitute the core of our concept of egalitarian planning for LDCs:[9]

(a) production and consumption of goods and services must be for the 'common good', and satisfy both efficiency *and* equity criteria;
(b) anti-poverty planning and policy instruments should be utilised to eliminate excessively large disparities in incomes and living standards between individuals, groups and regions; and
(c) the political decision-making process must be reformed to permit expanded popular participation so that social choices reflect the needs and preferences of all social groups.

These three broad guidelines are derived from the utilitarian principle of the 'greatest good of the greatest possible number' and the socialistic-humanistic doctrine of 'from each according to ability'. While production of goods and services must be organised in the most efficient manner feasible, it is equally important to recognise that every member of a society has a valid claim to *a* share of the total output. This share need not be an equal share, especially in view of differentiation of economic roles and occupational specialisation, but it should be a just or fair share, defined according to some ethical norm (i.e. 'decent' share) or economic principle (i.e. 'equal pay for equal work') relative to a particular area.

The novelty of the concept of production for 'the common good' is that it attempts to *unify* economic equity with efficiency criteria. Such a unification entails some difficult trade-off problems as we shall shortly see, but its absence during the post-war planning exercises in LDCs was a major blunder. The exclusion,[10] sometimes by deliberate 'postponement', of equity considerations from development planning in the Third World can no longer be justified. While unifying equity with efficiency in economic planning is not an easy task, in recent years a number of economists have began to experiment with ways and means of doing so[11] and these might be applied in LDCs as well. In the meantime, the magnitude of disparities in consumption and living standards in LDCs is so large that the introduction of egalitarian, anti-poverty planning measures can and should be started without any delay, wherever feasible, with outside encouragement and assistance.

An Egalitarian Pattern of Consumption

Consumption is the ultimate objective of all production. The notion of production of goods and services for the 'common good' is a recognition of the value judgement that it should enhance the well-being of all, rather than merely certain groups, such as the privileged elites or foreign investors.

Equalisation of Consumption of Basic Needs

Regardless of differences in rank, status and income, basic wants in terms of food, shelter, clothing and medical care, essential for healthy survival, are remarkably uniform for every human being, although, of course, there are international differences in food intake, housing, clothing and health requirements due to climatic and environmental factors. As we have seen in Chapter 3, there are many problems of measurement in the estimation of 'poverty lines' or minimum consumption levels. Nevertheless, for many LDCs deficiencies in basic human needs are so pronounced, and disparities in living standards between the 'haves' and 'have-nots' so wide that policies designed to reduce these disparities, say towards those now prevailing in some of the advanced countries, are urgently required. The argument that the LDCs are too poor to undertake such redistributive measures is hardly acceptable in view of the severe wealth and income concentration at the top.

It is important to emphasise, once again, that our intention is minimisation of disparities in consumption levels between individuals, and not perfect equality.[12] This proposal implies that there should be both a *minimum* as well as a *maximum* level of income. While this double requirement is a relatively radical reform, it is logically and practically unavoidable if there is to be a progressive redistribution from the rich to the poor. For, if only *minima* were imposed on consumption or income levels, there would be no assurance that over time there would not be concentration at the top.

It is evident that implementing any redistributive measure to eliminate excessively large disparities in consumption and living standards would cause some 'welfare loss' for the elites. But to the extent that egalitarian reforms are financed out of future income growth, these losses need only affect relative distribution without requiring absolute reduction in the current wealth position of the rich. Additionally, if social investments in health, education and rural development effectively raised the productivity of land and labour, both the equity and efficiency objectives would be served. But increased food production, rural development and better utilisation of agrarian labour would be contingent upon major land reform in many LDCs, as we shall see in Chapter 11.

The proposition of equalising the consumption of basic needs can be justified on both subjective and objective grounds. One of the central theorems of economic theory is the Law of Diminishing Marginal Utility of Money Income, which is an intuitive reflection of the fact that one extra dollar confers more 'welfare' or 'utility' to a poor person than to a rich person, and that, therefore, a dollar transferred from a rich to a poor person would increase the 'aggregate welfare' since the incremental loss suffered by the rich person is more than offset by the poor man's incremental gain. This is the fundamental justification for income transfer programmes and social security schemes in industrialised countries. The second principle is the empirically testable fact of income inelasticity of demand for foodstuffs; that is, the evidence, supported by numerous international studies, that the proportion of income spent on foodstuffs declines as the level of income rises, suggesting that the rich and poor consumers differ more in terms of consumption of luxury items than in terms of basic needs. While these two theorems may warrant the wider egalitarian concept of 'equal capacity for satisfaction'[13] it is far more idealistic (and conversely less practical) than our proposal of equalisation of basic needs.

Public Goods and Luxuries

Since we are not concerned with perfect equality of consumption levels between individuals, certain differences must be reckoned with. These differences are most likely to stem from variability in human talents, preferences and capacities for whatever reason, and they would ordinarily be revealed in terms of consumption of non-essential goods and services. In the case of public goods and services, such as education, transport and communications for example, the paramount egalitarian requirement would be that everyone should have an equal opportunity or access for the enjoyment of such goods and services. In the case of public education, no one ought to be denied schooling opportunity in line with his abilities and desires for lack of the necessary means. These propositions have important implications for taxation and subsidy programmes, as well as for regional development, which will be discussed presently. In the case of private luxury consumer goods, consumption should be subject to progressive taxation based on ability to pay.[14]

Egalitarian Production

So far we have been concerned with consumption. No system of egalitarian development can ignore the vital importance of production of goods and services; after all, there must be production in order to satisfy human needs and wants.

Distribution v. Redistribution

It is useful to start with the important distinction between distribution and redistribution. The latter can be defined as income transfers between different individuals, at a constant level of aggregate income (assuming that a dollar has equal value for everyone). In this zero-sum game, income shares would necessarily change. Distribution, however, may or may not alter income shares, because it is associated with increased income. Additional income may be allocated according to the old sharing pattern, or a new one. In the usual case, egalitarian reforms would be financed out of additional income with a greater share going to the lower-income groups. In the case of land reform, however, redistribution of ownership is unavoidable.

Rewards and Incentives

The pursuit of egalitarian objectives in consumption needs to be counterbalanced with some scheme of rewards and incentives that does not unduly harm productive enterprise and private initiative. Our concept of egalitarian development is not to be equated with absolute levelling of socio-economic differences. Human nature, as revealed in terms of abilities, preferences and expectations, is too diverse to permit perfect standardisation. Rather than aiming at some Utopian restructuring of man and society, we wish to utilise economic planning and policy in LDCs as tools for enabling everyone, and not just a privileged minority, to enjoy the comforts and benefits of modern technology.

In this context there is no necessary conflict between the objective of efficient production and private initiative and reward. Socio-economic differentiation is not inconsistent with human nature. The important principle of equity is that every person ought to have equal opportunity for economic security, education and self-development, providing only that it precludes excessive income and wealth accumulation. Thus the traditional justification of income and differentials in terms of larger investments in human capital formation by the rich, could only be reconciled with an elitist education system that restricted access to the children of well-to-do parents.[15] It is untenable to argue that privileged minorities at the top of the income pyramid receive higher income owing to their greater volume of educational investments if and when educational opportunity is denied to the majority of school-age children. As we shall see in Chapter 10, this is precisely the type of educational policy adopted in most LDCs during the post-war period.

Conflicting Interests

Undoubtedly, egalitarian policies do often entail conflicts of interest between the various social, political and economic groups. Any redistribution of assets benefiting the low-income recipients would require a corresponding loss for the rich; likewise a nationalisation or expropriation of foreign assets, with or without compensation, would clash with the interests of non-resident investors. These conflicts, however, arise from legal, political or institutional factors rather than from conflicting technical or economic efficiency criteria. To the extent that egalitarian development entails a 'zero-sum game' in which losses and gains always add up to zero, the parties suffering losses can be expected to resist redistributive measures and reforms. Thus, the maximum limits on excessive wealth and income levels proposed above would be resisted strongly by the rich elites, while firms accustomed to exorbitant profits and underpayment of workers would be opposed to any scheme of profit squeeze.

The seriousness of elite resistance to egalitarian reform should not be underestimated. For, although numerically small, the entrenched elites control the political and governmental machinery and this control is of fundamental importance both in general terms and particularly for the formulation and conduct of economic policy. Thus, the ruling elites would be capable of mobilising, if and when deemed necessary, two economic 'weapons' calculated to weaken the economy: (1) they might cut down the flow of private and public investment expenditures, causing stagnation and unemployment; and (2) they could impose direct and indirect restrictions on wages, employment income and consumption, through fiscal, monetary or commercial policies, or in extreme cases as in Amin's Uganda, they could resort to a reign of terror and force.[16] It is almost certain that the social and economic hardships caused by such negative measures would fall inordinately on the poor, marginal and weak sections of the society and not on the privileged and affluent groups.

Thus, some of the root causes of the apparent trade-off between maximum rate of growth of production and equitable distribution are social, legal and political, emanating from institutional ownership of resources rather than from technical constraints. This, of course, is one of the principal insights of Karl Marx.[17] Here, we should hasten to add, we are not concerned with the ideological aspects of class struggle, but rather with the analytical basis of the equity-efficiency trade-off. To the extent that sociological and institutional factors constitute some of the root causes of this trade-off, their presence should be explicitly recognised rather than assumed away for ideological reasons. The important implication of the present argument is that the resolution of the trade-off problem must be sought primarily in the political decision-making process rather than in price-market theory. We shall return to this problem shortly.

The Efficiency-Equity Trade-off

In terms of a production function, economic equity and efficiency are not necessarily conflicting. That is, technically speaking, the two may well be reinforcing. The most obvious example is the case of unemployed labour mobilised to increase the total output of goods and services. This is of special importance for LDCs. While there may be limitations imposed by the supply of co-operant factors and infrastructural deficiencies, the potential for increased economic equity *and* higher output is of fundamental importance for an egalitarian development strategy inasmuch as elimination of poverty and unemployment can be accomplished without the necessity of drastic redistribution of existing wealth and assets.

Likewise, the conflict between consumption and investment (i.e. between current and future welfare) is a problem of choice laden with value judgements. For example, if investment activity, concentrated in the modern export-enclave sector, is causally linked to substantial net factor payments abroad or to exports of substantial 'capital flight' to industrialised countries, does such investment really generate higher future (aggregate) welfare for the population as a whole? Or take the case of military expenditures paid out of forced savings or sacrifices in current consumption: surely these represent counter-productive 'investments' with, at best, dubious benefits to future generations?

On the other hand, policies designed to create employment opportunities, as for example through land and irrigation schemes to increase food production, would improve the welfare of present *and* future generations. Public expenditure for human capital formation (for example, by a 'more butter and less guns' policy) clearly represent productive long-term investment. This last point is worth emphasising: the trade-off between consumption and investment often conceals a major trade-off between wasteful and socially beneficial public expenditures.

In the final analysis, it would appear that the apparent trade-off between efficiency and equity need not necessarily create a (net) social loss, but may actually cause the elimination of superfluous elite consumption and unproductive expenditure by governments more interested in military and/or prestige expenditures than social and economic development, as well as excessive profit-taking by multinational corporations.

Instruments of an Egalitarian Development: Decentralised Planning

If economic planning is to work as an egalitarian tool, it must aim at increasing the income share of the poor and marginal groups. Operationally, this implies that economic planning ought to satisfy the needs of these groups.[18] But what are these needs? Who is to define them? What is the most efficient or appropriate planning strategy to respond to these needs? Should a 'top-down' strategy be adopted delivering to the target populations what planners and bureaucrats at the centre perceive to be the most urgent and important needs? What about the price-market mechanism, can it play a role, any role, in the promotion of egalitarian objectives?

To begin with the last question. As stated earlier in this chapter, a system of rewards and incentives is an essential element of our concept of egalitarian production. Admittedly, the price-market system, by itself, may fail to bring about a socially optimal pattern of income distribution, but through fiscal policy and other progressive measures, listed below, it could be reconciled with egalitarian principles. In particular, as we have argued above, where the market system tends to concentrate income and wealth in few hands, causing widespread inequality and poverty for others, this tendency could be arrested by imposing ceilings on incomes, assets or consumption levels, just as minimum ceilings on incomes would be justified as means of preventing absolute poverty.

On the question of a 'top-down' strategy, it is evident that there is a hidden assumption here that the masses, perhaps because of illiteracy, are unable or unfit to define their needs in any rational or articulate manner; therefore, it would be quite pointless to let them participate in the process of determining planning objectives, priorities and investment choices. In this approach, which characterised much of the post-war planning efforts in LDCs, the role of the state planners is very much like that of a latter-day saint, deciding what is good for the masses. This is not only an arrogant approach to development planning, but it also plays right into the hands of the powerful elites dominating the political system at the centre.

Rather than a 'top-down' strategy of economic planning, we would advocate a fully decentralised approach reaching down to the regional and village level, so that all groups and citizens from all walks of life are given the opportunity to participate in the determination of targets, priorities and investment choices reflected in the Plan. In this 'bottom-up' planning process, the first task of the planning office is to act as the principal organ of the state receiving requests for development projects of all kinds from the various parts of the country, and then following up on these requests to determine their feasibility financially, physically and technically. Some requests may be too ambitious, too costly or based on inappropriate data. If, however, a meaningful follow-up stage were undertaken, in which direct consultations between the planning office representatives and the affected groups took place, it is certain that there would be considerable progress to minimise waste and duplication. Nevertheless, it is equally certain that there would be insufficient funds in the development budget to finance even the most urgent and basic needs of all groups and regions. Thus, the second major role of the planning agency must be the co-ordination of competing claims for limited development resources. Whatever projects are ultimately included in the Plan must be justified and fully documented to the satisfaction of the population residing in the affected regions. On the other hand, in cases where specific regions are granted zero allocations in the Plan, these decisions must be justified on the strongest possible grounds. While a zero allocation might be justifiable in a given year, it would hardly be equitable if the population of a given region were denied any development expenditure year after year.

Decentralised planning requires a new set of institutions, such as regional and sub-regional planning offices, budgetary and fiscal procedures. In addition, it requires effective local government agencies and expanded political decision-making based on nation-wide participation. Some of these matters will be discussed below, but political reforms are matters in which political scientists and other related specialists have more competence than economists.

Suppose that a decentralised system of planning were actually adopted, the masses were actively encouraged to specify their needs, and these needs were actually incorporated in the Plan. What would be some of the typical needs that would be expressed most urgently and extensively? While these needs can be expected to be relative to individual localities, nevertheless some of the most important ones are bound to relate to income security, political and legal rights, and generally the 'bread and butter' issues of earning a decent living. These are the issues with which an egalitarian planning process would be involved. We shall discuss some of them in greater detail in the following chapters, but first let us specify some of the specific fiscal and economic policy instruments to promote an egalitarian development. Since there is an extensive literature dealing with progressive taxation and public finance, education, and other policy instruments, a brief discussion here would suffice.

Progressive Taxation

An egalitarian system of public finance would be based on 'ability to pay' and would rely primarily on income tax rather than on indirect forms of taxation. In most LDCs, the share of income tax of total revenues is disproportionately small, while indirect taxes are excessively large and unfairly burdensome for the lower-income groups. This regressive pattern is made worse by extensive tax evasion and avoidance by the affluent and the powerful — another important evidence of elite control of economic and political institutions.[19]

Wealth and Inheritance Taxation

In many LDCs, elite power and affluence are intricately tied to land ownership (often as absentee ownership) and property income. Since wealth and inheritance taxes are generally non-existent or easily avoided by the privileged groups, there is an automatic inter-generational wealth concentration process, in effect creating persistent poverty for the masses and wealth accumulation for the few, growing exponentially over time. In the past, elites have often successfully resisted land distribution schemes designed to benefit the peasants and they have acquired substantial equity ownership in post-war industrialisation,[20] further adding to wealth concentration.

An egalitarian public finance system would have to include both an *income floor* consistent with minimum consumption levels, and an *income* ceiling to prevent excessive wealth accumulation.[21] This is not a static problem; it is a dynamic one, since elitist accumulation is a tendency which always exists. Excess incomes can be taxed and the proceeds used to finance future redistributive projects.

State Subsidy System

The provision of subsidies from state sources should be justified on the basis of net social benefits. Evidence on the creation of 'infant industries' strongly suggests that public subsidies in LDCs for this purpose have been socially counter-productive, raising domestic prices well above world prices of comparable goods.[22] Also, the well connected business groups have succeeded in deriving excessive economic advantage from influence peddling and bribery, as have many foreign firms. The latter in particular have secured direct tariff protection and various forms of subsidies from willing elites in LDCs. These policies have generally favoured capital utilisation and have discriminated against labour even in the most labour-surplus countries. Instead of an 'infant industry' for the accumulation of physical assets (mostly foreign-owned), there ought to be an 'infant industry' for human capital formation, especially in rural areas — a topic to be discussed in the following chapters.

Public Goods and Regional Balance

The supply of public goods (i.e. goods and services subsidised by general taxes) should, in general, be in accordance with the egalitarian principle of equal accessibility for all. In the case of public housing, health and welfare as well as educational facilities, there would have to be a balanced regional distribution of facilities and services in order to ensure equality of access for the rural inhabitants. Such a spread of social overhead capital may entail some subsidisation of low-income regions at the expense of the regions acting as 'leading sectors' or 'growth poles', but this would be fully warranted by the social and long-term benefits of an integrated economy freed from dualism and lopsidedness. For instance, if the rural-urban drift of population were arrested as a result of effective rural employment creation, there would be significant urban benefits due to reduced open unemployment, overcrowding and crime in the cities, as well as other important direct benefits.[23]

Public Education

Under an egalitarian development strategy, public education would be guided by the principle of nation-wide equality of educational opportunity. While this would also have the desirable effect of increasing the quality and productivity of the nation's manpower resources, educational policy and planning would not be limited to the provision of the manpower requirements of a growing economy, at the post-secondary level, as was generally the fashion in post-war years; rather the policy objective would be the development of a nation-wide accessibility to schooling, especially in rural areas, to combat illiteracy and ignorance while increasing the labour productivity of future workers. We shall return to the problems of educational planning in Chapter 10.

Equal Employment Opportunity

Non-discriminatory employment of labour is another important prerequisite of egalitarian development. In most LDCs, recruitment of labour involves extensive forms of discrimination, based on tribal, racial or social criteria, as we have seen.[24] Despite the fact that most countries have legal and international obligations against discrimination in employment practices, these are probably the most universally abused of human rights recognised in law.[25] So long as job scarcity persists, it is doubtful that such unfair and inefficient practices can be stopped; and job scarcity can be eliminated only through a deliberate programme of economic planning and policy that recognised employment creation as the leading objective. The next chapter is devoted to spelling out the elements of a comprehensive employment policy (CEP) designed with this objective in mind.

Food Production and Land Reform

The rural sector is the focal point of egalitarian development strategy, at least for the great majority of LDCs. This stems from the fact that it is in the rural areas that the various socially desirable development objectives converge, in particular the objectives of increased food production and job creation. As we shall see in Chapter 11 (where an integrated rural development strategy is offered), the rural sector has been treated as a 'milch-cow' during the post-war industrialisation drive.

Increased agricultural productivity is an essential precondition of economic development, a fact well borne out by the economic history of all developed countries. But agricultural productivity is dependent upon land and labour productivity. Raising yield rates per acre can be accomplished partly through the application of modern farm technology, such as the fertiliser-seed-tractor combination. It is also dependent on a more efficient use of available land — a fact which is yet to be fully recognised in many LDCs where excessive fragmentation and/or landlordism prevail. Land redistribution through effective reform legislation is an essential precondition for raising both the productivity of land and labour. For, by providing land and other means to landless peasants, they can be turned into productive farmers. The alternative method of higher labour productivity – i.e. by merely pushing large numbers of migrants into urban sectors – is an artificial remedy which, as we have seen, leads to urban poverty and unemployment.

Political Reform for Social Choice

Probably the single most important, yet difficult, economic task of a political leadership, whether in an LDC or advanced country, or in a capitalist or socialist state, is identifying the ways and means of maximising the aggregate 'social good'. In normative economics, this is the problem of specifying a social welfare function,[26] i.e. the rules for making *fair* and *efficient* social choices.[27]

Is it Possible to Construct a Social Welfare Function?

Specifying a social welfare function requires not only a strong dedication to justice and fairness, but also information about the weights to be assigned on the relative claims ('deservingness') of competing individuals and on the relative 'social worth' of scarce resources used up in the process of production. Under highly restrictive assumptions, known as the Pareto Optimum Conditions,[28] it can be demonstrated in an *abstract* way that it might be possible to have 'Ideal Output', optimally distributed, resulting in maximised collective social welfare.

Problems of interpersonal comparisons and aggregating group preferences make these ideal conditions a practical impossibility.[29] Even the theory of the second-best, designed as a weaker alternative route for public policy to enlarge the social good, has been a subject of intense controversy amongst theoretical economists.[30] These theoretical and measurement difficulties have been so influential that during the post-war period (when planning became fashionable in LDCs) many economists assumed, explicitly or implicitly, that the task of specifying a social welfare function is essentially a *political* task – outside the realm of serious economic analysis concerned only with alternative efficiency conditions in production. The problem of distribution was more the task of sociologists, political scientists and, above all, practical politicians. These, and not the economist, were regarded as experts in coping with the tedious process of bargaining in the political arena between competing (or in Galbraith's terms 'countervailing') groups.

The economist's professional disinterest in the making of social choices (contrary, it might be pointed out, to the long tradition of *political economy*) has been far more damaging in LDCs relying on Western advice and theory than in industrialised countries. Unlike the latter, few LDCs possess a broad popular participation in the political decision-making process. As a result, the specification of social priorities and planning choices have tended to mirror the wishes and interests of elites and ruling classes to a much greater degree than in industrialised countries, although the persistence of poverty amidst affluence is clear enough evidence of unequal political power distribution in the latter as well.[31] Conversely, while political reform is a great social requirement both for advanced as well as less developed countries, if true egalitarian development is ever to occur, clearly it is far more urgently required in the latter.

Interdependence of Well-being: the Choice of Ends and Means

Standard economic theory, based on Adam Smith's 'invisible hand' and 'consumer sovereignty' doctrines blended into the competitive market model, is concerned with individual utility maximisation. Every individual acts in a highly independent way, protecting his interests against all others, subject only to his own tastes and budget resources. In the extreme case, there is no room for 'fairness' or concern for others — not even for family members or neighbours: everyone is an 'island'.

While independent utility maximisers may also maximise profits and outputs, the means they could utilise to achieve these ends are relevant only to the extent that they affect costs and prices. Unfair means of exploiting others are subordinated to economic ends. For example, slavery or forced labour practices[32] would be quite consistent with the end of maximum profits, as would organised destruction of competitors[33] within an elitist system enriching the privileged few at the top. The elite could easily use its political power to pass enabling laws to suppress any conflicting interests. The important inference is this: if and where political power is concentrated in a small group, economic ends pursued in even the most efficiently organised economic system may quickly create large and increasing inequalities in incomes and living standards. This is one of the most fundamental 'lessons' of colonialism, with its free trade and comparative advantage rationalisations.[34]

The above may be an extreme situation, although by no means unknown even today in many LDCs.[35] But consider the following — apparently a more tolerable case. In Figure 8.1, we depict rising

Figure 8.1: Income Growth and Shares

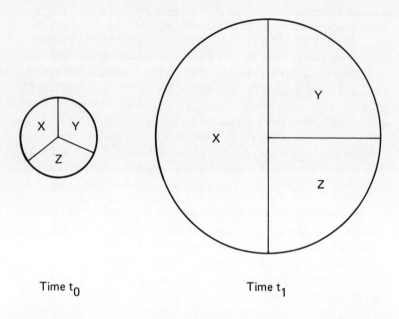

Time t_0 Time t_1

aggregate income during the time interval t_0 to t_1, such that the
income shares of three individuals, X, Y and Z, rise in absolute terms,
although X's share rises faster relative to Y's and Z's. Since all three
realise higher income levels, they are evidently better off in t_1 as
compared with t_0. This improvement would appear to indicate that
income growth is benefiting all three individuals; the fact that X is
gaining relatively more is immaterial *so long as Y and Z are unconcerned
about how and why X's income rises faster*: so long as the utility
functions of Y and Z are independent of X's, everyone is better off in
t_1 and, as economic planners, we need not worry about the means of
distribution.

But the means of distribution are critically important for the
stability of the system. Suppose that X possesses excessive political
power relative to Y and Z; as a result, suppose that he secures a large
subsidy from the state bank or enters into lucrative partnerships with
foreign firms, employing Y and Z as labourers at exploitative wage rates
set by legislation biased in favour of X. In the resulting growth process,
all three increase their income levels, although X's share has increased
from a third to a half, while Y's and Z's declined from a third to a

quarter each. These results may or may not be stable, i.e. acceptable to all three individuals and last a long time. Much depends on the degree and intensity of X's domination, and the political consciousness of Y and Z. If X happens to be a political monopolist (i.e. a dictator), and Y and Z are utterly inert or fatalistic, then the unfair growth pattern in Figure 8.1 may nevertheless persist for a long time. If, however, the level of consciousness of Y and Z is high and/or they feel intensely oppressed, the survival chances of X's supremacy would be quite limited. But how limited? And can we predict the timing of Y's and Z's 'revolt' against X? Finally, what are the factors that move Y and Z to challenge X's supremacy? These are difficult questions to answer with any exactness. In a large measure, the determinants must be highly subjective motives, including a conviction (real or imaginary) of mistreatment, under-payment, fear, risk-aversion, etc. They reflect the important fact that human relations, especially in economic transactions, are interdependent, and income growth *per se* is not a sufficient condition of a successful (i.e. equitable as well as efficient) development process.

The recognition that economic relations are characterised by envy and malice is of vital importance for egalitarian planning.[36] For if individuals are indeed interdependent utility maximisers, the planning process of maximising social (aggregate) income should in reality be a collective process of weighing alternatives and of choosing ends and means. The vector of choices ultimately chosen must therefore reflect the preferences of all groups. While unanimous expression of preferences is in practice impossible, the denial of the opportunity to the bulk of citizens of participating in the social choice process is unjustifiable and may ultimately generate unrest and conflict. The impossibility of an optimum social welfare function cannot justify an elitist growth process in which the masses are excluded.

In terms of economic planning, the collective choice process implies that the expenditures and projects that are ultimately included in the Development Plan must reflect the needs of all groups of citizens. This is essential if the means utilised (e.g. mobilisation of savings) are in fact justifiable in terms of the ends achieved (e.g. higher GNP). Thus, when a specific project is financed through an imposed sacrifice on rural masses, such as extra taxes or forced savings, the sacrifice can be regarded as tolerable or intolerable depending on the element of equity in the distribution of income generated by the project, and on the agreement of the masses with this distribution pattern. If such an agreement is not forthcoming, the material results ultimately achieved might be quite impressive in the aggregate, but may nevertheless destabilise the existing socio-economic order. The prospects of securing such an agreement, which would contribute to an orderly and equitable implementation of the project, would improve greatly if the masses (1) can anticipate an actual benefit from the project to compensate them for their sacrifices, and (2) have all the relevant information and political rights essential to the making of an informed and rational choice.

Realistically, however, it should be realised that an elite could attempt to 'bribe' an inert and fatalistic mass into accepting a process of income growth depicted in Figure 8.1. The elite may even use force to ensure that the pattern of income growth is significantly biased in its own favour. However immoral this elitist growth process may be, there is no reason why (as in colonial times) it could not last a long time. Yet the probability of an uprising or a bloody rebellion against the elite would always exist.

The Social Costs of Revolutions

The final result may suggest that revolution and rebellion offer the only option for egalitarian development in LDCs. After all, as Part Two showed, many countries in the Third World are characterised by conditions more in accord with the last paragraph than the previous one. Such an inference, though, would be hasty and unwarranted. However lofty the declared objectives of revolutionary leaders may be, rebellions — even some relatively non-violent take-overs — generate considerable suffering and great social cost both in human lives as well as material terms. The case of Uganda, discussed in Chapter 7, clearly demonstrates how a perfectly peaceful 'National War for Economic Independence' can subsequently turn into a prolonged state of economic chaos and a catastrophic reign of terror. In more general terms, Peter Wiles, in a highly interesting study,[37] has calculated the expected time periods of different types of revolutions (Soviet/Polish model, Western mixed economy model, Latin American populist model, Chicago school capitalist model, etc.) before the redistributive gains achieved by the masses can compensate their sacrifice and loss incurred for and during a successful revolution. His results suggest that it is most unlikely that the masses can expect to realise net welfare gains during their own life-time. Yet, it might be asked: what about Cuba and Fidel Castro? Assuming that Cuba is indeed a success story, surely the important question is whether the Castro-style revolution has any *prediction* value — whether it can be replicated elsewhere? Che

Guevara's attempt was hardly encouraging! The fact (which also applies to Russia or China) is that revolutions, like constitutions, are poor export items.

International Social Justice: New International Economic Order

If rebellions are too uncertain or costly for the poor, and the elites see no short-run gains in egalitarian reforms to increase the income share of the poor, aren't we in a cul-de-sac? This would appear to be so for a 'closed' economy, seen in a static context. From a dynamic perspective, and in an international setting, there is perhaps a ray of hope. For example, the new international economic order (NIEO), discussed in Chapter 12, affords a unique opportunity for launching a process of egalitarian development in LDCs. For while elites in the exceptional LDC may realise the long-run advantages of egalitarian reforms, it is perhaps more hopeful to think that the industrialised countries, and especially a reformed United Nations system, can and should seize the opportunity afforded by NIEO discussions to redress the unequal distribution of global wealth in such a way that the benefits of a more equitable international trade system are passed on to the underprivileged poor masses in LDCs. Thus, the Western countries, who originally initiated and financed much of the early industrialisation efforts in LDCs, may now play another important role, this time to promote economic and social justice within LDCs. This they can do by insisting that any reforms made in the international trade, exchange and monetary system as part of NIEO negotiations during the ongoing north-south dialogue[38] should be passed on to the poor masses — through egalitarian reforms — and not hoarded by the ruling elites themselves. This, of course, is by no means easy. Apart from problems of international diplomacy, there will undoubtedly be objections to NIEO from protectionist industries in advanced countries (e.g. labour-intensive, low-wage textiles and footwear manufacturing sectors) against 'cheap imports' from LDCs.[39] Additionally, the multinational firms, with their 'footloose' profit-maximising behaviour based on virtual freedom to transfer capital-intensive technology as well as profits and remittances globally, might resist restrictions on their activities resulting from an egalitarian development strategy.[40]

The role of the United Nations in the promotion of social justice through NIEO, as well as other channels, is especially vital since the UN assistance to LDCs was originally conceived as an instrument for the promotion of human rights and social justice.[41] In the past, these objectives have been followed largely in a passive way through silent diplomacy. In fact, the UN's large technical assistance programme (i.e. sending experts and advisers to work in LDCs) now appears to be *structurally* in conflict with the human rights and social justice objectives since these are subordinated or abandoned in the event of any potential criticism of elites and ruling classes for fear of jeopardising the technical assistance projects leading to the expulsion of the UN personnel. As a result, often corrupt and self-seeking politicians and officials in LDCs are indirectly protected against public exposure. Moreover, as we shall argue in Chapter 12, the experts and advisers in most LDCs are largely ineffective because they are obliged to work as government *functionaries* serving the dominant elites, having little or no contact with the needy and underprivileged populations. Finally, the UN experts and advisers often displace local manpower. Unlike 25 years ago, many LDCs now possess many qualified and competent technicians and professionals, some trained in top institutions around the world.[42] Therefore, if technical assistance programmes tend to conflict with the social justice and human rights objectives of the UN, then perhaps the former should be reorganised to become a more effective instrument of the latter. Perhaps the UN should become a dynamic and impartial international ombudsman, speaking out publicly and factually on inequalities, poverty and injustice in the world, especially in LDCs where these problems are acutest.

Conclusion

This chapter's central theme is that economic and social development in LDCs is a process of change affecting everyone — rich and poor; therefore, all should benefit from the results achieved. A process of development benefiting all constitutes egalitarian planning; a process based on collective social choices made voluntarily and rationally. We have seen, however, that egalitarian planning is likely to be resisted by the powerful elites controlling the economic and political institutions of many LDCs. These elites have successfully utilised planning and industrialisation during the post-war period for enrichment and self-aggrandisement; and they perceive little material benefits *in the short run* from egalitarian reforms increasing the income share of the poor. Such long-term benefits as may follow from increased social, economic and political stability are too distant and remote for the typical tough-minded elite member.

Such a conclusion may encourage a violent revolution. However, we feel this would be hasty and unwarranted on account of the substantial social costs that would follow. A more realistic inference is that the elites and ruling classes, living in a world increasingly becoming a 'global village' open to uncontrollable international 'demonstration effects', may come to realise that they are truly living on 'borrowed time' — that their monopoly status is fast eroding.

A further line of hope for the introduction of egalitarian reforms in LDCs lies in external influences: partly from a reformed United Nations system itself dedicated to the promotion of social justice ideals in the developing world, and partly from the industrialised countries, as part of the formation of a new international economic order. We shall return to these issues in Chapter 12.

The following chapters will be devoted to detailing some of the more essential elements of an egalitarian planning and policy instruments, such as an employment policy, educational restructuring and agrarian development. Needless to say, this approach is based on the assumption that egalitarian planning *as a non-violent revolution* is both feasible and relevant, given the will to attack the problems of poverty, marginalism, unemployment and inequality.

Notes

1. It may be useful to make an explicit distinction between value judgements and ideology. This chapter, while relying on value-judgemental assertions, is intended to refrain from Marxist, Leninist, Maoist or any other kind of ideology. This last term is defined in a standard dictionary as '1. the body of doctrine, myth, symbol, etc., of a social movement, institution, class, or large group. 2. such a body of doctrine, myth, etc., with reference to some political and cultural plan, as that of fascism, along with the devices for putting it into operation. 3. *Philos.* a. the study of the nature and origin of ideas. b. a system which derives ideas exclusively from sensation. 4. theorizing of a visionary or impractical nature.' Jess Stein and Laurance Urdang (eds.), *The Random House Dictionary of the English Language* (Random House, New York, 1973) (the unabridged edition).

2. One of the most authoritative recent studies of this subject is John Rawls, *A Theory of Justice* (Harvard University Press, Cambridge, Mass., 1971). See also Nicholas Rescher, *Distributive Justice, A Constructive Critique of the Utilitarian Theory of Distribution* (Blackwell, London, 1974). An useful collection of papers on the subject is presented in J. Roland Pennock and John W. Chapman (eds.), *Nomox IX: Equality* (Atherton Press, New York, 1967).

3. Hugo A. Bedeau, 'Egalitarianism and the Idea of Equality' in Pennock and Chapman, *Nomox IX.*

4. Gunnar Myrdal, 'What is Development?', *Journal of Economic Issues,* Vol.8, No.4 (December 1964). See also the important comment by Paul Baran on Colin Clark's definition of economic progress: *The Political Economy of Growth* (Monthly Review Press, New York, 1957), p.18, footnote 6.

5. ILO, *World Employment Programme* (Geneva, 1969). *Idem, Employment, Growth and Basic Needs* (Geneva, 1976).

6. *Guardian* (Manchester, England), 22 August 1971, commenting on the ILO Kenya Report, *Employment, Incomes and Equality. A Strategy for Increasing*

productive Employment in Kenya (Geneva, 1972). See also the companion country reports, including *Toward Full Employment. A Program for Colombia* (Geneva, 1970); *Matching Employment Opportunities and Expectations. A Programme of Action for Ceylon* (Geneva, 1971).

7. K. Popper, *The Open Society and its Enemies* (Routledge and Kegan Paul, London, 1945).

8. John Plamenatz, 'Diversity of Rights and Kinds of Equality' in Pennock and Chapman, *Nomox IX.*

9. These three guidelines are formulated partly in conformity with the elements of distributive justice (cf. Rawls, *A Theory of Justice,* p.275; Rescher, *Distributive Justice,* p.87) and partly in conformity with Pareto optimality conditions (cf. E.J. Mishan, 'A Survey of Welfare Economics 1939-1959', *Economic Journal,* Vol.70, No.278 (1960)).

10. For a critique of similar tendencies in industrialised countries, see Maurice Dobb, *Welfare Economics and the Economics of Socialism, Toward a Commonsense Critique* (Cambridge University Press, London, 1969), esp. Ch.5.

11. Illustrative empirical studies are G.M. Von Furstenberg and D.C. Mueller, 'The Pareto Optimal Approach to Income Redistribution: A Fiscal Application', *American Economic Review,* Vol.LXI, No.4 (September 1971); R.C. Fair, 'The Optimal Distribution of Income', *Quarterly Journal of Economics,* Vol.LXXXV, No.4 (November 1971).

12. It may be useful to quote Arthur M. Okun's concept of economic equality. He speaks 'of more or less equality as implying smaller or greater disparities among families in their maintainable standards of living, which in turn implies lesser or greater disparities in the distribution of income and wealth, relative to the needs of families of different sizes. Equal standards of living would not mean that people would choose to spend their incomes and allocate their wealth identically. Economic equality would not mean sameness or drabness or uniformity, because people have vastly different tastes and preferences.' *Equality and Efficiency, The Big Tradeoff* (The Brookings Institution, Washington, DC, 1975), p.3 and esp. Ch.3.

13. This is a central idea of A.C. Pigou whose book, written in the early twentieth century, remains one of the classics on welfare economics: *The Economics of Welfare* (Macmillan, London, 1920). The quote is from one of his last writings, 'Some Aspects of Welfare Economics', *American Economic Review,* Vol. XLVI, No.3 (June 1951). For an extended discussion of this point, see M. Dobb, *Welfare Economics,* esp. Ch.5.

14. Outright bans are unlikely to be effective since they would generate black market transactions.

15. Cf. Jean-Pierre Jallade, 'Education Finance and Income Distribution', *World Development,* Vol.4, No.5 (1976). A good survey is provided in Gary S. Fields, 'The Private Demand for Education in Relation to Labour Market Conditions in Less Developed Countries', *Economic Journal* (December 1974).

16. See Chapter 7.

17. According to the classical economists, production was unaffected by the ownership of resources or the institutional framework within which production was carried; 'that is, relations between men were treated as irrelevant for an explanation of distribution (of income). It was Marx's insight that this separation is invalid, even in the world of pure logic. . .' G.C. Hartcourt, 'Some Cambridge Controversies in the Theory of Capital', *The Journal of Economic Literature,* Vol.VII, No.2 (June 1969), p.395.

A neo-Marxist discussion of the social ownership of resources is given in Chapter 2.

18. R. Jolly, 'The World Employment Conference: The Enthronement of

Basic Needs', *ODI Review,* No.2 (1976).

19. Cf. Richard M. Bird and De Wulf, 'Taxation and Income Distribution in Latin America: A Critical Review of Empirical Studies', *IMF Staff Papers,* Vol.20, No.3 (1973); Richard M. Bird, *Taxation and Development, Lessons from Colombian Experience* (Harvard University Press, Cambridge, Mass., 1970); Gunnar Myrdal, *Asian Drama* (Pantheon, New York, 1968), esp. pp.2098 *et seq.*

20. One of the most clear-cut examples of this is Pakistan, where a mutually profitable alliance between the new class of *émigré* entrepreneurs and politicians after partition in 1947 created fortunes for a handful of 'families'. The details of this, and other countries, are discussed in Chapter 7.

21. As discussed above on p.178.

22. Cf. I. Little, T. Scitovsky and M. Scott, *Industry and Trade in Some Developing Countries, A Comparative Study* (Oxford University Press for the OECD Development Center, Paris, 1970).

23. These may include additional food production, but equally important, there may be positive complementarity effects. For example, the construction of a farm-to-market feeder road in a previously isolated region would increase trade and commerce both inwards and outwards. This type of complementarity is of critical importance for LDCs. If, for instance, a super-highway were built joining two major cities only, the new traffic generated might be relatively small owing to the inability of low-income farmers and users to purchase expensive cars to use the highway; however, if an appropriate low-cost consumer good were produced then significant local value-added or multiplier effects may be generated — a pattern which can be observed in some rural communities in Indonesia and elsewhere.

24. Chapter 4, p.86.

25. ILO, *Equality in respect of Employment under Legislation and Other National Standards* (Geneva, 1967).

26. A standard textbook treatment of this subject is Tibor Scitovsky, *Welfare and Competition: The Economics of a Fully Employed Economy* (R.D. Irwin, Homewood, Ill., 1971). Another important study is William J. Baumol, *Welfare Economics and the Theory of the State,* 2nd edition, (Harvard University Press, Cambridge, Mass., 1967).

27. A.K. Sen, 'Social Choice Theory: A Re-examination', *Econometrica,* Vol.45, No.1 (January 1977). This study has an up-to-date bibliography on the problem of social choice, i.e. the aggregation of individual preferences. It was originally posed by K.J. Arrow, *Social Choice and Individual Values* (John Wiley, New York, 1951).

28. Dobb, *Welfare Economics,* Ch.4.

29. A.K. Sen, 'The Impossibility of a Paretian Liberal', *Journal of Political Economy,* Vol.78 (1970); *idem, On Economic Inequality* (Clarendon Press, Oxford, 1973).

30. E.J. Mishan, 'Second Thoughts on Second Best', *Oxford Economic Papers* (October 1962).

31. A.B. Atkinson, *The Economics of Inequality* (Clarendon Press, Oxford, 1975); Lester C. Thurow, *Generating Inequality in the US Economy* (Basic Books, New York, 1975).

32. As we have seen in the case of Liberia, Chapter 6.

33. E.g. the Dutch in Indonesia. For details, see B. Higgins, *Economic Development, Principles, Problems and Policies,* rev.ed. (Norton, New York, 1969), p.683 *et seq.*

34. Arghiri Emmanuel, *Unequal Exchange: A Study of the Imperialism of Trade, with additional comments by Charles Bettelheim* (Monthly Review Press, New York, 1972). Also see P. Baran, *The Political Economy of Growth;* James D.

Cockcroft, Andre G. Frank and Dale L. Johnson, *Dependence and Underdevelopment, Latin America's Political Economy* (Anchor Books, New York, 1972).

35. See Chapter 6, note 28, p.139.

36. Allan Feldman and Alan Kirman, 'Fairness and Envy', *American Economic Review,* Vol.LKIV, No.6 (Devember 1974); H. Varian, 'Equity, Envy and Efficiency', *Journal of Economic Theory,* Vol.9 (1974).

37. *Distribution of Income – East and West* (North Holland, Amsterdam, 1974).

38. UN General Assembly, *Declaration and Program of Action on the Establishment of the New International Economic Order* (May 1974); *Charter of Economic Rights and Duties of States* (December 1974), 7th Special Session of the UN General Assembly, resolutions adopted in September 1975. Jan Tinbergen (ed.), *RIO: Reshaping the International Order* (the second report to the Club of Rome) (E.P. Dutton, New York, 1976).

39. An interesting study of US tariff concessions (items 806.30 and 807.00) for LDCs imports is G.K. Helleiner, 'Manufactured Exports from Less Developed Countries and Multinational Firms', *Economic Journal*, Vol.83 (March 1973).

40. Richard J. Barnet and Ronald E. Muller, *Global Reach: The Power of the Multinational Corporations* (Simon and Schuster, New York, 1974).

41. Cf. Arthur H. Robertson, *Human Rights in the World* (Manchester University Press, Manchester, 1972); Rosalind S. Pollock, *The Individual's Rights and International Organization* (Smith College, Mass., 1966).

42. An interesting type of international technical assistance, which relies heavily on LDC experts, is the Commonwealth Fund for Technical Cooperation (CFCT). See the publication, *Commonwealth Skills for Commonwealth Needs,* (CFTC, London, June 1977).

9 AN EGALITARIAN EMPLOYMENT POLICY BASED ON MANPOWER PLANNING

If the leading objective of egalitarian development is to increase the income share of the poor groups, the principal policy instrument to promote this objective must be an employment policy designed to create productive job opportunities for the mass of job-seekers. The alternative strategy of raising the earnings of workers already employed is unlikely to make a significant contribution towards income levelling in view of the large volume of unemployment already prevailing in most LDCs. In fact, as we have seen in Chapter 4, high-wage policies have often worked to minimise employment creation by encouraging capital substitution, and future measures to raise earnings substantially can be expected to result in labour displacement.

Neither is it desirable to pursue the objective of income levelling by means of huge income transfer programmes; hand-outs to a permanent and growing army of unemployed can only lead to social polarisation and conflicts between the supporting and dependent groups. Employment is both an end and a means: as an end, it generates self-respect and a sense of dignity; as a means, it provides a stream of earned income needed to pay for human wants and overcome poverty. Employment in this context must be understood in the sense of a productive, full-time job resulting in a level of income which ensures an adequate standard of living relative to a specific labour market. Thus, where there are underemployed persons, or the so-called 'working poor', unable to earn an adequate level of income, we would regard these conditions as signs of a deficiency in employment opportunity in addition to the problem of open unemployment.

The International Labour Organization's World Employment Programme[1] was useful in drawing world opinion to the critical unemployment problem in LDCs, but what is now required is an action strategy in these countries to make employment creation a leading objective of economic planning. In this chapter a comprehensive employment policy (CEP) is proposed, aimed at evaluating and approving every new development project on the basis of the number of new jobs it generates. While fiscal, monetary and industrial development policies could be utilised towards this end, the major source of employment potential in most LDCs must be found in the agricultural sector as will be discussed below.[2]

Past Prescriptions for the Unemployment Problem

Neoclassical growth theory lacked an employment orientation, as we have seen in Chapter 1, and the extent to which the theory is applicable to LDCs is a debatable question in view of the enormous differences in terms of structure, socio-economic conditions and institutions.[3]

The relevance of Keynesian stabilisation policies, too, is questionable — and not only because most LDCs lack well-developed fiscal and monetary institutions. Fine tuning of aggregate demand, as implemented in industrialised countries, is unlikely to solve the unemployment crisis of LDCs since it is caused more structurally than by a deficiency of demand. Moreover, even in industrialised countries, fine tuning policies are increasingly ineffective due to cost-push and administered prices. We have seen[4] that in the post-war period, many LDCs relied on tariff and fiscal incentives to investors to stimulate industrial growth, but these measures failed to generate adequate employment opportunities. Therefore, in future selective fiscal measures (as discussed in the following pages) may be utilised in order to accelerate job-creation in the modern sector, although this is virtually certain to be a limited contribution.[5]

CEP and Manpower Planning

Our proposal for a comprehensive employment policy in LDCs gives added importance to manpower planning and human resource development. In the past, manpower planning in LDCs generally played a subsidiary role in overall economic planning. This reflected the general preoccupation of economic planners with physical capital formation, and the neglect of human resources. However, it was also due to the failure of manpower planners themselves to deal with the basic question of how to accelerate job creation. As a rule, they were more interested in making long-range manpower forecasts of high-level personnel needed for industrialisation in the modern sector; they neglected the large and important agricultural sector.

If manpower planning is to play a central role as a tool of CEP, it must be considerably strengthened and its aims redefined. In many LDCs, the manpower planning function should become a major activity of economic planning offices, and development plans should explicitly state the number and type of jobs to be created during the plan period. Equally important, during the implementation stages, performance of the plan ought to be appraised, not just in terms of GNP growth rates, but on the basis of employment creation and the reduction in the level of unemployment.

As we have already noted in previous chapters, there are major conceptual and statistical problems surrounding employment and labour utilisation in LDCs.[6] But the magnitude and severity of the unemployment crisis necessitate a new and concerted planning strategy that places human resource development and utilisation at the top of development priorities.

What is Manpower Planning?

It is now necessary to define and spell out the unique role of manpower planning. At the highest level of generality, manpower planning is a systematic and co-ordinated approach to the (1) development, and (2) utilisation of human resources. Its long-term objective is the employment of every job-seeker at a wage rate which supports an adequate living standard in a given labour market.[7] This objective, however, can be considered as a feasible policy target in most LDCs only *after* large-scale human capital formation is undertaken by the government in order to raise the quality and productivity of the population, as workers, consumers and citizens.

Essentially, there are two compelling reasons justifying CEP based on manpower planning: (1) human capital formation is a time-consuming process of major social investment justifying an 'infant industry' approach; and (2) nation-wide employment creation promotes social justice and a fairer distribution of income.

The 'Infant Industry Argument' for Human Capital Formation

Skills and technical know-how, embodied in human beings, are a country's most valuable assets, as clearly demonstrated by the post-war reconstruction of Europe with the aid of the Marshall Plan. Human capital, however requires a long gestation period since schooling, training and skill acquisition take years.[8] Furthermore, unless the quality and supply of first-level schooling is nationally adequate, human capital formation will be deficient and limited. There will then be potential human capital loss, involving wasted future income as well as frustrated individual capacity.

In economic theory, the classical 'infant industry argument' is a powerful justification for social investments in deferred income growth. During the post-war industrialisation drive, the argument was effectively utilised to channel resources into new domestic industries to allow their growth from infancy towards a level of maturity, at which stage they could effectively compete in world markets. Thus, investment in infant industries was investment in trade as an 'engine of growth' leading to sustained long-run development. As we shall see in Chapter 12, this is a rather unlikely prospect.

The 'infant industry argument' in favour of investment in human capital formation is a much sounder approach because it opens up infinite opportunities for individual enterprise and participation in the development process. Providing citizens with the opportunity to equip themselves with education, skills and know-how is allowing each one of them to contribute to, and play a part in, future social and economic development. Denying them this opportunity is denying them the right to participate in the development process.

But what kind of educational and skill development opportunity should be provided? How much is it likely to cost, and is it financially feasible? These are some of the central concerns of educational planning to be investigated in the next chapter. At the moment, it is necessary to examine an equally important question: how to maintain a dynamic balance between human capital formation (supply) and jobs (demand)? This is the purpose of manpower planning. It implies that the role of the manpower planner and that of the economic planner must be fully co-ordinated and the two activities linked functionally. In the past, the manpower planner and the economic planner worked in separate fields pursuing separate objectives. Functional harmonisation of the two functions would imply that (a) the manpower planner would determine the supply of manpower to be delivered to the labour market by the institutions charged with the development of human capital, and (b) the economic planner would determine the number and types of jobs to be provided by the planned investment expenditures. As a matter of necessity, both would have to be involved in the process of balancing supply and demand of manpower, and work towards a long-term labour market equilibrium.

Income Distribution and CEP

If economic planning is utilised as a policy instrument for raising the living standards of the population, employment opportunity is the functional link for levelling personal incomes. The positive link between employment of labour and income distribution follows from the fact that increased labour utilisation expands the share of wages and personal income, relative to property income. Increased income share of the low-income groups can be expected to generate beneficial effects in the product mix as well as labour productivity. Since poorer families spend a greater proportion of their income on consumption of food than higher-income groups, increased personal income share at the lower scale of the income pyramid is likely to stimulate aggregate demand for basic consumer goods.[9] To the extent that food and consumer goods are locally produced (rather than imported), greater income equality in LDCs can also be expected to result in higher domestic value-added than before, with a major boost to agricultural production. Increased food supply however may be contingent on major land reform and other reforms, as we shall see in Chapter 11. Finally, increased income and improved consumption levels among the lower-income groups would improve labour productivity and worker efficiency due to better nutritional standards.[10] Thus, on balance, we can regard employment creation as a strategy of planning and development, meeting two cardinal objectives simultaneously: providing productive jobs and distributing the benefits of economic progress across the entire nation.

A Critical Review of Past Manpower Planning

It is now necessary to review past manpower planning efforts in LDCs against the objectives outlined above. It will be seen that past efforts were faulty and inadequate. Guidelines for future manpower planning must be defined in such a way as to avoid the mistakes of the past.

Narrow Scope and Undue Emphasis on Long-Term Forecasting

In the first place, the scope of manpower planning was highly restrictive; it was typically conceived as a tool of forecasting long-term manpower requirements of industrialisation.[11] Projections of ten years or longer were quite commonly attempted, usually on unrealistic assumptions and poor data bases. In one sense, long-term projections were quite logical: educational plans for producing high-level manpower called for long-term budgeting and preparation. In addition, Development Plans, spanning upwards of 5 years, justified equally long-term projections of manpower needs, if only for the sake of consistency.

Long-term manpower forecasting, however, involved a high degree of abstraction from the existing realities of LDCs. It simply assumed away the pressing short-term and immediate problems of unemployment and underemployment. A further shortcoming was that agriculture was generally ignored. While this is understandable in view of the general preoccupation with industrial growth in LDCs, it has resulted in biases and distortions that, together with other factors, have helped to create the present unemployment problem. In particular, the stress on industrial manpower requirements was merely another argument for creating an urban-rural disequilibrium. While the manufacturing sector is an important source of wage employment and provides jobs for many skilled craftsmen and technicians, the neglect of the agricultural sector could hardly be reconciled with the fact that often upwards of 70 per cent of the population of LDCs live in rural areas and depend on agriculture for their livelihood; moreover, these nations will remain essentially rural for generations to come despite high rates of migration from rural to urban areas.

Macro Approach

Generally speaking, past manpower forecasting efforts in LDCs can be described as macro-planning inasmuch as they aimed at deriving manpower requirements for economic growth from certain macro-economic data such as planned investment and aggregate input-output relationships.[12] For example, one of the earliest and influential manpower forecasting exercises was the OECD's Mediterranean Regional Project which endeavoured to derive long-term manpower needs in Turkey, Greece, Yugoslavia, Spain, Italy and Portugal, on the basis of aggregate labour productivity and GNP growth rates.[13] The purpose of this exercise, and numerous others that followed, was to identify manpower shortages which could hamper future economic growth so that corrective measures might be taken in the meantime by 'gearing' education/training sectors to future manpower requirements. Despite critical opinion to the contrary,[14] manpower forecasting quickly became a global fashion. It became so popular that there is hardly an LDC without some sort of manpower study or survey providing statistical projections of its long-range needs.[15]

Unreliable Statistical Data

Aggregative manpower planning represented the ultimate example of 'planning without facts'. In view of inadequate statistical data needed for forecasting, the manpower planners often utilised what became known generally as 'guesstimating' — i.e. arbitrary and conjectural estimating, sometimes camouflaged by highly sophisticated econometric techniques,[16] but more often by dubious surveys of employers' intentions or opinions.[17] In some cases, statistical data from one given country were transplanted on the basis of weak arguments borrowed from Rostow's stages of growth theory.[18] In addition to poor data, forecasts were often based on exceedingly unrealistic assumptions. For instance, it was assumed that production functions are subject to constant returns to scale implying fixed input-output ratios,[19] and it was assumed that the education sectors could be 'geared to' or harmonised with the economy so that educational expansion would, in due course of time, effectively remove any shortages in the labour market. Under these circumstances, it is hardly surprising that manpower forecasts in the past were highly unreliable. An *ex poste* assessment of 18 African manpower studies, for example, found that all were significantly inaccurate, with seven cases underestimating requirements by no less than 50 per cent and eleven overestimating by over 100 per cent, in some cases by as much as 300 per cent to 800 per cent.[20]

False Rationalisations

Yet the manpower studies were utilised in some highly important policy decision-making. General magnitudes of future and existing shortages of high-level manpower were taken as justification for major university expansion programmes or large-scale foreign scholarship schemes of sending students to universities in the USA or Europe. As a short-term solution to the pressing manpower shortages, increased reliance on expatriate manpower was recommended. Thus, manpower planners in effect helped to rationalise expansion of technical assistance programmes from aid donors and UN agencies. Although reliance on expatriate personnel was conceived as a temporary measure until LDCs could become self-sufficient in manpower, in actual fact it increased quite rapidly, especially under the stimulus of the UN's Development Decade. Thus, a large and more or less permanent body of international bureaucracy has been created to manage the United Nations Development Programme and the programmes of many affiliated agencies of the UN.[21] Additionally, inflows of direct investment funds, attracted by policies providing tax incentives and tariff protection to multinational corporations, have generally stimulated inflows of foreign manpower imports as well, in some cases as a direct result of concession agreements entered into with the governments of LDCs. Partly because of increased reliance on expatriate manpower, higher educational expansion programmes, embarked upon at about the same time, failed to generate, as originally expected, an expansion of indigenous employment. Instead, they merely created an over-production and wasted resources, leading to intellectual unemployment and the school-leaver problem, which are discussed further in Chapter 10.

All in all, past manpower planning efforts in LDCs cannot be regarded as having aided egalitarian development. They were more beneficial to foreign interests participating in the industrialisation process than to the inhabitants of the developing countries.

Elements of a New Approach to Manpower Planning

The past record of manpower planning in LDCs is hardly encouraging as the preceding pages amply demonstrate; it may be quite surprising, therefore, that we are nevertheless proposing that manpower planning can indeed make a significant contribution to the solution of the unemployment problem in LDCs. It must be noted, however, that our concept of manpower planning is radically different from past experience in this area, both in scope and substance. In the following pages we spell out the elements of this new approach to manpower planning, first in the modern sector, and then in the traditional.

Modern Sector

The modern sector in most LDCs is relatively small, both in terms of actual and potential employment. It is unlikely that the secondary and tertiary sectors alone can generate sufficient labour absorptive capacity to overcome the unemployment problem, although there may be significant employment creation in these sectors as a result of appropriate fiscal, commercial and manpower policies.

Industrial Training and Matching Jobs and Workers

Skilled manpower for wage employment in the modern sector is a function of vocational and technical training. Expansion of these forms of training is an essential step in increasing the level of employment in this sector. Training *per se,* however, cannot guarantee employment of trained persons, even though their employability is actually raised.[22] Employment opportunities are created by investment and public expenditure projects. If, however, the pattern of development planning and policy is so regulated as actively to maximise employment, then training may well be matched to specific employment. This matching of jobs and workers requires some very careful co-ordination between the scale of training and the number of jobs to be created by new investment. Helping with the matching process at the micro-level is a key function of the manpower planner, and it implies that he has to operate as a linking co-ordinator between the economic planner, designing the investment projects, and the training agency undertaking the skill development.

Micro v. Macro Forecasting

While the matching process described above implies that long-range forecasting of manpower requirements is necessary, it is vitally important to be clear about the nature of these forecasts. In the past, they tended to be highly aggregative, at the macro-level; as a result they were unrelated to planned expenditures. The manpower planner worked quite independently of the economic planner. If, however, manpower forecasts are conducted at the level of specific projects (at the micro-level) then manpower training activities can be tailor-made according to job creation. Such a co-ordination of manpower training with given expenditure projects at the micro-level is highly efficient in terms of cost of training as well as in terms of placement of trained personnel in productive employment.

Product Mix and Choice of Technique

Perhaps the most critical link in the matching process proposed here is the selection of industrial projects to be included in the Development Plan. This in turn, is determined by the kinds of products which are desired, and the choice of techniques that can be utilised in the production activities. While costs and prices of inputs and the availability of alternative technologies are important considerations — and they are normally included in pre-investment feasibility studies — the number of jobs that can be expected to be created ought to be an explicit criterion as well. This is especially valid for public-sector projects, although, in the face of the unemployment crisis, there would be very rational reasons for LDCs to rewrite their tariff and trade regulations in order to encourage labour-using techniques of production while deliberately minimising capital-intensive methods in the private sector as well.[23]

Ex-Ante Project Appraisal

Benefit-cost analysis is a well known technique of project appraisal.[24] In the past, it has been used primarily for promoting efficient utilisation of physical and financial resources, in line with the central planning assumption of capital shortage in LDCs. There is, however, no reason why it cannot be applied to manpower utilisation as well, since manpower, too, is a factor of production requiring planned utilisation.

The suggested benefit-cost analysis for employment creation is an *ex-ante* appraisal of specific projects from the standpoint of their employment creation, i.e. the number of jobs which they will generate.

It has been shown elsewhere[25] how this application can be undertaken, demonstrating with a hypothetical example that under certain assumptions, a labour-intensive highway project would be socially more beneficial, compared to a capital-intensive alternative method of construction, the chief difference being the number of jobs created by the alternative techniques. There has been impressive progress in recent years in the methodology of benefit-cost appraisals with special reference to LDCs[26] and, from a planning point of view, a planner capable of undertaking *ex-ante* appraisal of proposed development projects can make a significant contribution to the objective of employment creation.

Fiscal Measures for Job Creation

In future, LDCs should rewrite tariff and fiscal policies which encourage capital use while minimising employment generation. There are several alternative measures that can be adopted. The period of tax holidays offered to foreign multinational firms can be tied to the volume of employment created instead of capital investment. Similarly, high rates of depreciation of business capital or investment allowances should be replaced by appropriate fiscal incentives linked to employment generation. Tariff policies encouraging imports of capital-intensive equipment should be stopped in cases where labour-intensive methods are available. For example, the construction of public highways, rural irrigation and land development schemes, in the past performed by heavy-duty earth-moving equipment imported from industrialised countries, often can be undertaken (as in China) by intermediate technology maximising labour use. Doing this might sometimes be resisted by engineers accustomed to Western procedures and equipment, but it is a temptation that must be curtailed to combat unemployment.

As an additional incentive to private employers in the modern sector, it may be desirable to introduce appropriate labour subsidy schemes to boost employment.[27] While such a subsidy will be costly for the government,[28] the social benefits may be sufficiently large to warrant it. A more serious objection to the labour subsidy proposal is that it is virtually certain to have limited impact because the modern industrial sector is typically a small fraction of the total economy. Even if modern-sector employment were doubled or trebled as a result of selective fiscal measures, many LDCs would still have severe unemployment levels. The resolution of the unemployment crisis necessitates that agricultural and rural development are assigned the top priority in future economic planning and policies both for food production and employment creation.

Financing Industrial Training Through a Levy

In view of the financial constraint prevailing in most LDCs, it may be desirable to impose an industrial training levy on manufacturing and industrial firms in order to finance manpower training in the modern sector. In fact, some LDCs already have alternative forms of levies along this line.[29] The UK's Industrial Training Boards, created under the 1964 Act, provide perhaps the most comprehensive example of this system.[30] The rates of levy, its coverage, administration and the type of training activities to be financed under this scheme will, of course, vary from one country to the next, reflecting differences in circumstances, but the initial step to legislate for the levy and the training function must be taken by the government.

The training function in the modern sector cannot be satisfactorily undertaken unless complemented with adequate and systematic labour market research and analysis. This research work, seriously neglected in the past, is essential for several reasons, the most obvious being the determination of training requirements. However, it should be comprehensive enough to analyse, on a regular basis, the workings of, and the changing conditions in, the labour market and generate up-to-date information about employer needs, wages and employment conditions. There is no reason why this research function should not be financed out of the training levy.

The Traditional Sector

This is where the principal source of future employment opportunities must be sought. The potential of agriculture in LDCs exists not only for food production, but also for employment. The fundamental fact is that today the great majority of the Third World population live in rural areas and depend on agriculture for their livelihood. Despite rapid urbanisation in the post-war period, this fact will remain for several decades to come. Concern with their economic and social welfare necessitates that economic and development policies must give top priority to land reform, appropriate farm technology, extension and credit facilities and other reforms designed to transform rural communities into productively employed farmers producing marketable food surpluses.

There are a number of countries which have successfully adopted these types of progressive agrarian reforms. One such example is Taiwan, which, soon after the Second World War, redistributed land by decree,

putting a maximum limit of 8 acres on the size of farms. Since 1949,
Taiwan has achieved a remarkable agrarian development, subsequently
leading to impressive industrial expansion.[31] Not surprisingly, much of
the success in Taiwan was due to complementary measures designed
by the government to provide agricultural credit to new farmers,
introduction of fertilisers, pesticides and other modern farming
techniques, and adequate marketing and storage facilities. Under proper
political conditions, there is no reason why similar successful agrarian
reforms cannot be introduced in several LDCs.

Youth Employment and Agriculture

In view of high and rising youth unemployment in LDCs, special
attention is necessary to accelerate job creation suitable for youth
manpower. It has been argued elsewhere[32] that, with proper incentives
and effective administration, agricultural development schemes may
offer substantial employment opportunity for young persons, provided
that a major restructuring of the traditional education system is undertaken
to expand rural education and training along with job placement
opportunities.

Such a restructuring undoubtedly would represent a bold step, but
bold steps are needed to overcome the youth unemployment problem.
Traditionally, education systems in LDCs have neglected agricultural
education and training. Even the technical or vocational institutions
have produced graduates fit only for urban employment. What are
needed are rural training centres and schools teaching curricula oriented
strictly toward rural skills and living conditions. Such centres should be
very closely tied to rural development projects so that graduates could
be utilised in these projects immediately upon graduation. Rural
development projects of this kind may include large-scale land
development schemes or rural public works programmes. But the
beneficiaries must be the young settlers themselves, as in the Malaysian
approach referred to in the last footnote.

Some LDCs are actually endeavouring to implement this type of
restructuring of their education systems. For example, Tanzania has
given rural education and training top priority in its Second Five-Year
Development Plan.[33] Recognising that 97 per cent of the country's
population live in rural areas, the Plan is formulated to restructure the
rural community around *Ujamaa* (fatherhood) villages featuring self-
reliance and co-operation, and by reorientation to achieve two
objectives: first, to promote 'socialist and rural development' by
making school an integral part of the rural community instead of an

elitist institution; second, to produce a class of educated and trained farmers and persons whose standard of living will depend mainly on the level of productivity of their farming activities. It is hoped that these changes will help to check rural-urban migration of young school-leavers by producing graduates who do not shun manual work on the land.

The restructuring of the education system is based on the realistic premise that transformation of an essentially rural country like Tanzania into a modern society will, of necessity, be a time-consuming process and that, in the meantime, the economic well-being of the rural population cannot be ignored. The basic orientation of the Plan is, therefore, agricultural and rural development, of which educational restructuring is an integral part. The Plan proposes the creation of *ujamaa* villages and a range of policies aimed at improving or extending rural credit facilities, village irrigation schemes and livestock production, as well as the rural physical infrastructure.

Rural youth schemes are by no means new. They have been tried in many countries, usually with disappointing results.[34] However, these discouraging efforts are often due to lack of sufficient financial and governmental support indicating low priority assigned to such projects. Given the mounting unemployment problem in LDCs and the existing crisis in education in most of these countries, it is necessary to undertake the necessary reforms of agricultural and rural development. The next chapter elaborates on the educational imbalances and needs of LDCs.

An Agriculture-Based Employment Policy: Training Farmers and Farm Workers

Youth land schemes with proper incentives is one way of creating productive employment opportunity in rural areas. An even larger volume of rural jobs could be generated as a result of large-scale training and education programmes specifically designed to raise the productivity of farmers and farm-workers. The way to solve the problem of low agricultural productivity in LDCs is through investment in rural manpower development. The human capital model is no less valid for rural communities than for urban groups. The provision of training and education opportunities for rural communities can most efficiently be done in the context of the integrated rural development strategy outlined in Chapter 11. This follows from the fact that training, *per se,* is not enough since it would only expand the supply of trained rural manpower. To convert this manpower supply into farmers and farm-workers producing food and income would require a number of related reformist interventions.

The principal requirement is an egalitarian land redistribution programme aimed at maximising the number of self-employed and viable smallholders. That small is not necessarily inefficient is clearly demonstrated by the experience of Japan and Taiwan, to cite two well known cases.[35] The cardinal rule of egalitarian land redistribution is that the mean farm size should be no less and no more than what would be required to generate an income stream considered adequate for an average rural family in a given area. The question of what is 'adequate' is an empirical question that can only be determined in relation to a particular area, taking into account soil fertility, water supply, climatic conditions, etc. For these reasons, a certain variance about the mean is unavoidable. The critically important task of determining the mean farm size is a basic planning function, and it should be based on careful field studies designed to test the pay-off streams, crop suitability and intermediate technology in various localities. It is a function which forms a necessary part of the decentralised planning strategy outlined in Chapter 8.

There is a necessary trade-off between agricultural output and employment implicit in the land redistribution stated above. Under an efficiency-oriented capitalist farming system, plantation techniques of production could be applied to food production as well (as the 'Green Revolution' experience in Pakistan and elsewhere clearly illustrates) in order to maximise the average productivity per acre of land. This, however, would result in labour displacement and elitist income concentration since the efficient scale of land for the application of capital inputs would necessitate large farms. If the output of these plantation-farms is drained away, the poverty of the landless and marginal farmers becomes inevitable.

The egalitarian land redistribution suggested above (and aimed at maximising the number of viable smallholder farms) is designed to avoid these negative social effects of capitalist farming. In effect, our proposal is to convert the landless peasants and marginal farmers into self-employed producers – producing for their families and for markets. The quantity of marketable surplus in this context would depend, besides the average farm size, on relative farm prices and the availability of credit, extension and marketing services to these smallholders – again, matters best managed within the integrated rural development strategy of Chapter 11.

Land reform, thus, emerges as a critically important determinant of employment policy in LDCs – quite apart from the conventional argument for it as a means of expanding food production for industrialisation. For this reason, land reform must become *plannable* in the sense that it should be implemented in an orderly manner as part of the development plan and linked to targets of food production *and* employment.

Notes

1. ILO, *World Employment Programme* (Geneva, 1969). See also the country case-studies undertaken under this Programme: *Toward Full Employment: A Programme for Colombia* (Geneva, 1970); *Matching Employment Opportunities and Equality: A Strategy for Increasing Productive Employment in Kenya* (Geneva, 1972). Subsequent country studies included Sudan and Iran. In addition to these case-studies, the ILO has undertaken very useful applied research directed at problems of employment, income distribution and appropriate technology in LDCs.

2. See pp.210-13 below and also Chapter 11.

3. See pp.24-5 in Chapter 1.

4. See p.55 *et seq.* and also Part Two, especially the cases of Malaysia (Chapter 5), Liberia (Chapter 6) and Brazil (Chapter 7).

5. D. Morawetz, 'Employment Implications of Industrialization in Developing Countries: A Survey', *The Economic Journal*, Vol.84 (September 1974); H.W. Singer, 'International Policies and Their Effect on Employment' in Ronald Robinson and Peter Johnston (eds.), (HMSO, London, 1971), pp.194-202; David A. Morse, 'The Employment Problem in Developing Countries', ibid., pp.5-13.

6. See, esp. pp.77-8. See also ILO, *Concepts of Labour Force Utilization* (Geneva, 1971); Frederick H. Harbison, *Human Resources as the Wealth of Nations* (Oxford University Press, New York, 1973), esp. pp.19-51.

7. Wage and income policy is an important integral part of employment and manpower policy, and it should serve two objectives: first, it should restrain unrealistically (or artificially) high wage rates which minimise job creation, and second, it should promote an effective ceiling on earnings to prevent a dynamic process of income concentration. This last requirement, discussed in Chapter 8, is an essential element of an egalitarian employment policy. On wages and incomes policy in LDCs, see A.D. Smith (ed.), *Wage Policy Issues in Economic Development* (Macmillan, London, 1969).

8. G. Becker, *Human Capital* (National Bureau of Economic Research, New York, 1964); T.W. Schultz, 'Investment in Human Capital', *American Economic Review* (March 1961).

9. Recent empirical studies or rural income consumption patterns in LDCs provide confirmation of this. Thus, Mellor and Lele, analysing the consumption of increased cash income of Indian farmers, concluded that agricultural families spend about 75 per cent of incremental income on highly labour-intensive agricultural commodities. Kilby and Johnston, using data from Taiwan and Uttar Pradesh, India, reached similar conclusions. Cline, working with data from Mexico and Brazil, found that land redistribution, accompanied by policies to terminate price distortions favouring mechanisation and capital-intensive farm technology, tend to increase the income share of labouring and rural classes and generate favourable consumption impact on the local economy. All these empirical findings are summarised in G. Hunter, 'The Food Research Institute's Fiftieth Anniversary Conference: Strategies for Agricultural Development in the

1970's: A Summary and Critique', *Stanford University Food Research Institute Studies,* Vol.XII, No.1 (1973).

10. For evidence, see P. Belli, 'The Economic Implications of Malnutrition: The Dismal Science Revisited', *Economic Development and Cultural Change,* Vol.20 (October 1971). This matter is also discussed in Chapter 3 above.

11. An influential study is the report of the Ashby Commission in the early 1960s which estimated the high-level manpower requirements of Nigeria's modern sector: Nigeria, Federal Ministry of Education, *Investment in Education, the Report of the Commission on Post-School Certificate and Higher Education in Nigeria* (Eric Ashby, Chairman) (Federal Government Printer, Lagos, 1960). See also UNESCO, *An Asian Model of Educational Development: Perspectives for 1965-80* (Paris, 1966).

12. For good examples of macro-planning covering the experience of a large number of developing countries see C. Hsieh, 'Planned rates of employment increase in development plans', in *International Labour Review,* Vol.97, No.1 (January 1968), pp.33-71, and *idem,* 'Approaches to fixing employment targets in development plans', ibid., No.3 (March 1968), pp.273-96.

13. OECD, Mediterranean Regional Project, *An Experiment in Planning by Six Countries: Greece, Italy, Portugal, Spain, Turkey and Yugoslavia* (country reports published individually for each country, mimeographed) (Paris, 1964); OECD, *Occupational and Educational Structures of the Labour Force and Levels of Economic Development* (OECD, Paris, 1970); H.S. Parnes, *Forecasting Educational Needs for Economic and Social Development* (OECD, Paris, 1962).

14. R. Hollister, *A Technical Evaluation of the First Stage of the Mediterranean Regional Project* (OECD, Paris, 1966). S.E. Harris (ed.), *Economic Aspects of Higher Education* (OECD, Paris, 1964); M. Blaug, 'Approaches to Educational Planning', *Economic Journal* (June 1967).

15. For representative country studies see F. Harbison and C.A. Myer (eds.), *Manpower and Education* (New York, McGraw-Hill, 1965); B. Ahamad and M. Blaug (eds.), *The Practice of Manpower Forecasting* (Jossey-Bass, Amsterdam, 1973). (This book contains an excellent bibliography.)

16. The pioneering econometric model-builders included Tinbergen, Correa and Bos. Their model with critiques by Parnes, Balogh, Sen and others is presented in J. Vaizey (ed.), *The Residual Factor and Economic Growth* (OECD, Paris, 1964). Also, see S. Bowles, 'The Efficient Allocation of Resources in Education', *Quarterly Journal of Economics,* Vol.81, No.3 (1967).

17. For a critical analysis of various manpower forecasting techniques see O. Mehmet, *Methods of Forecasting Manpower Requirement* (Centre for Industrial Relations, University of Toronto, 1965).

18. The most ambitious such study is M.A. Horowitz *et al., Manpower Requirements for Planning* (2 vols.) (Northeastern University, Boston, Mass., 1966). Also see P.R.G. Layard and J.C. Saigal, 'Educational and Occupational Characteristics of Manpower: An International Comparison', *British Journal of Industrial Relations,* Vol.4 (July 1966).

19. See the comments by A.K. Sen on the Tinbergen model in Vaizey, *The Residual Factor.*

20. R. Jolly and C. Colclough, 'African Manpower Plans: An Evaluation', *International Labour Review,* Vol.106 (August-September 1972), p.232.

21. See Chapter 12.

22. This is one of the major 'lessons' of the debate between structuralists and deficient demand theorists in the early 1960s preceding the passage of the Manpower Training and Development Act of 1962 in the USA. See the US Congress, Joint Economic Committee, *Higher Unemployment Rates, Structural Transformation or Inadequate Demand* (Washington, DC, 1961).

23. See G.E. Lent, 'Tax Incentives for the Promotion of Industrial Employment in Developing Countries' in *Fiscal Measures for Employment Developing Countries* (ILO, Geneva, 1973). This is a very useful study containing excellent papers by leading authorities in the field.

24. There is a large volume of literature on benefit-cost analysis. A comprehensive survey, somewhat dated now, is given in A.R. Prest and R. Turvey, 'Cost-Benefit Analysis: A Survey', *Economic Journal,* Vol.LXXIV (December 1965). An important contribution, especially from a social standpoint, is I.M.D. Little and J.A. Mirrlees, *Project Appraisal and Planning for Developing Countries* (Basic Books, New York, 1974).

25. O. Mehmet, 'Benefit-Cost Analysis of Alternative Techniques of Production for Employment Creation', *International Labour Review,* Vol.104, Nos.1-2 (July-August 1971).

26. See the earlier study of Little and Mirrlees, *Manual of Industrial Project Analysis in Developing Countries, Vol.II: Social Cost-Benefit Analysis* (OECD, Paris, 1968) and the revised 1972 edition of the same study.

27. A.R. Prest, 'The Role of Labour Taxes and Subsidies in Promoting Employment in Developing Countries' in *Fiscal Measures.*

28. On its administrative costs, see A. Peacock and G.K. Shaw, 'Fiscal Measures to Create Employment: The Indonesian Case', *Bulletin for International Fiscal Documentation,* Vol.27, No.11 (November 1973).

29. A notable case is the national training scheme SENA in Colombia financed by a 2 per cent training tax levied on salaries and wages in the public and private enterprises whose capital exceed 50,000 pesos or employing more than ten workers. SENA operates a vast array of apprenticeship and industrial training for workers in commerce, industry, agriculture, hotel management, medical services, etc. As a semi-autonomous organisation within the Colombian Ministry of Labour, SENA is a large, efficient agency; its 1971 expenditures exceeded 500 million pesos. Training agencies similar to SENA exist in other Latin American countries. See Frederick H. Harbison, *Human Resources as the Wealth of Nations,* pp.85-9.

30. United Kingdom, Ministry of Labour, *Industrial Training: Government Proposals,* Cmd. 1892 (HMSO, London, December 1961); *idem, Industrial Training Act: General Guide – Scope and Objectives* (rev.) (1965). D. Lee and B. Chiplin, 'The Economics of Industrial Training', *Lloyds Bank Review* (April 1970).

31. In the years following land redistribution, the country's development has been remarkable: its annual growth rate during 1951-61 is estimated at between 7.0 per cent and 7.5 per cent; agricultural output's growth rate during 1953-60 was 23 per cent and agricultural productivity rose by almost as much. See A.Y.C. Koo, *The Role of Land Reform in Economic Development: A Case Study of Taiwan* (Praeger, New York, 1968).

32. O. Mehmet, 'Youth Unemployment in Developing Countries: The Need for Restructuring the Education System', *International Development Review,* Vol.XIV, No.4 (1972).

33. United Republic of Tanzania, *Tanzania Second Five-Year Plan for Economic and Social Development, 1st July 1969 to 30th June, 1974* (Dar-Es-Salaam, 1969).

34. Countries where such schemes have been attempted, usually with limited success (though mostly due to the types of incentives offered), include: Ivory Coast, Jamaica, Malagasy Republic, Malawi, Mali, Senegal, Zambia. See ILO, *World Employment Programme* (Geneva, 1969). For a more detailed study (not limited to youth schemes) is Philip H. Coombs with Manzoor Ahmed, *Attacking Rural Poverty, How Nonformal Education Can Help* (Johns Hopkins University Press, Baltimore and London, 1974).

35. E.F. Schumacher, *Small is Beautiful, A Study of Economics as if People Mattered* (Blond and Briggs, London, 1973).

10 EDUCATIONAL PLANNING: SHIFTING FROM ELITIST TO EGALITARIAN PRINCIPLES

The unemployment crisis of LDCs also mirrors an educational crisis,[1] reflecting the fact that educational mismanagement in the past bears a heavy responsibility for the problems of labour utilisation.[2] Consistent with the strategy of a comprehensive employment policy (CEP) proposed in the preceding chapter, this one develops the theme that educational restructuring is essential to replace elitist values generated by traditional colonial schooling, with egalitarian principles based on universality and equality of access. Thus the task of educational planning needs to be fully co-ordinated with the overall framework of egalitarian planning.

The chapter begins with a review of past educational policies in LDCs and then suggests, in outline, a restructuring strategy with major emphasis on expanded educational opportunity in rural areas.

Misplaced Priorities

During the post-war period, many LDCs (especially the newly independent ones) embarked on ambitious educational expansion programmes in response to demographic pressures for school places and 'rising expectations'. Unfortunately, however, this expansion usually reflected misplaced or misguided sets of priorities. University and higher education levels were given top priority, and primary and rural education needs were ignored. Table 10.1 shows that during 1960-71, enrolments in universities and higher education institutions in LDCs as a whole increased twice as fast as total enrolments. Furthermore, virtually all of the educational expansion was concentrated in urban areas. As a result, illiteracy rates in rural areas remained excessively high, and for some LDCs reached 80 per cent in 1971 (Table 10.2). In addition, technical, vocational and agricultural education and training were seriously neglected, despite general manpower shortages (and costly imports of expatriates) in these fields.

Despite rapid enrolment growth, budgetary allocations in general lagged behind requirements. Public expenditure on education as a percentage of GNP for all LDCs combined remained stationary at 3 per cent during 1965-71 (compared to 6 per cent for developed

Table 10.1: Percentage Increase in Enrolments, by Level 1960-71

	Total[b]	1st Level[c]	2nd Level[d]	3rd Level[e]
World total[a]				
1960-5	4.9	4.2	6.4	10.0
1965-71	3.1	2.6	3.8	7.9
Developed countries				
1960-5	3.5	2.3	4.9	9.5
1965-71	1.2	0.2	1.9	7.3
Developing countries				
1960-5	6.7	6.0	9.9	12.4
1965-71	5.1	4.4	7.6	10.2

a. Excluding China, the Democratic People's Republic of Korea and the Democratic Republic of Vietnam.
b. Not including pre-primary, special and adult education.
c. Not including pre-primary education.
d. General, vocational and teacher training.
e. Universities and other institutions of higher education.
Source: UNESCO, *Statistical Yearbook 1973* (Paris, 1973), Table 2-1.

countries)[3] despite rapid GNP growth rates in many LDCs. Consequently, the quality of education was sacrificed for quantity. As one observer put it, the results were often 'shockingly high drop-out and repeater rates, or. . .over-crowded class-rooms and (what goes on in there) in the name of education'.[4]

In Latin America, where independence had come earlier than in Africa and Asia, national literacy levels were relatively higher, except in such countries as Haiti, Guatemala, Honduras and Bolivia. Nevertheless, in common with other LDCs, Latin American countries possessed education systems manifesting glaring inequalities, regional imbalances, official inertia and resistance to reform and incredible inefficiency — factors closely related to a long tradition of elite control favouring classical university education at the expense of skill development and rural education.

Lack of Educational Opportunity

Despite the post-war emphasis on enrolment growth, lack of educational opportunity is still a widespread problem for most LDCs. In fact, estimates by UNESCO indicate that, because of a rapid parallel population growth, there has been an increase in the aggregate number of adult illiterates in the world, virtually all living in LDCs: amongst UNESCO's member countries, no less than 460 million adults were

Table 10.2: Illiteracy Rates in Selected LDCs by Sex and Rural/Urban
Areas (population 15 years and over)

Region/Country	Year	Total	Male	Female
Africa				
Morocco	1971			
Total		78.6	66.4	90.2
Urban		50.5	45.6	45.6
Rural		88.5	78.1	98.7
S. America		(including persons of unknown		
El Salvador	1961	literacy status)		
Total		51.0	46.1	55.1
Urban		28.8	21.0	35.0
Rural		66.3	61.3	71.5
Chile	1970			
Total		11.9	11.1	12.8
Urban		7.6	6.4	8.6
Rural		27.2	25.1	29.7
Ecuador	1962	(excluding Indian jungle population)		
Total		32.5	27.9	36.9
Urban		11.9	8.1	15.2
Rural		44.5	38.4	50.7
Asia				
Indonesia	1971	(population 10 years and over)		
Total		40.4	29.2	51.0
Urban		20.9	11.5	30.2
Rural		44.7	33.2	55.5
Malaysia	1970	(population 10 years and over)		
Sabah Total		55.7	44.8	67.6
Urban		30.9	21.2	42.1
Rural		61.1	50.1	73.0
Sarawak Total		61.7	51.4	72.1
Urban		35.9	25.2	46.5
Rural		67.4	57.1	77.7
W. Malaysia Total		39.2	27.9	50.4
Urban		31.8	21.6	42.1
Rural		42.4	30.7	54.0
Sri Lanka	1969			
Total		19.4	10.6	27.6
Urban		11.7	—	—
Rural		20.7	—	—
Thailand	1970			
Total		21.4	12.8	29.7
Urban		12.3	6.3	18.1
Rural		22.9	13.9	31.6

Source: UNESCO, *Statistical Yearbook 1973,* Table 1.4.

classified as illiterate in the mid-1960s – a figure representing 60 per cent of their active population.[5] According to UNICEF no less than 500 million children of compulsory school age in the world lack access to any type of schooling. As shown in Table 10.3, as late as 1967/8, of all the children in Africa between 5 and 15 years of age, only 40 per cent were attending a school; 55 per cent did so in Asia; 75 per cent in Latin America; and 50 per cent in the Arab states. While there has been some progress since 1960, it must be noted that these figures are regional averages, and taken in conjunction with those presented in Table 10.2, they actually imply a severe lack of educational opportunity in the rural areas, especially so far as female children are concerned. In the words of a recent UNESCO report on literacy:

> For many school-age children there are no schools at all, nor are all the children who do attend school staying there long enough to acquire permanent literacy; thus new generations of illiterates continue to join the adult population . . . A closer look at statistics on illiteracy reveals further injustices. Almost universally, more women are illiterate than men; recent growth in literacy has favoured men over women, thus widening this differential. Rural dwellers are more apt to be illiterate than those living in urban areas, especially in many countries that depend largely on agricultural production for their income. There is a dangerous possibility that educational differentials between these groups will widen unless women and rural populations receive special attention.[6]

The opportunities for acquiring higher education are even more restricted. For example, just under 10 per cent of the young people are able to enter a secondary school and a mere 1 per cent are at the university.[7] Yet large amounts of scarce resources have been spent on higher education causing over-investment, while primary and rural education have been neglected. Ivan Illich, the originator of the 'De-Schooling' movement, commenting on the steep educational pyramids in Latin American countries, noted that 'Nowhere in Latin America do 27 per cent of any age group get beyond the sixth grade, nor do more than 1 per cent graduate from a university.'[8]

Universal *v.* Elitist Education

That education improves labour productivity and contributes to economic growth has been recognised by classical economists since Adam Smith. However, it was not until about 1960 that the acquisition

Table 10.3: Percentage of Children of Primary School-Age Attending
School,[a] 1960-1 and 1967-8 (Provisional)

Region	1960-1	1967-8
World total	63	68
Africa	34	40
N. America	98	98
L. America	60	75
Asia[b]	50	55
Europe	96	97
Oceania	95	95
(Arab states)	(38)	(50)

a. Primary school has been defined in each country's school system.
b. Excluding China, the Democratic People's Republic of Korea and the
   Democratic Republic of Vietnam.

Source: UNESCO, *Literacy 1969-71* (Paris, 1972), Table 6.

of skills and specialised knowledge through education and training was
recognised as an investment process in human capital formation.
Schultz's pioneering work, supplemented by the findings of others
including Denison, Abramovitz, Becker, Harbison, Myers, Kuznets and
Balogh, helped to break the 'capital-is-everything' approach to economic
development.[9]

But the human capital model had a generally elitist impact on
educational planning and priorities in LDCs. While it tended to justify
university expansion on grounds of eliminating high-level manpower
shortages in those countries, it was actually undertaken more for
prestige and self-interest reasons on the part of ruling elites. Building a
university was far more prestigious than a village primary school and,
besides, it enhanced the educational careers of privileged children in
circumstances where attendance at university is primarily a function of
family income and social status.[10] In addition, bureaucratic inertia
provided a further motive for inaction and resistance to reform.

For all of these reasons, governments in many LDCs in the post-war
years tended to ignore essential reforms needed to make education
more relevant to social and economic needs, and more responsive to
egalitarian principles. As a result, many LDCs continue to remain
burdened with elitist and colonial educational structures characterised
by outmoded curricula and teaching methods, and gross inefficiencies.

It is hardly surprising, therefore, that recent empirical research is finding that public educational expenditure in the Third World is often regressively redistributing income from the poor to the rich with a social rate of return close to zero or, in some cases, negative.[11] In specific terms, primary schools generally prepare pupils, fortunate enough to attend, for secondary schools which, in turn, prepare students either for university education or white-collar jobs in urban centres, preferably in the civil service carrying generous fringe benefits. Even in rural areas, primary schooling has a strong, built-in anti-rural bias, and education is hardly regarded as terminal, leading to an agricultural occupation. Instead, it encourages out-migration to urban areas.[12] Pro-urban and white-collar biases are inculcated even in vocational and agricultural schools.[13]

Thus, by merely expanding the scale of traditional education systems, without altering its instructional content or its elitist orientation, governments in LDCs have actually contributed to the emergence of youth unemployment. They failed to recognise that the colonial and classical education is essentially elitist, designed for the benefit of a select and privileged few, and that it functions best for producing office workers for the civil service or urban white-collar occupations. It is unfit for mass production, and is highly wasteful in countries with small salaried and wage-employment sectors.

School-Leavers Problem

Many LDCs today are faced with a grave problem of 'school-leavers'. These are drop-outs as well as graduates who are unable to find jobs for which they have been educated.[14] Confined mostly to urban centres, but often consisting of rural migrant job-seekers, they are predominantly young persons with considerable educational qualifications.

At first sight, the 'school-leavers' problem suggests that the economic value of education in LDCs is marginal, if not actually zero or negative. It appears as a problem of over-production and over-investment in the education system. In fact, however, it simply reflects misguided educational policies and priorities in the past. In the first place, it demonstrates the irrelevance of traditional forms of education with emphasis on urban, civil service jobs. Conversely, it reflects the mistake of early post-war plans and policies which ignored rural education and agricultural training, while limiting educational expansion to towns and cities. Widening rural-urban educational as well as wage disparities merely lead to an efflux of young persons from the countryside in search of schooling as a passport to higher-paid government or urban jobs. Second, emphasis on classical, generalist educational programmes generates a mismatch between the economy's manpower needs and the qualifications of job-seekers. The typical unemployed school-leaver possesses virtually no technical or vocational skills which the employers need most. Therefore, vacancies for technical and skilled jobs coexisted with a surplus of 'generalists'.

Under-Investment in Skill Development and Agricultural Education

It may be paradoxical that LDCs which made industrialisation the leading objective of post-war development policies should, at the same time, fail miserably in taking steps to increase the supply of skilled and trained manpower to meet the requirements of industrial growth. There are several reasons for this. In the first place, it reflected the anti-manpower bias of the government leaders, their failure to regard educational and training expenditures as a significant form of social investment. Second, since much of the industrialisation projects relied on technology and management as well as investment capital mostly imported from abroad, they could do likewise so far as technical and middle-level manpower categories were concerned. Such a reliance on expatriate manpower would immediately solve any manpower shortage, rather than prolong it for several years until domestic production could be forthcoming. Also, much of the technical advice given to the LDCs strongly recommended reliance on foreign manpower resources as a temporary measure until domestic manpower supplies could be produced.[15]

In some countries, such as Liberia,[16] governments deliberately under-invested in technical, vocational and agricultural education, substituting expatriate personnel for domestic manpower even though the wage differential may be as much as ten times that of local workers in similar occupations.

Differences in labour productivity provided the major reason for the wide wage differential between expatriate and domestic workers. In turn, these productivity differences reflect under-investment in skill development in LDCs. This is equally valid for industrial and agricultural sectors. For example, a recent study found that the difference in average agricultural output per worker between a group of 11 LDCs and a group of 9 advanced countries was as much as 83.5 per cent in favour of the latter, with the differences in the quality of human capital accounting for 35 per cent of the productivity difference.[17] Differences in land resources per worker accounted for only 2 per cent, livestock 19 per cent, and technical inputs such as fertiliser and farm machinery 29 per cent. These are extremely important findings, indicating serious under-investment in agricultural education and training facilities in LDCs. Such investments are capable of high returns both in food production as well as employment generation in rural areas. Equally important, these results demonstrate convincingly that appropriate investment in human capital formation is productive both socially (i.e. in raising literacy levels, for example) as well as in output terms.

Over-Investment in Universities

Neglect of technical, vocational and agricultural education in LDCs was counterbalanced with an over-investment in university education. In many countries, this was due to prestige reasons rather than economic needs or financial capabilities. For instance, the prospectus of the University of Zambia, established in 1965, was probably quite typical of many new universities in LDCs when it declared what it was 'determined to earn the respect and proper recognition of the international university community'.[18] In other words, it would strive to become a prestige institution. In line with this objective, and quite aside from financial limitations,[19] many new universities in LDCs relied on expatriate faculty, sometimes for as much as 30 per cent of the total teaching staff, provided under foreign aid programmes and United Nations technical assistance. Even where provided at the expense of donor agencies and countries, expatriate faculty create severe financial as well as cultural problems, such as conflicting ideas and orientation about teaching procedures, aims of a university, and substantial salary differentials relative to local faculty members. In addition, the cost of providing fringe benefits — such as housing — normally borne by the LDCs can be quite substantial.

Another type of resource misallocation in the university sector resulting from the pursuit of prestige objectives, is to be seen in the development of high-cost, ultra-modern medical schools and technology which nevertheless have limited social value. In many Latin American countries, for example, large sums have been spent to equip university medical schools with sophisticated technology imported from abroad for heart and organ transplants, which are used only sparingly but with much publicity, while there is a severe shortage of general practising physicians needed for basic preventative and curative medical services and health delivery programmes, especially in rural areas.[20]

As with the problem of 'school-leavers' already discussed, many LDCs suffer from an excessive number of university graduates, especially those from arts and humanities fields of study, typically anticipating public service employment. Writing about India, Mark Blaug has made the interesting observation — valid for many other LDCs as well — that the Indian public service is actually *hoarding* large numbers of university graduates, in the sense that their remuneration exceeds the value of their marginal productivity. Despite serious intellectual unemployment in the country, the problem of over-production of Indian university graduates is expected to continue rising: by 1986, 1.5 million unemployed graduates and no less than 4 million unemployed matriculants are projected.[21] Such conditions naturally lead to a 'brain drain', while those who are unable to migrate abroad remain idle. In both cases, there is social waste of public resources used in providing expensive education to such persons.

The phenomenon of the 'brain drain' exemplifies the great social waste of the traditional university system of LDCs.[22] In the first instance, emigration of college graduates to industrialised countries mirrors the limited professional opportunities available in their native countries; but it also reflects the discriminatory employment practices which are prevalent in those countries. Thus, the Pearson Report quoted UN estimates relating to 1967 that 40,000 trained specialists, such as physicians, engineers, etc. had left LDCs for advanced countries,[23] while at the same time, these same countries relied heavily on expatriate technical and advisory personnel from abroad. 'The number of qualified people going from the poor countries to the rich is larger than that of the technical advisers from industrialized countries moving in the other direction.'[24] Baldwin has observed: 'The less developed countries are not being stripped of manpower they badly need; more often than not they are being relieved of manpower they cannot use.'[25] This over-production of university-trained personnel reflects serious misallocation of resources in universities in LDCs and calls for careful reappraisal of educational priorities. Educational resources must be reallocated in the light of realistic estimates of the absorptive capacity in the industrial and urban sectors. Simultaneously, there should be a major expansion of agricultural education and non-formal rural schooling geared to the present and future needs of farming communities. The values and student expectations generated in rural educational and training institutions should be heavily and deliberately biased toward an agricultural way of life, rather than urban-oriented.[26]

Aims of Educational Policy: Expansion or Restructuring?

On the basis of the experience acquired during the post-war period, three main guidelines can be inferred for future educational planning and policy in LDCs. These three guidelines represent a major institutional restructuring of the existing, elitist education systems, rather than merely expanding them by linear extrapolation. They are: (i) literacy programmes in rural areas designed to provide universal accessibility to first-level education, if need be through cost-saving (but well organised) non-formal methods; (ii) agricultural and rural education and training programmes planned as terminal rather than feeding higher levels of education; and (iii) middle-level technical/vocational polytechnics and institutes for skill and craft development in rural as well as urban areas. Given the budgetary constraints under which education systems in most LDCs have to function, the restructuring outlined above (and discussed further below) implies that future university programmes should be curtailed, and public resources be re-diverted to finance educational activities under (i) to (iii) above. In this way, educational restructuring need not create intolerable financial burdens on the development budget.

Low-Cost Universal Literacy

In LDCs with high illiteracy rates, development of a nation-wide, universal literacy must be a leading policy objective. This is desirable not only for higher productivity of workers, but also for increased social and political consciousness of the target groups so that public decisions, including expenditure programmes and planning priorities, are based on the widest possible participation in the decision-making process.

Universal literacy according to conventional methods of schooling, however, would be too costly for the majority of LDCs suffering from illiteracy. For example, how could an LDC with an average GNP *per capita* of $100, up to half of which may be non-monetary, hope to provide universal primary schooling for its entire school-age population, when the typical primary school teacher's salary is likely to be 10 to 15 times the average GNP *per capita*? |

Innovations in a number of poor LDCs during the last decade offer some encouraging possibilities for low-cost, often non-formal literacy programmes, at least for early-stage experimentation. For example, the West African countries of Upper Volta, Niger, Mali and Mauritania are among the poorest with only 10 to 20 per cent of primary school-children able to enroll in conventional primary schools. With World Bank assistance, they have recently started a low-cost network of rural education centres designed to provide illiterate rural youths with a mix of practical training in agriculture, crafts and elements of literacy and numeracy.[27] These centres can accommodate 30-40 youths for about three years of study, training and practical work. The programme has met with much success in arresting the efflux of young persons to towns. A key factor is that instruction is in the vernacular, often the tribal language instead of English or French. Furthermore, instruction is attuned to the technological methods and cultural values locally predominant rather than to some outside, foreign elements of modernity. Instead of tractors (which are too expensive anyway), emphasis is placed on purchasing a pair of oxen to plough and farm. Of critical importance is the fact that former trainees are assisted to set up small farmers' co-operatives, pooling their resources. Also, the literacy programmes are co-ordinated with the work of other development projects, for example, those under the Ministries of Agriculture, Health, etc. A side-effect of rural functional literacy programmes can be illustrated from Mali, where the official language is French: it has been discovered that after the rural trainees became literate in their own tribal languages, they started to write to government officials, who used to work exclusively in French but now have no choice but to learn to read and write in their own languages themselves. The cost per trainee of rural literacy programmes is no more than 25 per cent of the cost of providing 4 grades of primary education to each pupil.[28]

The World Bank's experiment in West Africa is by no means the only case of low-cost, non-formal literacy projects. UNESCO's World Educational Literacy Programme[29] is another multi-country experiment which may lead to some encouraging results, particularly if these efforts receive support and financial backing from domestic leaders. Low-cost functional literacy programmes deserve every support, both inside and outside LDCs, although they cannot meet all the educational needs of the target groups.

Urban-Rural Imbalance

The task of educational restructuring in LDCs is complicated by the traditional pro-urban bias of educational policy. This pro-urban bias has resulted in the concentration of Ministries of Education, administrative headquarters, universities and colleges, the largest and best equipped secondary and primary schools, the bulk of teachers and libraries in urban centres. Unequal and inferior educational opportunity in rural areas constitutes one of the most important causes for the drift of school-age population into towns in the post-war period.

Consequently, a more balanced regional distribution of educational facilities would contribute to arresting the migration of youth into towns. Linear expansion of the traditional system of classical/liberal arts types of education would be counter-productive. In fact, instead of removing the existing regional imbalance in the education system, such an expansion might even accelerate out-migration. What is required is an *integrated* approach in which educational programmes in rural areas are complemented with other rural and agricultural development projects.[30] While expanding educational opportunity in rural areas, curricula and teaching methods should be changed from traditional arts orientation towards skill and craft development, and students encouraged, through rural values and proper incentives, to seek a rural occupation. One of the highest priority objectives must be the creation of training and education centres designed to produce self-employed farmers, rural artisans and skilled workers in the light of the needs of rural communities. A unique feature of rural education and training policies must be that they should function as terminal rather than merely feeding some urban higher education institution. In addition to appropriate curricula, teachers in rural areas must have qualifications relevant to a rural environment. The importance of properly qualified, adequately paid and motivated teachers in rural areas cannot be overstated in view of their critical influence in shaping the values and expectations of individual students.

An obvious handicap of the educational restructuring favouring rural areas is that it runs contrary to the conventional job preferences and urban biases of the youth in LDCs. There exists considerable evidence, compiled through surveys of students' attitudes and career preferences, indicating that most students aim at a white-collar desk or office job primarily because of a general association between manual and rural work and low social status.[31] These negative values, reinforced by colonial elitism, were uncritically accepted by post-war educational and economic planners, who presumed that educational expansion policies ought to reinforce traditional job preferences, however unrealistic or counter-productive they might be in the context of LDCs. While the task of altering these anti-manual and anti-rural values is difficult, if proper and adequate incentives were offered to the students (in particular land), then educational restructuring could go a considerable distance in changing these values. The educational history of such ideologically different countries as Japan and the People's Republic of China contain striking similarities in the degree of emphasis attached, in the early stages of industrialisation, on technical, vocational and agricultural training, based on the principles of accessibility and practical relevance.[32]

Notes

1. Philip H. Coombs, *The World Educational Crisis, A Systems Analysis* (Oxford University Press, New York, 1968).

2. M. Blaug, *Education and Unemployment Problems in Developing Countries* (ILO, Geneva, 1973).

3. UNESCO, *Statistical Yearbook 1973* (Paris), Table 2-6.

4. P.H. Coombs, *What is Educational Planning?* (UNESCO, Paris, 1970), p.27.

5. UNESCO, 'UNESCO's Contribution to the Promotion of the Aims and Objectives of the United Nations Development Decade: Report by the Director-General', General Conference, 14th Session, 25 October-30th November 1966 (Paris, September 1966, 14C/10).

6. UNESCO, *Literacy 1969-71* (Paris, 1972), p.10.

7. World Bank, *Education* (Washington, D.C., 1971), p.9.

8. 'The Futility of Schooling in Latin America', *Saturday Review*, 20 April 1968, p.59. Also see his more recent study: *Limits to Medicine, Medical Nemesis: The Expropriation of Health* (McClelland and Stewart, Toronto, 1976) where Illich notes (pp.238-9) that 'In all of Latin America, except Cuba, only one child in forty from the poorest fifth of the population finishes the five years of compulsory schooling. . .'

9. For a convenient collection of pioneering works on this subject see M. Blaug (ed.), *Economics of Education* (2 vols.) (Penguin, Harmondsworth, 1968).

10. Jean-Pierre Jallade, 'Education Finance and Income Distribution', *World Development,* Vol.4, No.5 (1976); Douglas M. Windham, 'Social Benefits and the Subsidization of Higher Education: A Critique', *Higher Education,* Vol.5 (1976); C. Jencks *et al., Inequality: A. Reassessment of the Effect of Family and Schooling in America* (Basic Books, New York, 1972).

11. Recent discussions of the relationships between education and labour markets in LDCs are presented in Blaug, *Education and Unemployment Problems in Developing Countries.*

12. C.R. Frank, 'Urban Unemployment and Economic Growth in Africa', *Oxford Economic Papers,* Vol.20, No.2 (July 1968); S.V. Sethuraman, 'Urbanization and Employment: A Case Study of Djakarta', *International Labour Review,* Vol.112, Nos.2-3 (August-September 1975); Blaug, *Education and Unemployment Problems in Developing Countries.*

13. Thus, virtually all of the agricultural scientists are employed in urban centres, usually in Ministries of Agriculture and other public sector agencies. According to a UNESCO report in 1965, 'Of India's 2,600 agricultural scientists, 90 per cent are in the public sector [i.e. civil servants mainly in offices of the Ministry of Agriculture], whereas the country's agricultural production is almost entirely in the hands of private cultivators. Hardly 1 percent of the scientists are engaged in farming or farm management, while less than 3 percent are in these occupations in the food and dairy industries combined. . .' Quoted in Coombs, *The World Education Crisis,* p.95. Similar evidence from other LDCs confirms the view that agricultural schools function primarily as a transfer mechanism leading to white-collar jobs rather than as terminal intended for cultivators and farmers.

The misplaced role of technical/vocational institutions is discussed in P.J. Foster, 'The Vocational School Fallacy in Development Planning' in C.A. Anderson and M.S. Bowman (eds.), *Education and Economic Development* (Aldine, Chicago, 1966). Reprinted in Blaug (ed.), *Economics of Education 1.*

14. A.J. McQueen, 'Unemployment and Future Orientation of Nigerian School-Leavers', *Canadian Journal of African Studies,* Vol.3, No.2 (Spring 1969); A. Callaway, 'Unemployment Among School Leavers', *Journal of Modern African*

Studies, Vol.1, No.3 (1963); Blaug, *Education and Unemployment Problems in Developing Countries.*

15. See Chapter 9.

16. See Chapter 6.

17. V.M. Ruttan, *The Future of Agriculture (A/D/C Reprint,* Agricultural Development Council, New York, December, 1974).

18. Quoted in C.A. Coulson, 'The Problem of Higher Education in Africa', *African Affairs,* Vol.70 (July 1971), p.284.

19. It has been estimated that in the early 1970s it cost roughly $3,000 to keep a student at an African university for a year, while the bulk of the population of Africa earns less than $100.

20. See Chapter 3, esp. pp.68-70. Also Ivan Illich, *De-Schooling Society* (Harper and Row, New York, 1971).

21. Quoted by M. Blaug in 'Education, Economic Situation and Prospects of India 1971', *Bulletin of the Institute of Development Studies,* University of Sussex, Vol.3, No.3 (1971).

22. W. Adams (ed.), *The Brain Drain* (Macmillan, New York, 1968).

23. Lester B. Pearson *et al., Partners in Development* (Praeger, New York, 1969), p.202.

24. G. Wulker, 'Education and Training in Development', *Intereconomics,* No.9 (1974), p.285.

25. G. Baldwin, 'Brain Drain or Overflow?' *Foreign Affairs,* Vol.48, No.2 (1970), p.359.

26. The problems associated with this are briefly discussed below on p.228.

27. Francis J. Letham, 'Innovation in Education in Western Africa', *Finance and Development,* Vol.11, No.4 (December 1974).

28. Ibid., p.28.

29. See the various country case studies published by UNESCO: B. Dumont, *Functional Literacy in Mali: Training for Development* (Paris, 1973); P. Furter, *Possibilities and Limitations of Functional Literacy: The Iranian Experiment* (Paris, 1973); M. Viscus, *Literacy for Working: Functional Literacy in Rural Tanzania* (Paris, 1971).

30. For an inventory of rural and out-of-school programmes (in addition to sources cited in the previous footnote), see J.R. Sheffield and V.P. Diejomaoh, *Non-Formal Education in African Development* (African-American Institute, New York, 1972); P.J. Foster and J.R. Sheffield (eds.), *Education and Rural Development* (The World Yearbook of Education 1974) (Evans Bros. Ltd, London, 1973); Philip H. Coombs with Manzoor Ahmed, *Attacking Rural Poverty: How Nonformal Education Can Help* (Johns Hopkins University Press, Baltimore, 1974).

31. See Coombs, *The World Educational Crisis,* pp.93-7.

32. For an account of Chinese educational policy in the post-war period, see Immanuel C.Y. Hsui, 'The Impact of Industrialisation on Higher Education in Communist China' in F. Harbinson and C.A. Myers (eds.), *Manpower and Education, Country Studies in Economic Development* (McGraw-Hill, New York, 1965). A brief account of the Japanese educational development is presented in Y. Hora and M. Yano, 'Changes in Education in Post-war Japan', *Developing Economies,* Vol.VII, No.4 (December 1969).

11 EGALITARIAN PLANNING AND RURAL DEVELOPMENT

In future, the 'engine of growth' for most LDCs should be agrarian development, but the fruits of this growth should not be drained away into urban sectors; instead, they should be utilised for meeting the needs of rural communities and for sustained development of agriculture. Urban poverty and unemployment can most effectively be remedied by action directed at rural areas, the source of post-war migration into the urban ghettos and slums. This pro-rural planning strategy, detailed below, is fully consistent with the egalitarian principles outlined in Chapter 8 in which a decentralised process of determining priorities, reflecting regional and village needs, was advocated.

We begin with a brief discussion of the rural-urban disequilibrium generated by the post-war industrialisation strategy, and then consider the shifts in planning priorities and reforms in the decision-making process for a pro-rural development approach. The principal issues in this approach are: (1) the question of farming techniques which are appropriate for small-scale holders whose limited working capital and resources severely constrain their investment choices; (2) the question of land reform; (3) how to mobilise rural communities for egalitarian reform rather than for rebellion; and (4) the feasibility and stability of an integrated rural development (IRD) strategy designed to improve rural living standards in the most efficient manner possible.

Rural-Urban Disequilibrium

The post-war theory of 'Big Push' industrialisation was based on the notion of draining rural surpluses and resources into non-agricultural sectors. In the standard two-sector model,[1] the rural sector, represented as primitive and stagnant, was the source 'from which labor, savings, food, foreign exchange, and taxes [were to be] squeezed in order to develop imposing but inefficient urban industries'.[2] This notion was theoretically justified by means of two arguments: (a) income elasticity of demand for non-agricultural products was considered to be relatively high, and (b) 'growth poles' were perceived to lie in modern sectors. The array of policy instruments utilised to relegate agriculture to a subservient position in planning priorities included tax and credit incentives for domestic manufacturing, 'infant industries' sheltered by over-valued currencies and high tariffs,[3] not forgetting the negative impact of surplus 'food aid' from foreign donors.[4] Donor countries and international aid agencies generally have been reluctant to become interested in the intricate systems of traditional agriculture and have avoided tackling complex social, political and institutional problems that have long handicapped the efficiency and productivity of the smallholder.[5] The focus on technical problems (e.g. tractorisation, pesticides, high-yielding seeds) has diverted attention from the political cultural and social determinants of food production, while, at the same time, the concern with large-scale farm technology ignored the need for an appropriate intermediate technology to upgrade the smallholder's operations.

Future agricultural development policies and strategies must be based on the premise that the role of the smallholder should be strengthened and upgraded. He must become the central objective of plans to arrest the rural-urban disequilibrium created by the post-war industrialisation drive. Such a strategy would have far-reaching implications. It would tend to combine economic growth and food production with greater social justice for the rural masses; it would put a stop to the exploitation of the rural sector 'as a milch-cow'[6] and retain agricultural surpluses and resources in the rural sector; and it would greatly improve economic and non-economic incentives available to rural communities. Food production on typically small farms need not be inefficient. Marketable surpluses need not be reduced as rural consumption levels are raised, especially if the barter terms of trade move in favour of agriculture. On the other hand, dependency on outside markets, with their destabilising price and income fluctuations, would be lessened.

Intermediate Agricultural Technology

As with industrialisation strategy, past efforts aimed at increased agricultural output relied heavily on the transfer of highly capital-intensive Western technology, often as a result of aid programmes.[7] To some extent this was occasioned by the neo-Malthusian fears of over-population and the urgency of solving the perceived global food shortage; these fears were probably overstated.[8] At any rate, the 'extension bias'[9] characterised in the US and foreign agricultural aid programmes in the post-war period reflected the oversimplified view that readily available innovation and technical know-how, developed in temperate climatic zones, could be adapted in tropical agricultural environments to replace primitive farming methods and to promote more efficient resource allocation and greater output. Whenever these 'extension' strategies failed to function as originally expected, it was explained away with yet another oversimplification: the traditional farmer was simply too resistant to progress because of ignorance and irrationality.

In recent years, micro studies of smallholders and traditional farmers have demonstrated that these cultivators are far from being irrational; they are quite responsive to favourable price and market incentives[10] and may adapt appropriate new technology under acceptable risk conditions.[11] Furthermore, these studies are finding out that the real constraints to improved farm output and productivity are the social and institutional factors, and the alleged resistance of traditional farmers to modernisation is actually a reflection of the failure of extension workers and agricultural technical advisers to take into account the negative effect of these institutional factors on the motivations and risk-taking behaviour of the cultivators. What is needed is low-cost technology, suitable for the smallholder, whose financial resources and social circumstances dictate a relatively modest and conservative investment strategy. The mere availability of tractors, fertilisers and seeds, on commercial terms, is not an incentive for small farmers, with low working capital and with competing family obligations. 'It is ironic that the peasant is accused of ignorance of which society is guilty.'[12] While expensive imported technology assisted the large and wealthy landowners, who benefited from the 'Green Revolution', in many LDCs the position of the smallholder deteriorated.[13] Impressive rises in output levels achieved in some countries[14] were often accompanied with displaced smallholders, rural unemployment and underemployment, and increasing poverty.[15]

Reliance on capital-intensive farming technology in labour-abundant economies is not only inconsistent with factor endowments, but it also generates income inequality by augmenting property incomes (which accrue to landowners and speculators) and reducing the income share of the rural masses. Supporting evidence of these trends from Pakistan,[16] Ethiopia and elsewhere suggest that the political and economic power of peripheral elites is the chief reason for the inequitable consequences of inappropriate farm techniques. Thus, the question|of the agricultural technology most suitable for LDCs is more a political problem than a technical or financial one. This is hardly surprising given the fact that farm technology represents a specific form of rural change, and, as such, is a potential threat to the entrenched provincial elites. In purely technical terms, the prerequisites of an intermediate farm technology can be spelled out quite readily.

Thus, agricultural technology must be aimed at producing inexpensive farm implements and equipment that can be widely used on small farms, operated by farmers with limited purchasing power. In the words of agricultural economists, farming technology must be 'unimodal', that is to say, 'aimed at the progressive modernization of the bulk of the nation's cultivators, as contrasted to a "bimodal" crash modernization effort concentrated upon a small subsector of large-scale mechanized farms'.[17] This is the important lesson emerging from the experience of Japan and Taiwan where a wide range of simple, inexpensive farm implements of good design have long been used extensively by the bulk of the farmers.[18] Home-made, inexpensive farm implements have several important advantages worthy of consideration. They reduce the foreign exchange requirements of an expanded food production; they create a rising demand in the agricultural sector for industrial products, thereby contributing to the domestic value-added content, and thus generating beneficial external economies for the non-agricultural sectors. Appropriate farm technology of this type can best be acquired through research and development activities located in the LDCs themselves. Reliance on transfer of technology from abroad, or even on expatriate personnel, is unlikely to lead to appropriate innovations. Experience acquired over several decades of technical assistance programmes, whether bilateral or multinational, is generally a dismal record of repeated failures to introduce inappropriate (imported) technology from temperate climates into tropical or other environments.[19] Unfortunately, mounting an effective agricultural research and development programme, adequately funded and staffed by qualified local personnel, is a major investment undertaking, requiring foresight and commitment on the part of the political leadership to the needs of agricultural development.

The Complex Issue of Land Reform

Many LDCs suffer from severe maldistribution of land, reflecting highly complex institutional arrangements governing ownership and utilisation of agricultural land. Consequently land reform occupies a central place in efforts to expand food production and stimulate rural development. As we shall see, however, land reform represents a truly herculean task requiring far-reaching transformation of traditional and deep-rooted relationships between men and land as well as the rights and obligations of several classes: landlords and tenants, peasants and serfs, middlemen and rent-collectors, chiefs and tribes, and so on.

These institutional complexities were largely ignored during the post-war planning exercises which were preoccupied with urban-centred industrialisation. Land reform resulted more from *coups/d'état* and populist revolutions than piecemeal planning, and passive involvement in this field by the United Nations had little impact.[20] Only in very recent years have economic planners become interested in the issue of land reform and, given its complexity, it is hardly surprising that there are wide differences of opinion on the subject.[21] What should be the aims of land reform: increased food grains and marketable surpluses for urban markets and/or exports? Redistribution of land to peasants and landless so they can feed themselves, or to large-scale capitalist farmers who would be capable of producing a surplus? When, in addition, questions relating to land taxation, tenancy and rent and land-use practices, and the nature of conflicts between various classes are considered, the range of difficulties emerge as a truly overwhelming challenge. Sometimes Utopian visions or revolutionary options *appear* to make it far easier to break with the burdens of history and start afresh than to tackle a non-violent programme of land reform. Despite differences of opinion on whether land reform is 'plannable', one central fact commands general consensus: land reform has now become an essential recipe for social justice in most LDCs, if only because the well-being of the bulk of rural communities depends on agriculture. Let us now examine the issues behind land reform.

Essentially, maldistribution of land refers to two interrelated problems: (1) the possession of a large amount of farmland by a few, and often absent, owners; and (2) the sharing of a small, fragmented farmland by a large number of peasants, usually on the basis of feudalistic and highly inequitable tenancy arrangements. In its narrow sense, land reform relating to high concentration of land ownership 'means the redistribution of property or rights in land for the benefit of small farmers and agricultural labourers'[22]; in the case of excessive fragmentation it refers to consolidation of uneconomic small farm units into more efficient farms. More generally, however, land reform may be understood to mean 'an integrated programme of measures designed to eliminate obstacles to economic and social development arising out of defects in the agrarian structure'.[23] This general definition of land reform emphasises the need for a whole range of policies dealing not only with redistribution of property rights in land, but also with other complementary measures, including improvements in tenancy conditions, farm credit, co-operative and marketing organisations, agricultural education and extension services. Because land ownership in many LDCs is a source of political and economic power, land reform is fundamentally a political question, involving deep-rooted social conflict, with many interrelated dimensions. Maldistribution of land can exist in several forms: (1) high concentration of ownership; (2) absentee ownership; (3) excessive fragmentation; and (4) inequitable tenancy arrangements.

High Concentration of Land Ownership

The agrarian structure often mirrors a rigid pyramid of rural hierarchy: at the bottom there is a large class of landless peasants subsisting in poverty; at the top is the provincial elite composed of the affluent class of big farmers and landowners; and in between there is a broad range of underemployed smallholders and tenants. In this age-old elitist, caste-like social organisation, land is the source of wealth and status. The problem of rural poverty and underdevelopment stems from the fact that the bulk of the rural mass is politically weak *because* the peasants are either landless or possess farms too tiny for even subsistence living. The case of India is by no means unique. The National Sample Survey of 1954-5 revealed that 61 per cent of households were landless or had holdings under 2½ acres; yet, collectively these households owned only a mere 6 per cent of the total land. At the other extreme, just 7 per cent of households owned 62 per cent of the total land.[24] As we shall see shortly, the roots of this tenure system go back a long way in Indian history. In Iran, prior to the land reform in the early 1960s, a mere 1 per cent of the rural population possessed about 60 per cent of total arable land, while less than 5 per cent of the nation owned 90 per cent of the land. In West Pakistan, land ownership in the mid-fifties was so feudalistic that one-tenth of 1 per cent of total owners accounted for 15 per cent of the land. In the Philippines in the early 1950s about 3 per cent of the landowners owned no less than 42 per cent of the land. In fact, in one region alone (Central Luzon), a total of 500 estates, ranging from 150 to 12,000 hectares, accounted for an aggregate area amounting to more than one-third of the total land in the region.[25]

In Latin America, unequal land distribution has long been a topic of bitter debate. On the one hand, there are the *latifundia* or excessively large estates owned by the descendants of Hispanic Conquistadors; and, on the other, there are the *minifundia* or tiny parcels of land, generally too small for economic viability. The statistical dimensions of the *latifundia-minifundia* pattern can be spelled out easily. In Uruguay in

1966, just 3,860 farm units ranging from 1,000 hectares and over accounted for less than 5 per cent of the total farm units in the country, but 58 per cent of the land. At the same time, there were 23,453 *minifundia* farms, ranging from 1 to 9 hectares in size, and these collectively accounted for about one-third of all farm units and for less than 1 per cent of total land. The case of Argentina is even more dramatic. In 1960, there was a total of 457,173 farm units in the country, of which 11,459 were in the *latifundia* category with sizes of more than 2,500 hectares: these accounted for about 60 per cent of the total farm land. In fact, if farm units of more than 1,000 hectares are included in the *latifundia* category, then 5.9 per cent of farm units accounted for three-quarters of the total farm area. At the other extreme, farm units of less than 5 hectares, representing 15.7 per cent of the total farm units, accounted for just 0.1 per cent of the land. This highly inequitable and inefficient land use is a major cause of the well known Latin American model of domestic dualism and the associated structural weakness of the economy. The *latifundia-minifundia* pattern repeats itself in Brazil, Bolivia (where agrarian structure caused the 1952 revolution), Colombia, Peru, Ecuador, Paraguay, Chile and the Central American republics.[26] In countries with a relatively high proportion of indigenous population − such as Ecuador, Guatemala and Peru − the *minifundia* pattern is even more widespread, sometimes in the form of *microfundia*, i.e. farms which are so tiny that they cannot produce adequate output to support one family at the minimum subsistence level.

An important concomitant of high concentration of land ownership is the problem of absentee landlordism. Many owners live in luxury far away from their holdings and estates. They delegate the supervision of land and rent-collecting functions to appointed middlemen − a system which is wide open to abuse and exploitation. The *Zamindari* system in British India is a classic example. Under the original system, instituted in 1793, the *Zamindaris* were revenue collectors for the colonial administration. They were allowed to retain 10 per cent of the monies they collected, as compensation for their services. In due course of time, the *Zamindars* emerged as a land-owning class itself, primarily as a result of usurious money-lending and land repossession. Subsequently, they delegated rent collection to agents, and did neither any agricultural work nor lived on their farms. The *Zamindaris* lived, in effect, as a parasitical social class of *rentiers*. The burden of the system in rural India was so heavy and ruinous to the country that 'for all practical purposes, land reform in independent India has meant the end of the

Zamindari system'.[27]

Fragmentation

Uneconomic, tiny farm units represent a sharp contrast to the
concentration of ownership of large estates. Fragmentation of land
stems from several causes, social, cultural, historical and religious. In
the Moslem countries of the Middle East, Asia and elsewhere, it is
primarily due to the provisions of the Islamic law of inheritance which
requires that the land holdings of the deceased be subdivided among
his descendants. In densely populated Asian and Latin American
countries, fragmentation can also be explained in terms of shortage of
cultivable land. For example, in the North-West Frontier Province of
Pakistan, the landlord holdings had a mean size of 13 hectares, which
is by no means a large unit. Yet, this holding was subdivided, on the
average, into 5.2 plots of 2.5 hectares each.[28] In Colombia, during
1954-60 there was an increase of 32 per cent in the number of farm
holdings, but a reduction of 25 per cent in the mean size. The number
of holdings under 1 hectare rose in this period from 18 per cent to
33.3 per cent of all farming units. In India, during 1954-60/1, the mean
size of holdings fell by 10 per cent while the number of holdings under
1 acre rose by 8.6 per cent. Similar statistical data can be cited from a
number of heavily populated countries in the Third World. They all
reveal the same pattern of inefficient land use, and they all underline
the importance of land and tenure reform. The difficulties and
complexities of these problems can hardly justify inaction.

Inequities of Tenancy Arrangements

'Tenancy in itself is socially admissible if the rentals are not exhorbitant
and if the tenant has a reasonable security and stability, especially if
the form of tenancy does not preclude final acquisition of land.'[29]
However, the history of tenancy arrangements in LDCs is a long and
bitter record of social injustice and exploitation of the politically weak
and economically insecure tenants and peasants by greedy landlords
and their zealous agents, often surpassing the worst evils of the medieval
lord-serf relations. In fact, until very recently, in Iraq, Persia and India,
landowners were able to impose customary levies and/or exact free
labour from peasants who, even though not serfs in law, were obliged
to make these payments in deference to the political and social power
of the landlords.[30] Indeed, similar practices, sometimes overtly, still
exist in certain places. In some Latin American countries the status of
farm labourers on large estates is virtually akin to serfdom because even

though legally not bound to land they work on, they are nevertheless wholly dependent for their source of livelihood on the pleasure of the landowner. Thus, until recently the *mestizos* of Bolivia held land in return for labour supplied to the landowner on the basis of informal tenancy arrangements. For this reason, they could be evicted at the landowner's will. In some Andean countries, the condition of indigenous peasants, called *yanaconas,* remains practically identical to that of feudal serfs on the manor since they are legally bound as chattel to the estates of large landowners.[31]

Agrarian Movements: Power-Houses for Egalitarian Planning

Serfdom and feudalism may not exist in the rural sectors of most LDCs, but mass poverty does, and the roots of rural poverty often extend back to feudal times. Post-war planning efforts turned a blind eye to the problem of rural poverty. In fact, as we have argued before, the pro-urban bias of industrialisation policies actually helped to worsen the plight of the bulk of the peasantry of the Third World. In many respects, the peasants in LDCs are truly the 'wretched of the earth',[32] surviving at the margin of subsistence as if they were condemned by fate to a life of toil and misery, and forced by the institutional system to submit to inequitable land tenure, oppressive landlords, usurious money-lenders and many other forms of injustice, not forgetting a physical environment often niggardly and hostile.

How can this virtually hopeless situation be turned around? How can the rural poverty trap be broken? Should the peasants be mobilised into revolutionary movements to dispossess the landlords and throw out the exploiters? This is, at first, an appealing option. But how feasible is it in reality? Given the political as well as the intellectual underdevelopment of the peasants (caused by centuries of neglect and exploitation by the landowning elites), the chances of a successful revolution *of* the peasants *by* the peasants and *for* the peasants are very slim indeed. The populist and peasant movements in Latin America provide ample evidence of this.[33] But what if intellectuals from urban centres, dedicated to peasant ideals, could be recruited to organise and lead the peasants? These intellectuals could start with the political education of the peasants. For example, they might follow Freire's methods of raising the level of consciousness among the Brazilian peasants by teaching them to forget about learning 'the cat sat on the mat' but to remember that 'the landlord sat on the peasant'.[34] This is the path to violence and rebellion and the peasants would have to receive not only political instruction, but also guns and training in revolutionary strategy. Even if the outside intellectuals were to remain true and incorruptible leaders of the peasants to the very end (by no means a safe bet), the end results are unlikely to justify the costs and sacrifices of the peasants made for the revolution. Suppose, for example, that the landlords and all the other rascals are thrown out, and the peasants take over the farmlands. Without seeds, fertilizers, farm equipment, marketing and warehousing facilities, and, above all, farm credit, how can the poor peasants achieve success?

A pragmatic way to eliminate rural poverty is through economic planning dedicated to egalitarian objectives and attuned to basic needs. Instead of mobilising peasants and rural communities into militant organisations to prepare them for a rebellion, they could be mobilised into power-houses for participation in the dynamic process of economic planning. Since rural communities constitute the majority in most LDCs, their potential political impact on planning and policy is a force not to be underestimated. Even in such centralised economies as Russia and China, the leadership at the centre has preferred to impose moderate levies of surplus extraction on peasants rather than run the risk of political unpopularity with excessive or extreme methods.[35] If peasant movements *for* egalitarian planning could be introduced in LDCs, the planning process would become increasingly responsive to the needs of rural communities. In this 'bottom-up' approach, problems and needs will be specified by the communities themselves in a dynamic process of bargaining and consultation with the planners, officials and technicians from the planning agency. To a large extent, therefore, overall designs or blue-prints regarding, for example, the aims to be served by land reform would be invalidated, unless they were drafted in response to specific needs of specific communities and with the active participation of these communities in all phases of the drafting.[36]

While it is true, as we have argued before, that post-war economic planning in LDCs was generally elitist, it is also evident that the rural communities and peasants contributed to this result by default: due to inertia, indifference and ignorance, they failed to demand and insist that economic plans should be responsive to their needs. The draining of rural surpluses for the enrichment of urban sectors and foreign markets could be arrested and reversed if rural communities could mobilise and exploit their potential political strength, and this could be done through non-violent means.

One dimension of the problem of rural poverty that must be kept in proper perspective is the fact that it is essentially a rural-urban conflict. The challenge therefore is: how to reverse the flow of resources in favour of rural areas? In Lipton's language, this is the problem of 'urban bias'.[37] But there is no implication in this strategy that a reversal of resource flow is a sufficient condition for eliminating all forms of rural poverty with equal urgency. In view of the tremendous magnitude of the problem, and, given the equally complex sets of needs of such diverse rural groups as the landless, share-croppers and smallholders, to name only a few, it is clear that serious issues of competing claims will still remain under a decentralised, egalitarian planning strategy. The crucial point, however, is that under this strategy the long-overdue attack on rural poverty would have been launched. Then it would be possible to consider the complex issue of land reform, for example, in the context of the regular planning process.[38]

But how can such a strategy of planning ever gain acceptance from those powerful urban elites and the provincial polities including the rich landlords and other vested interests who derive great benefits from the existing unequal *status quo?* Even in a fully 'closed economy', with no external trade and relations with the rest of the world, there are non-violent alternatives. For example, peasant organisations might be able to win some success in political bargaining with central and provincial elites. To the extent that the power bases of the elites in the capital and provincial centres have different or conflicting interests, the peasant organisations would be quite capable of striking beneficial bargains and deals. Given the reality that income distribution is something largely determined in the political arena, then the way to increase the income share of a specific target group, such as the rural poor, is to organise them for participation in that arena. Citizen's clubs, community halls, labour groups and other local organisations for community action are neither too costly to form, nor too visionary. There will, no doubt, be difficulties at first, but growing pains are always part of new institutional change.

There is a further prospect: in a world rapidly becoming globally integrated, thanks to modern means of communication and technology, no single country is entirely isolated in a 'closed economy'. Nor is the leadership in LDCs entirely insensitive to world opinion and pressures from such bodies as the United Nations as well as donor countries. Even Idi Amin is conscious of his international image. Therefore, appropriate external pressure, especially with compensating aid, could work as a critical catalyst in the pursuit of egalitarian and pro-rural objectives. In Chapter 12, we shall return to a discussion of the role of aid and technical assistance in egalitarian development. At the moment, we turn our attention to a possible method of developing rural areas in LDCs based on institution-building and economic planning.

Integrated Rural Development

The importance of institutional reform is critical to a new strategy of integrated rural development (IRD). This comprehensive 'systems' approach incorporates land reform, intermediate farm technology, human resource development, and a wide range of agrarian support services, packaged to emphasise the complementary nature of rural development projects.[39]

The implementation and financing of IRD would be feasible only if development priorities and financial resources are deliberately shifted from urban-centred to rural-based projects. For example, rather than concentrating educational and training facilities, public housing projects, industrial sites and physical infrastructure in and around urban centres, they would have to be dispersed regionally, partly according to resource endowments and partly on the basis of regional needs.

Defining the concept of IRD presents some difficulties that should be noted; indeed, it may carry alternative notions for macro- and micro-economists and other social scientists. We use the concept in the micro-economic sense, to emphasise the complementary or inter-dependent nature of the specific development projects which would be capable of generating economies of scale and output and external benefits. This is done, not because the macro approach, based on multi-sectoral interdependence, is technically inferior, but rather because, from an administrative and operational standpoint, implementation and financing can be expected to prove more manageable at the project level than at the sectoral level. For example, since ministries and departments in most countries are functionally organised (e.g. agriculture, education, health), it would be practically an impossible task to insist on a comprehensive education plan, a comprehensive agriculture plan, etc., all properly integrated within a macro perspective. On the other hand, it would be more feasible, in financial as well as administrative terms, to co-ordinate specific development projects planned for a given rural area or target population so that maximum efficiency and maximum impact are attained. The Ministry of Agriculture, for instance, could handle a land development scheme in region X, while the Ministry of Education builds a rural training centre there, and the Ministry of Labour arranges for the placement of trained workers on the land scheme. The Ministry of Finance or some other credit institution could provide settler credit to the new farmers, while the marketing and extension service agencies provide the relevant assistance. If some irrigation works or farm-to-market roads are required, then the Ministry of Public Works could be called upon to participate in the appropriate stage of the IRD. The planning agency would act as the co-ordinating agency.

The unique feature of IRD is its overall objective: the raising of the living standards of the rural communities who, as a rule, were neglected by post-war planners and policy-makers preoccupied with industrialisation. Much of the current problems facing LDCs now can be traced to this neglect. Conversely, eliminating poverty and underdevelopment implies that the welfare of the rural populations must be the focal point of future development policies and strategies.

As we have seen in Chapter 3, poverty is a multi-variate human condition, requiring simultaneous attack on several fronts — improved education, health, housing and nutrition, as well as higher incomes for the target population. Within the IRD approach three main subsets of specific prospects can be delineated.

Firstly, the IRD set should contain some income-generating projects (i.e. in conventional terminology 'productive' projects) which are also labour-intensive so that the rural poor may be able to raise their *per capita* income levels through gainful employment or economic activity. The specific mix of outputs and activities that could be undertaken would necessarily depend on soil, climate and economic conditions, but the importance of cash-cropping, vegetable growing, animal husbandry on small and medium-sized farms cannot be understated. Equating productive efficiency with large estates is a serious strategic miscalculation.[40]

It is important to note here that projects that are merely income-generating (without creating opportunity for greater labour utilisation) might be inappropriate, since income maximisation can be pursued through large-scale, capital-intensive methods, as the 'Green Revolution' experience demonstrates. It is also important to add that income generation through IRD approach might contain a significant non-cash component. For example, production for own consumption or payments in kind in rural communities may greatly assist in raising rural real incomes, despite the fact that they may not be recorded as transaction income realised from marketable outputs.

The second subset of IRD projects are those directed at human resource development and utilisation. They would include education and training programmes, as discussed in Chapter 10, health and sanitation schemes, and community and recreational activities appropriate to rural living conditions. These projects should be regarded as social investments in balanced regional development and in the future productivity of rural labour. Equally significantly, these human resource investments can be expected to enhance incentives for a rural way of life and contribute toward rational political participation by the rural communities. The post-war obsession with urban values, and the associated 'rising expectations' culture, can best be offset by reversing the flow of development resources so that an effective strategy of employment and income generation in rural areas could reduce the glaring rural-urban disparities.[41]

The third subset of IRD projects relate to major institutional and structural reforms, including land reform and decentralised political processes, which are by far the most challenging and difficult reforms to implement and maintain. Rural areas in LDCs, however stagnant they might be in the two-sector models of post-war economists, are actually very dynamic and diverse in a social and political sense, and the socio-economic structure is typically under the domination of provincial elites, made up of feudal barons, rich merchants and farmers, money-lenders and civil and military ruling classes. The rural masses, too, are by no means homogeneous, and cover a wide range of diversity in terms of income, access to land, status, and, therefore, needs. The resulting problems of conflicting interests and competing needs cannot be resolved by economists alone. There are important roles for the political scientist, anthropologist and other specialists of the development process. But to create the maximum impact, these specialists have to be fully co-ordinated and 'teamed up' within a common planning framework designed for a common overall objective: to eliminate mass poverty and inequality in rural areas. The economist could study the responsiveness of farmers to market incentives, costs of inputs, taxes and rents, and he may evaluate the effectiveness of farm credit and marketing facilities, etc., but determining feasible political reforms in given situations to promote wider popular participation in the dynamic process of planned development is a matter to be left to the political scientist. And, as we have argued above, this is also an area in which domestic elites are quite sensitive to external pressure, which, when properly applied, may contribute to highly beneficial results.

Consequences of IRD and Land Reform

Finally, what can be said about the possible results of the pro-rural strategy, IRD projects and land reform? Are these suggested remedies likely to create stable egalitarian conditions in rural areas? For example, giving titles to landless peasants may be an essential first step in promoting social justice in rural areas, but what about future prospects? There are numerous cases of legislated land redistribution schemes in LDCs in which land was transferred from big landlords to landless peasants, but subsequently it was repossessed by the original owners and the peasants reverted to their status of hired hands.[42] While these negative consequences often result from loopholes in the reform legislation, expressly placed for safeguarding the interests of the elites, they also result from lack of complementary reforms to provide farm credits, seeds, implements and marketing assistance to the new farmers. It is in these kinds of situations that a 'systems approach' along the lines of the IRD strategy manifests its relative advantage over past methods of modernising agriculture. The experience of Green Revolution in Pakistan, discussed in Chapter 7, clearly demonstrates that a capitalist approach to food production is elitist because the benefits are likely to be concentrated in the hands of the big landowners, merchants and speculators, in a process which also creates more landless peasants and mass poverty. These results are also confirmed by the experience of large-scale settlement and land development schemes in Ethiopia, Pakistan, Sudan and other LDCs.[43]

Therefore, if the IRD strategy is to introduce *and* maintain egalitarian development in rural communities, it would be necessary to ensure that the requirement for ceilings as well as floors on incomes (as discussed in Chapter 8) be effectively incorporated as part of the strategy. Without this requirement, any pattern of growth is likely to generate future income and wealth concentration. However, this danger can be avoided if the procedure stated in Chapter 9 is followed and a mean farm size determined for a given area.[44] While this may conflict with the objective of maximum output due to economies of scale, there would be compensating gains in employment, social cohesion and economic equity.

Notes

1. W.A. Lewis, 'Economic Development with Unlimited Supplies of Labour', *The Manchester School,* Vol.22 (May 1954), reprinted in A.N. Agarwala and S.P. Singh (eds.), *The Economics of Underdevelopment* (Oxford University Press, London, 1958); J.C.H. Fei and G. Ranis, *Development of the Labor Surplus Economy* (Richard D. Irwin, Homewood, Ill., 1964).

2. P. Streeten quoted by G. Hunter in 'Strategies for Agricultural Development in the 1970's: A Summary and Critique', *Stanford University Food Institute Research Studies in Agricultural Economics, Trade, and Development,* Vol.XII, No.1 (1973), p.60.

3. I. Little, T. Scitovsky and M. Scott, *Industry and Trade in Some Development Countries: A Comparative Study* (Oxford University Press, London, 1970), especially Chs. 4-5.

4. T.W. Schultz, 'Value of U.S. Farm Surpluses to Underdeveloped Countries', *Journal of Farm Economics,* Vol.42 (1960); L. Dudley and R.J. Sandilands, 'The Side Effects of Foreign Aid: The Case of Public Law 480 Wheat in Colombia', *Economic Development and Cultural Change,* Vol.23, No.2 (January 1975).

5. W. Peterson, 'An "Optimist's" Pessimistic View of the Food Situation', *Social Science Quarterly,* Vol.57, No.2 (September 1976).

6. Streeten in Hunter, 'Strategies for Agricultural Development', p.61.

7. B.F. Johnston *et al.,* 'Criteria for the Design of Agricultural Development Strategies', *Food Research Institute Studies,* Vol.XI, No.1 (1972).

8. Of course, the world food situation and prospects are characterised by a full range of views from complete Malthusianism to the alternative extreme position of long-run optimism. Paul R. and Anne Erlich argue that 'There unquestionably is enough food produced to feed today's four billion adequately if it were more equally distributed. Whether enough can be produced to support the six to seven billion expected to live on Earth in the year 2,000 or a minimum ultimate population of eight to ten billion, regardless of distribution is another question.' *Social Science Quarterly,* Vol.57, No.2 (September 1976), p.380.

9. Johnston *et al.,* 'Criteria for the Design of Agricultural Development Strategies', p.55.

10. R. Krishna, 'Agricultural Price Policy and Economic Development' in J.N. Southworth and B.F. Johnston (eds.), *Agricultural Development and Economic Growth* (Cornell University Press, Ithaca, New York, 1967).

11. C.R. Wharton, Jr. (ed.), *Subsistence Agriculture and Economic Development* (Aldine, Chicago, 1969), especially the article by G. Castillo,   : 'Comment: A Critical View of a Subculture of Peasantry'.

12. J. Mellor, 'Toward a Theory of Agricultural Development' in Southworth and Johnston, *Agricultural Development and Economic Growth,* p.50.

13. H. Kaneda, 'Economic Implications of the "Green Revolution" and the Strategy of Agricultural Development in West Pakistan', *Pakistan Development Review* (Summer 1969); E.H. Jacoby, 'Effects of the "Green Revolution" in South and South-East Asia', *Modern Asian Studies,* Vol.6, No.1 (1972).

14. For data on wheat and rice production during 1953-70, see Eric M. Ojala, 'Impact of the New Production Possibilities on the Structure of International Trade in Agricultural Products', *Food Research Institute Studies,* Vol.XI, No.2 (1972), Table I. During 1970-4, *per capita* food production in LDCs fell steadily, due to crop failures caused by drought conditions, the most dramatic famine conditions being in the Sahelian countries. Fears of emerging food shortages and famine in many LDCs, including the Indian sub-continent, were prominent motivations leading to the 1974 World Food Conference sponsored by FAO in Rome. See FAO, *Assessment of the World Food Situation* (Rome, 1974).

15. W. Ladejinsky, 'The Green Revolution in Punjab, A Field Trip', *Economic and Political Weekly,* Bombay, Vol.IV, No.26 (June 1969); C.R. Wharton, 'The Green Revolution: Cornucopia or Pandora's Box?', *Foreign Affairs* (April 1969).

16. The case of Pakistan was discussed in Chapter 7.

17. P. Kilby and B.F. Johnston, 'The Choice of Agricultural Strategy and the Development of Manufacturing', *Food Research Institute Studies,* Vol.XI, No.2 (1972), p.156.

18. Kilby and Johnston, 'The Choice of Agricultural Strategy'; B.F. Johnston, 'Agricultural and Structural Transformation in Developing Countries: A Survey of Research', *Journal of Economic Literature,* Vol.VIII, No.2 (June 1970), p.395 for additional references.

19. A.H. Moseman, *Building Agricultural Research Systems in Developing Nations* (Agricultural Development Council, New York, 1970).

20. United Nations, *Progress in Land Reform* (various reports) (New York).

21. G.Hunter, 'Strategies for Agricultural Development'; D. Lehmann (ed.), *Agrarian Reform and Agrarian Reformism* (Faber and Faber, London, 1974), especially the articles by C. Bell, T.J. Byres and M. Lipton.

22. Doreen Warriner, *Land Reform in Principle and Practice* (Clarendon Press, Oxford, 1969), p.xiv.

23. UN, *Progress in Land Reform,* Third Report (New York, 1962), p.vi.

24. Warriner, *Land Reform,* p.142.

25. The statistics in this paragraph, excepting India, are from Hung Chao Tai, *Land Reform and Politics: A Comparative Analysis* (University of California Press, Berkeley, 1974), pp.24-5.

26. R. Farley, *The Economics of Latin America* (Harper and Row, New York, 1972), pp.176-7.

27. Warriner, *Land Reform,* p.156.

28. Hung Chao Tai, *Land Reform and Politics,* pp.29-30.

29. W. Froehlich, quoted in ibid., p.30.

30. Warriner, *Land Reform,* p.27 *et seq.*

31. F. Chevalier, 'Problèmes agraires des Amériques latines de tradition indigène' in CNRS, *Les problémes agraires des Amériques latines* (Paris, 1967), p.29; and Warriner, *Land Reform,* pp.6-9. Also see Farley, *The Economics of Latin America,* pp.174-5.

32. F. Fanon, *The Wretched of the Earth* (MacGibbon and Kee, London, 1965).

33. Henry A. Landsberger (ed.), *Latin American Peasant Movements* (Cornell University Press, Ithaca, New York, 1969). A radical approach to the subject is G. Huizer, *Peasant Rebellion in Latin America* (Penguin, Harmondsworth, 1973).

34. Quoted in M. Lipton, *Why Poor People Stay Poor* (Temple Smith, London, 1977), p.332.

35. Lehmann, *Agrarian Reform and Agrarian Reformism,* p.20, and the paper by Geoffrey Shillinghaw in the same volume.

36. This decentralised planning approach is discussed in greater detail in Chapter 8.

37. Lipton, *Why Poor People Stay Poor.*

38. Thus, B. Higgins argues that economic planning is 'more like "social medicine" than "social engineering" in that it should concentrate on particular maladies in specific cases, rather than on a general theory of development': 'Economics and Ethics in the New Approach to Development', *University of Ottawa Research Paper,* No.7801 (1978), pp.30-1.

39. See the special issue of *CERES, FAO Review on Development,* No.51 (May-June 1976), devoted to institutional reform in rural sectors in LDCs, with a number of country case studies. Montague Yudelman, 'Integrated Rural Development Projects: The Bank's Experience', *Finance and Development,* Vol.14, No.1 (March 1977). For other related studies, see Philip H. Coombs with Manzoor Ahmed, *Attacking Rural Poverty* (A World Bank Publication) (Johns Hopkins University Press, Baltimore and London, 1974); G.H. Axinn and S. Thorat, *Modernizing World Agriculture, A Comparative Study of Agricultural Extension Education Systems* (Praeger, New York, 1972); A.T. Mosher, *Creating a Progressive Rural Structure* (Agricultural Development Council, New York, 1969); D.G. Green, 'Non-Formal Education for Agricultural Development: A System Perspective' in P. Foster and J.R. Sheffield (eds.), *Education and Rural Development,* The World Yearbook of Education 1974 (Evans Brothers Ltd, London, 1973).

40. This is demonstrated by the experience of Japan and Taiwan.

41. It is relevant to point out that in some plantation-economies, estate workers in large numbers move back into the 'traditional' sector during the harvesting and planting seasons (causing seasonal labour shortage on the estates) in response to peak-season employment opportunities and 'pull' incentives. In fact, similar patterns of labour migration *away* from urban centres into rural sectors may be observed in some countries, including West Africa. All this suggests that the attachment to land and rural areas in many LDCs is by no means a dying phenomenon.

42. In the Indian State of Maharashtra, for example, it is reported that 1.7 million acres were repossessed by the original owners, displacing 101,000 tenants out of a total 150,000 given land under reform legislation; many landless peasants were then rehired as farm labourers. G. Hunter, *Modernizing Peasant Societies, A Comparative Study in Asia and Africa* (Oxford University Press, New York, 1969), p.151.

43. John M. Cohen, 'Rural Change in Ethiopia: The Chilalo Agricultural Unit', *Economic Development and Cultural Change,* Vol.22, No.2 (July 1974); K. Griffin, *The Political Economy of Agrarian Change: An Essay on the Green Revolution* (Macmillan, London, 1974).

44. See p.212.

12 GLOBAL EQUITY: REFORMING THE INTERNATIONAL TRADE AND AID SYSTEM

Egalitarian planning and development in LDCs have crucial international dimensions, least of all because the post-war stimulus for planned industrialisation in LDCs originated largely in Western countries, which must therefore bear considerable moral responsibility for the imbalances and inequalities which this strategy has created.[1] More fundamentally, however, the trade and aid relationships between the rich and poor countries have long been conspicuous by the absence of a common concern for social justice for the masses in the Third World — the poorly paid estate workers, the jobless and marginal workers in urban slums, the landless peasants and underemployed rural communities. These relations, dominated by small groups of powerful elites in LDCs, and foreign interests, typically as unequal parties, have created an inequitable system of global economic order which concentrates income in favour of the rich. It is therefore evident that prospects for egalitarian development within LDCs rest significantly on appropriate reform in the international economy.

This chapter investigates briefly four interrelated issues. We begin by looking at the global maldistribution of income among nations and observe that, if the existing world economic order is not changed drastically, the year 2000 will witness a widening international inequality between the rich and poor nations. Then we examine the pattern of international trade to identify some of the basic inequities structured into the present system which bias it in favour of the rich countries. This may suggest that in future LDCs perhaps should become more self-reliant and less dependent on foreign trade to achieve growth; but the north-south dialogue currently under way as part of the new international economic order offers a unique opportunity for reform of the system for greater global equity. Finally, we examine the effectiveness of the foreign aid system, with special reference to UN technical assistance operations as instruments of egalitarian development.

The Widening Global Gap

There was a feeble trend during 1950-62 towards equalisation of global income distribution when the overall GNP growth rates in LDCs (viz. 4.2 per cent p.a.) exceeded that of the developed countries (viz. 3.8

per cent p.a.).[2] The equalising trend, which represented a significant reversal in the economic history of the world at least since the start of the Industrial Revolution, was brought about partly by the post-war enthusiasm in LDCs — many in the process of achieving independence — to take advantage of new technological and economic opportunities for growth, and partly because of the generosity of rich countries to provide aid and technical assistance to LDCs in a concerted effort at launching a global attack on economic backwardness, disease and hunger.

While the global GNP growth rates in the fifties inched towards equalisation, *per capita* incomes in the rich and poor nations actually widened owing to the unprecedented population explosion in the latter. With a population growth rate of 2.5 per cent, the LDC's GNP growth of 4 per cent actually meant that income *per capita* increased by only 1.5 per cent, while in the rich countries, where the population growth was only 1.5 per cent, income *per capita* rose at close to 2.5 per cent.

More disturbingly, after 1962 global income growth trends took a turn for the worse. The UN Development Decade I failed to achieve its 5 per cent annual growth of GNP in LDCs, and it also failed to stimulate increased aid inflows to these countries. During 1963-8, the GNP of all LDCs rose by 4.5 per cent[3] compared with 5 per cent for developed countries, and the already huge gap in *per capita* incomes began to widen. Some of the reasons for this were the increasing disenchantment, both in donor and recipient countries, with the consequences of foreign aid, the realisation that the real benefits of aid were significantly reduced by tied aid, rising burdens of external debts, and conflicting priorities in aid allocation between donors and LDCs.[4] At the same time there was growing recognition that there are no 'instant developments' and no short-cuts available for LDCs, as some observers appeared to believe in the immediate post-war years.

Prospects to the Year 2000

More fundamentally, there are major structural inequities in the existing pattern of international trade and economic relations between the rich and poor nations, and persistent poverty and underdevelopment in the latter are intricately connected with these built-in inequities of the world order. Consider the following global scenario to the year 2000.

In 1965, 70 per cent of the world's estimated 3.3 billion population lived in LDCs, but they accounted for a mere 15 per cent of the global GNP, measured in US dollars. According to the 'moderate' projections of Kahn and Weiner,[5] |the LDCs' population share in the year 2000 will increase to 78 per cent and their GNP share to 18 per cent. Income *per capita* in the rich and poor nations will worsen relatively from the 1965 ratio of 1:13 to 1:14 in the year 2000. Looking at specific countries, the gap in average *per capita* income of India is expected to reach $270 compared with USA's $9,650 (in 1965 US dollars) – i.e. a mere 1/36th. An absolute income level per person of $270, in 1965 purchasing power terms, would represent a significant economic progress for India, indicating that she would break out of the internationally accepted poverty line of $200 *per capita.* However, since these figures refer to *national* averages, they would be perfectly consistent with large *domestic* income inequalities between economic elites and the masses. Thus, unless egalitarian redistributive measures are effectively introduced by the end of the century, India may still be characterised by enormous socio-economic inequities in the year 2000, as she is now.

Domestic egalitarian reforms are urgently and vitally required in LDCs. However, such reforms would not be adequate to offset the great inequalities in the global distribution of wealth and income. According to Kahn and Weiner's projections, even in China, perhaps the extreme model of egalitarianism, *per capita* income in the year 2000 is expected to increase to $320, or just 1/30th of the USA average, assuming that the existing world order is maintained. This clearly implies that the international economic system and the underlying global income distributive mechanism are generating economic inequalities and disparities between the nations and inhabitants of the world. Income concentration in the rich countries is matched by rising poverty in the poor nations, this, of course, being fully consistent with growing income disparities in the latter.

Widening international inequality in income distribution is hardly conducive to world stability and peaceful relations, any more than widening internal disparities between privileged elites and the masses is tolerable. It is quite unthinkable that, in an age of 'global village', there can be economic security and stable political order in a world in which a few privileged nations can exist as an 'island of wealth surrounded by "misery"'.[6] Nor is it feasible to expect that the rich countries can continue to enjoy conditions of full or near-full employment of labour, while the poor nations are bedevilled by mounting unemployment, marginalism and mass poverty.

Redistributing Global Income: Trade or Autarkic Development?

Ultimately, there are two alternative methods of redressing unequal global income distribution: (1) through a reformed system of trade and monetary arrangements between the rich and poor countries, as for example along the lines of the ongoing dialogue over the new international economic order (NIEO) proposals, to be discussed below; (2) through increased income creation in LDCs themselves, based on greater self-reliance and reduced dependency on external trade and technology. In the long run this strategy would ensure that the wealth and resources are increasingly kept within the LDCs themselves, as a result of deliberate autarkic development strategy.

Of course, these two alternatives are by no means entirely exclusive. Nevertheless, the second approach would imply a major reorientation in LDC planning, quite possibly leading to world-wide economic chaos.

Inequities of the 'Old International Economic Order'

In order to understand the current NIEO debate, it is first necessary to dwell briefly on the workings of the 'old', colonial system of trade ⸴ between primary producing countries and the industrial economies. The brief historical sketch of Malaysia, presented in Chapter 5, is highly relevant in this context. The main conclusion there was that the Malayan economic model was designed, first and foremost, in order to create a dual economy based on cheap labour policy and free trade in primary products, and to transfer the surpluses realised from the ordinary budget and trade account to England.

The gap between classical theory and policy practice has seldom been greater than in the field of international trade. The early trade models relegated LDCs to the status of primary producers in line with the classical doctrine of comparative advantage. The fact that free trade existed only in primary products, while the import trade in manufactured goods was subject to various import duties and indirect taxes, was hardly noticed. Likewise, virtually no attention was paid to administrative restrictions imposed by colonial authorities, in such places as Indonesia and India, prohibiting domestic import-substituting industries in order to protect the national economic interests in the colonial country. Persistent underdevelopment and poverty in LDCs were generally explained in terms of Euro-centred theories, such as the backward-sloping supply curve hypothesis. Even the more recent debate over the instability of export earnings tended to divert attention from the more fundamental causes of the problem.[7] The mainstream literature of development economics generally ignored modern forms of mercantilism and the possibility that the poverty of primary producers might be causally linked to large net outflows of resources to industrialised countries. Despite extensive evidence of adverse secular movement in the barter terms of trade for primary producers, the dominant view was that trade acted as an engine of growth.

The structure of trade with LDCs in the post-war period retained its colonial origins. The International Monetary Fund (IMF) and the General Agreement on Tariffs and Trade (GATT) were conceived as institutions primarily for rich countries.[8] Industrialisation and development planning in LDCs were preoccupied with domestic efforts to maximise GNP growth rates: there was relatively little attention given to structural reform in the international economic order until 1964, when the United Nations Conference on Trade and Development (UNCTAD) was created.[9] Initially, the 'most favoured nation' tariff reductions introduced under the Kennedy Round of multilateral trade negotiations were limited to trade between industrialised countries. During the period from UNCTAD I in 1964 to UNCTAD III in 1972, tariff and non-tariff barriers in developed countries constituted a variety of obstacles to the expansion and diversification of exports from LDCs.[10] Repeated attempts by the group of 77 countries to obtain trade concessions from the group B countries resulted in failure and confrontation.[11]

The idea that the exports of LDCs should be accorded preferential tariff treatment did not gain any acceptance among the developed nations until the late 1960s. While articles 36-38 of the 1965 GATT chapter set forth a number of trade and development policy objectives aimed at a larger share of world trade for LDCs through non-reciprocal trade liberalisation, the results of the Kennedy Round negotiations in 1967 were disappointing for the LDCs. During 1967-70 negotiations between the rich and poor countries, at the UN General Assembly and such organisations as the OECD, attention was focused on the creation of a generalised scheme of preferences (GSP).[12] In October 1970, agreement was reached among members of UNCTAD and the UN General Assembly for certain GSP proposals providing for legislated preferences by willing donors. Limited concessions were granted by the EEC, Japan and Norway in late 1971, and on 1 January 1972, the United Kingdom, Ireland, Sweden, Denmark, Finland and New Zealand introduced their own version of GSP. Canada joined the scheme in July 1974. The largest industrial country, the USA, did not act until the Trade Act of 1974 (which did not take effect until late 1975), largely owing to resistance by protectionist forces and growing US trade and balance of payments problems.[13]

Preferential tariffs to LDCs, giving them advantageous access to the rich markets in developed countries, represent a limited but positive step in the right direction. To date, however, the actual tariff concessions granted have generated little visible benefit to LDCs. This is due to several reasons. In the first place, only about 39 per cent of the total trade flow from LDCs to rich countries is subject to tariff treatment, and the bulk of the trade, consisting of primary products and raw materials, enters on a duty-free basis. Processed agricultural and fishery products, potentially expanding categories of LDC exports, are excluded from GSP arrangements, as are selected manufactured and semi-manufactured products such as textiles and footwear. In addition, there have been a number of administrative regulations — such as 'certificate of origin' — tending to frustrate the objective of GSP arrangements.[14] Even more importantly, there are many non-tariff obstacles, ranging from tight health and safety regulations, packing and labelling specifications, to quota ceilings and other quantitative restrictions,[15] acting as trade barriers.

At any rate, the gradual progress towards trade liberalisation, based on multilateral trade negotiations, was finally overtaken and overshadowed by the oil and energy crisis beginning in 1973, and leading to the dramatic call by LDCs for the establishment of a New International Economic Order (NIEO) to rectify the inequities of the old order. The issue of trade liberalisation, based on preferential access of LDC exports to the markets of rich countries, remains a subject of intense and prolonged discussions, as are numerous other issues which have emerged as part of the NIEO debate. The problems of inflation and rising unemployment in many industrialised countries, creating new pressures for protectionist policies, limit the prospects of trade liberalisation, at least in the short run, and make the chances of any dramatic gains by LDCs highly unlikely.

What is NIEO?

The principal premise underlying NIEO is that sustained domestic development in the Third World cannot be achieved until the existing mercantilist system of international trade is restructured drastically to promote equitable global distribution of incomes and resources. NIEO is the product of the Sixth Special Session of the General Assembly of the UN which itself was an outgrowth of the Algiers Conference of 1973. The Declaration and Programme of Action on the Establishment of a New International Economic Order, proclaimed in the UN General Assembly Resolutions Nos. 3201 and 3202, were subsequently amplified through a number of companion documents and declarations, such as the Charter of Economic Rights No.3362 adopted during the Seventh Special Session of the General Assembly.

The NIEO declarations cover a great number of issues, including commodity stabilisation schemes, indexation of the prices of primary products, compensatory financing to offset the oil deficits of poor countries, and trade liberalisation advantageous to LDCs. Initially conducted within a general atmosphere of political confrontation between the rich and poor countries, most visibly exemplified in the UN General Assembly debates, the NIEO claims appeared to have been bogged down in an impasse, in part due to the dramatic success of the OPEC cartel and the 1973-5 general commodity boom, both of which tended to create a mood of new-found power for the primary producing countries.[16] In more constructive terms, however, three major areas of structural reform can be identified within the NIEO context (apart from the problem of trade liberalisation already discussed above): (1) stabilising commodity trade and export earnings of primary producers; (2) international monetary reform and the matter of linking it to the development financing needs of LDCs; and (3) the activities and power of multinational corporations.

Although the Third World commodity trade represents only about 20 per cent of total world trade in commodities, export earnings of several LDCs — needed to pay for their essential imports of capital goods and in recent years oil — are heavily dependent on a handful of commodities. Thus, in 1973 exports of primary products accounted for about two-thirds of the total export earnings of LDCs; in many individual cases, this proportion is much higher.[17] The cyclical decline of the LDCs' share of world trade, the oligopolistic powers of the multinational corporations over the global marketing and distribution system, the development of substitutes for many primary products, as well as the unpredictable effects of weather on supply — all of these factors tend to reduce the power of primary producers (with the important exception of OPEC countries) over the pricing and marketing of their commodities. With little control by LDCs over international terms of trade it is hardly surprising that the relative prices of primary products have long been declining.[18] The additional problem of the instability of export earnings also generates economic insecurity within LDCs and a 'boom-bust' pattern of growth, as we have seen in the case of Brazil in Chapter 7.

Methods of stabilising international commodity trade and the export earnings of LDCs have long occupied the attention of international organisations, principally at UNCTAD. There has been much lip-service paid to the cause of commodity stabilisation but little effective results have been forthcoming. Generally, the rich countries have shown a preference for a commodity-by-commodity approach rather than the integrated, comprehensive approach favoured by UNCTAD. The corner-stone of the integrated approach is the creation of a sufficiently large buffer stock of a number of commodities, including wheat, sugar, rice, coffee, cocoa beans, tea, cotton, jute, wool, rubber, copper, lead, zinc, tin, bauxite and iron ore. However, the creation of such a vast international marketing scheme can only become feasible if the exporting and importing countries agree to finance and operate it effectively, with the support of international organisations.

A second area of institutional restructuring proposed as part of NIEO is the creation of a new link between current efforts of global monetary reform for additional liquidity and the practically unlimited needs of LDCs for development financing over and above their already heavy external debt burdens, made worse in recent years by world inflation and oil deficits. The link proposal aims at shooting two birds with one stone: update the old Bretton Woods system of international monetary order, designed when most of the LDCs did not even exist, and at the same time enlarge the flow of development assistance to the Third World. The principal monetary instrument for this is the IMF's Special Drawing Rights (SDRs) or 'paper gold', created originally in 1969. Since then SDRs have been a useful method of creating international liquidity, utilised both by developed and developing countries, and only 9 Fund members out of a total of 126 have declined to participate in the scheme.[19] There appears to be considerable agreement, for example in the discussions of such bodies as the Committee of Twenty of the IMF, that the SDRs should become the principal reserve asset, but the SDR/aid link remains a debating point.

Probably the most emotionally charged NIEO issue concerns the activities of multinational corporations (MNCs). With their parent headquarters in the USA and other rich Western countries, the MNCs pursue global profit maximisation, through pricing and marketing policies and production techniques, which often clash with the development policies of host LDCs.[20] For example, the MNCs may transfer modern, capital-intensive techniques to their branch plants in LDCs which minimise job creation; because of their extra-territorial nature, they may contravene foreign policy objectives of host countries; by the device of intra-corporate transfer pricing, they may understate actual profit margins and evade royalty and tax obligations; and through their oligopolistic market power they may exercise undue influence over the pricing, marketing and distribution of goods and services, and refuse to disclose corporate information about their activities. Coming in the wake of world-wide business scandals, the issue of MNCs often leads to charges of neo-imperialism and new forms of mercantilism, all designed to exploit the resources of LDCs and harm their efforts of achieving sustained domestic development. While these charges may sometimes be exaggerated, there can be little doubt about the inequities of the present system of international trade. This can best be described in specific micro-studies, and we may utilise the case of the world banana trade as an example.

The Banana Trade: A Commodity in Dispute

Bananas, grown exclusively in tropical countries, are an important part of the diet of these countries. It is not one of world's major export commodities: in the early 1970s, some 6 million tons were exported by producing countries, chiefly to the USA, EEC markets and Japan, this volume representing just 0.2 per cent of total world trade or 2.5 per cent of trade in agricultural products. Nevertheless, the export trade in bananas is an extremely important source of earnings for certain LDCs, principally some Latin American and Caribbean countries, such as Ecuador, Costa Rica, Honduras and Panama, together with the Philippines in Asia, and the Ivory Coast, Somalia and Cameroon in Africa.[21]

In the post-war period, the banana trade underwent substantial growth and change. Although the volume of exports expanded at an annual average rate of 5 per cent during 1950-73, prices declined by about 30 per cent. Coupled with steadily rising prices of manufactured goods, the terms of trade of bananas worsened by about 60 per cent over this period. Thus, whereas in 1960 a tractor cost the equivalent value of 3 tons of bananas, in 1970 no less than 11 tons of bananas were required to pay for the same tractor.[22]

As with many other primary products, the world banana trade is highly oligopolistic, and is dominated by three US transnational firms: United Fruit Company (with 35 per cent of world exports), Standard Fruit (25 per cent) and Del Monte (10 per cent). The organisation and operations of these firms represent the textbook model of vertical and horizontal integration, extending from the control of fruit-growing in the producing countries through transportation and shipping, insurance, storage, ripening, to wholesale and retail distribution in the consuming countries. Thus in Ecuador, the world's largest banana producer, 97 per cent of total exports are in the hands of two foreign firms. At the other end, the United Fruit's market share in consuming countries in 1973 ranged from a high 81 per cent in Switzerland to 12 per cent in Japan, and Standard Fruit's share was only 6 per cent in Switzerland, but 42 per cent in the USA, 31 per cent in Italy and 30 per cent in Canada. In fact, 100 per cent of the Canadian banana retail distribution was controlled by the three firms: United, Standard and Del Monte.[23]

Such an extensive control over supply, distribution and consumer markets creates ideal conditions for large monopoly mark-ups and profit margins. A recent study at UNCTAD into the banana dollar, and its allocation between growing countries and foreign interests, is highly revealing.[24] The study, based on selected trade flows making up about 40 per cent of the total value of world banana exports in 1971, found that 'the gains of the domestic growers are about 11.5 percent, those of the foreign enterprises are of the order of 88.5 per cent.'[25] Since in 1971 the estimated retail banana sales were valued at $2,114 million, only about $245 million can be regarded as the revenue share of domestic producers compared with $1,859 million accruing to foreign enterprises.

These findings are highly significant for a number of reasons. First, they indicate the inequities of the existing international marketing and industrial organisation dominated by MNCs. As a result of their oligopolistic power, these firms realise huge returns compared with the producing countries, which are cut off from lucrative marketing and distributive operations. Second, it appears that the major issue of world trade is not really greater access by LDCs to the markets of rich countries as a result of trade liberalisation *per se,* but rather structural reforms in international marketing and industrial organisation to permit *greater revenue-sharing* by the producing countries. For, under existing oligopolistic conditions, expanding banana exports, due to liberalised trade, would merely guarantee that the income disparity between the growing countries and foreign firms would actually become larger in absolute terms.

An even more fundamental issue raised by the inequitable banana revenue-sharing pattern is that it is by no means an isolated case, but on the contrary, quite typical of most commodity trade flows. Although micro-data is hard to obtain, in a large measure due to the strict secrecy rules observed by many MNCs, evidence now being gathered by UNCTAD, ECOSOC and other UN agencies, as part of the research activities of the NIEO, indicate that similar patterns exist in the trade in bauxite and other primary products.[26] Against the background of

OPEC's success as a producers' cartel, and with the assistance of the UN, several exporting countries have recently begun to create producers' associations in order to develop collective action and counterbalance the oligopolistic control of MNCs. In some cases, producers have imposed legislated royalties and levies on the revenues of these firms, some even resorting to outright nationalisation.[27] While these actions may be expected to generate more confrontation in the international trade arena, they also demonstrate the urgency for structural reforms in the existing order.

One of the central objectives of reform in the international trade and monetary system must be the promotion of egalitarian development within LDCs to parallel a more equitable global economic order. There is hardly any justification for increasing and stabilising income flows to LDCs if these flows result in even greater income concentration in the hands of the affluent and privileged groups with more poverty amongst the masses. Domestic reform, especially wider participation in the decision-making process and planning priorities more in accord with social justice principles, must be made an integral part of the NIEO negotiations between the rich and the poor countries.[28] As important participants in the NIEO debate, the UN and some of its affiliated agencies can play a vital role toward this objective. But the UN itself is very much in need of some major reforms, especially as a vehicle of multilateral aid to LDCs (see below).

A UN Levy on Multinationals

An effective, and relatively simple, method of improving the image of MNCs in the Third World would be to empower the United Nations to impose a moderate Development Levy on the volume of exports from LDCs to industrialised countries handled by the MNCs. In 1975, the total LDC exports to industrialised countries amounted to about US $150 billion, most of it no doubt handled by the MNCs.[29] In the same year, total official development assistance (ODA) transferred through the multilateral agencies was about US $4 billion.[30] Thus, a UN Development Levy of about 5 per cent would be capable of doubling the ODA flows channelled through the UN aid system.

The advantages of the proposed UN levy on MNCs are obvious. It would provide the UN system with a much-needed financial boost, enabling it to finance egalitarian development projects directly beneficial to target groups (see the next section); it would allow the MNCs to contribute to Third World development; and the nominal levy rate would hardly make any difference to profits or dividends.

The goodwill which such a scheme would generate for the MNCs would justify it as an investment in world development rather than just another form of tax. The levy scheme need not turn the UN into a tool of global corporatism since MNCs are not UN members. In the long run, the scheme might even lead to financial independence for the UN, freeing it from dependence on member-country contributions.

But the UN aid system first has to be streamlined and reorganised in such a way that it can truly function as a vehicle of egalitarian development. This is no simple task, as we shall see presently.

The International Aid System: Who is Helping Whom?

During the two decades preceding NIEO, bilateral aid from rich countries was provided to LDCs largely as a substitute for trade[31]; and multilateral aid, channelled through the UN system and other international agencies, evolved to avoid foreign policy conflicts between the donor and recipient countries.[32]   Both bilateral and multilateral aid programmes were premised on one fundamental assumption: that external assistance *can* play a positive and effective role in fostering development in LDCs within their existing political systems and the international economic order. Implicit in this assumption was the ready acceptance of the moral dedication and political commitment of leaders and ruling elites in LDCs to the goals of development and progress. Accordingly, despite the critical shortage of aid funds relative to development needs, efficiency criteria were seldom applied in the early process of aid-giving, and, similarly, the utilisation of aid, following receipt, was not rigorously scrutinised.

The UN Development Decade I witnessed a remarkable growth in the number and size of donor aid agencies. In several rich countries, new agencies of government were created to administer the aid work, designed to operate largely outside the domain of the traditional Ministries of Finance, Foreign Affairs, and Trade and Industry. In 1961, the largest single such agency was created: the American Agency for International Development (AID), operating as an autonomous agency within the State Department. In 1964, the Labour government in Britain set up a brand new Ministry of Overseas Development. Other countries followed suit with their own version: Sweden's SIDA, Canada's CIDA, Denmark's DANIDA, Norway's NORAD, all emerged during the course of the 1960s.[33]

There was a parallel expansion of the multilateral aid agencies as well. The United Nations Development Programme (UNDP) was set up to take over the Technical Assistance and Special Fund activities of the organisation. UNDP opened field offices in every member country, headed by a Resident Representative and assisted by a full complement of officials internationally recruited. Older specialised UN agencies, such as the Food and Agriculture Organization (FAO), International Labour Office (ILO), World Health Organization (WHO), the UN Education, Scientific and Cultural Organization (UNESCO) were significantly expanded, and new agencies were established, including the UN Conference on Trade and Development (UNCTAD), the UN Industrial Development Organization (UNIDO) and the World Food Programme (WFP). In addition, a whole new network of regional institutions came into existence: the Asian Development Bank (AsDB) set up under the auspices of the UN Economic Commission for Asia and the Far East (ECAFE), the African Development Bank (AfDB) likewise created under the wing of the Economic Commission for Africa (ECA), and the Inter-American Development Bank (IDB) created as an agency of the Organization for American States (OAS). The World Bank, too, joined in the expansion process by setting up in 1960 the International Development Association (IDA) to complement the other institutions in the Bank Group, namely, the International Bank for Reconstruction and Development (IBRD) and the International Finance Corporation (IFC).

This large and sudden burgeoning of the aid agencies brought into existence a huge international civil service of managers, loan officers, auditors, analysts of every description, book-keepers and clerks. Recruited internationally from the UN countries, according to designated national quotas and on highly attractive terms of service, these international civil servants were expected to assist LDCs in fostering domestic development.

Technical Assistance: Does it Work?

In addition to permanent staff employed in headquarters, regional and field offices, both the bilateral and multilateral aid agencies began sending increasing numbers of advisers, consultants and technicians — generally, but often misleadingly, referred to as experts — on various types of fixed-term assignments in LDCs.[34]

Technical assistance programmes have been criticised by many observers for a great variety of reasons. Some have pointed out the inter-agency duplication of functions and problems of co-ordination;[35] others have challenged the lavish pay and fringe benefits of experts;[36] many have criticised the recruitment and briefing practices of donors which may lead to 'culture shock' after arrival in duty stations.[37] Some have even argued that it represents a form of colonialism.[38] Sir Robert Jackson, after an extensive study of the UN aid system, recommended country programming based on an integrated, system approach,[39] and the Pearson Commission appealed to the humanitarian and idealistic motivations in donor countries to increase aid flows.[40]

In point of fact, a far more basic challenge can be levelled against the technical assistance system: it doesn't reach the target groups. Because experts tend to be concentrated in such urban sectors as education and public administration, they are unable to make any impact on the living standards of target populations, especially those living in rural areas. Experts are formally guests of the host government. Upon arrival they are assigned to individual Ministries and agencies of government, and they report to the political and bureaucratic elites controlling the political system. The typical expert has little or no dealing with the poor and underprivileged masses, and he is obliged to function within the existing administrative machinery, dominated by elites who are unsympathetic to criticism, even when based on compelling evidence. The rules of international diplomacy, and the doctrine of national sovereignty, strictly observed in the technical assistance system, seriously restrict the role and effectiveness of the expert. He is expected to remain silent even in the face of widespread corruption and misuse of aid funds by self-seeking officials and politicians. In many cases, the expert is not able to deliver assistance to target populations because the entrenched elite frustrates his attempts for reasons of political survival. A reform-minded expert working in the field with the poor and underprivileged groups may find that his project funds are withheld, or ultimately he may be expelled from the country.

Technical assistance programmes in the past have made several important contributions to the cause of development in many LDCs. Success, however, was often despite, rather than because of, local political leadership and domestic elites. There are numerous cases of promising rural projects that were started and abandoned when external assistance ceased, ruling elites simply cutting off funding from regular budgetary sources. In fact, sometimes technical assistance is tolerated by an influential Minister, not because of need or high priority assigned to the project by the host government, but merely to obtain equipment and machinery, such as cars and tractors, which may be provided as part of an aid package, or in order to secure overseas fellowships, again provided on the same basis, which would then be distributed through the Minister's well established patronage network. Food subsidy programmes, too, are liable to be misused by corrupt officials or they may be operated to benefit civil servants and army personnel rather than target poverty groups.[41]

The idea that technical assistance can operate successfully as a form of on-the-job counterpart training, similar to the traditional apprenticeship system, is subject to several major problems. Thus, in many instances the expert-counterpart relations fail miserably, often from the very beginning, simply due to cultural or personality barriers. In some cases, the counterpart may be technically just as proficient as the expert, especially if the latter is a retired official sent abroad more as a personal bonus for past service in the donor country, than as a reformer.[42] On the other hand, an expert who is technically competent may nevertheless fail totally if he lacks the necessary tact, patience and personal skill to function in different environments. Also, there is the fact that the sending of an expert to an LDC may displace a local job-seeker, especially in countries faced with a growing school-leavers and unemployment problem. Even a Peace Corp volunteer may fill a job which otherwise might go to a native graduate. The services of volunteer expatriates are not only provided at a social cost to the host country, but often they entail considerable financial costs as well since the host country is expected to provide various fringe benefits and even some cash compensation to the volunteer.[43]

Capital Assistance

Long-term capital loans and grants, and not technical assistance, represent the major form of official development assistance (ODA) to LDCs, whether provided bilaterally or multilaterally. We have focused on technical assistance above because technical assistance represents the most visible human link between the donor and recipient countries. Of course many of the structural and operational problems are common to all forms of foreign aid, whether they are bilateral, multilateral or whether they involve capital or technical assistance.

There are, however, some important aspects of capital aid which deserve mention. Traditionally, this form of aid has been provided to finance physical infrastructural projects intended to serve the needs of industrialisation. Even when provided on concessional terms, capital aid in fact represented an important avenue for the transfer of inappropriate technology. Long-term agricultural loans were, as we have seen in the case of Pakistan, utilised for capital-intensive farm mechanisation and land consolidation schemes promoting elitist growth. By tying their loans and grants, bilateral donors actually utilised capital assistance to LDCs as instruments of their commercial and export-promoting policies. Multilateral agencies specialising in capital funding, such as the World Bank and the concessional IDA credits, were indirectly serving the same objectives. In recent years, there has been a greater Bank emphasis on human resources and rural development, but the operational problems discussed below remain just as valid for the UN family and other donors.

The Aid and Social Justice Conflict

As presently structured, the international aid system is a wasteful and inappropriate mechanism for promoting egalitarian development in most LDCs because the supply of aid and technical assistance is channelled through governmental and political machinery not always dedicated to the ideals of social justice. Where this machinery is controlled by self-seeking elites *they* end up as the principal gainers of aid, rather than the poor and the needy groups. So long as the donors cannot *directly* approach and deliver aid to the target population, the international aid system is unlikely to become an effective instrument for egalitarian development.[44] In the case of bilateral aid, which is by far the largest source,[45] it may be impractical to make the supply of aid contingent upon detailed follow-up and close scrutiny of actual utilisation since bilateral aid is always suspect as a tool of the donor's foreign and military policies. Multilateral aid managed through the UN and its affiliated agencies (referred to as the 'UN family') has the important relative advantage of being *politically neutral,* since the UN family does not have foreign policy objectives or military and commercial interests.

In the past the UN family of organisations failed to capitalise on its relative advantage of political neutrality. Although the share of multilateral aid rose from 5 per cent to 28 per cent of total official DAC aid during 1965-75,[46] the performance of the multilateral aid system remained well below expectations, as reflected by a number of major evaluations of the system.[47] An important reason for this is the fact that the UN family operates strictly within traditional rules of international diplomacy. The UN experts are despatched to LDCs as if on political missions, and they actually work *for* and *with* the ruling elites rather than directly with target populations; the UNDP Resident Representative acts largely as an ambassador of the UN to the host government.

A Direct UN Aid Delivery System

A new reformist approach is to have the UN technical assistance

personnel function largely *outside* the existing political and
governmental machinery in LDCs.[48] Doing this would not only be
consistent with the principle of political neutrality of the UN family,
but also allow the system to reach and deliver aid to the target
populations in a more direct and effective way. The UNDP field office,
under the management of the Resident Representative, might serve as
the real centre of the UN technical personnel, and each expert,
equipped with a clear job description, would be linked to defined target
groups. Visible impact on the living conditions of target groups, and not
reports prepared for HQ consumption, should be the yardstick for
successful expert missions.

The UN technical assistance programmes cannot, of course, operate
in a vacuum: they require important contributions from the host
government. The all-important point is the *form* of this contribution.
While financial contribution — i.e. 'counterpart funds' — can be
important in some cases, it is argued here that *political and moral
support* of the project are even more important. For it is this type of
support that is required for bringing about institutional and legislative
reform necessary for egalitarian development. In general, UN aid and
technical assistance must be conditional upon explicit and contractual
obligation on the part of the host government to undertake the
necessary legislative and institutional reform. For example, in
agricultural aid schemes requiring some form of land reform, aid should
not be provided until effective reform legislation is enacted. Otherwise,
the aid can be expected to be wasted. Rather than accept such wasteful
aid allocation, these funds could be better utilised in some other LDC
more willing to help its poor and needy populations. The same
principles should apply to other UN schemes: the building of a
technical or vocational training centre by the ILO or UNESCO should
be linked to actual programmes of job creation so that the graduates
are provided with employment following training. Educational and
social infrastructural projects should be located in sites within easy
accessibility of the target populations — usually away from capital
cities — in order to offset the pro-urban bias of post-war planning
priorities.

One of the most counter-productive ingredients in the existing UN
technical assistance system is the contractual obligation placed on host
governments to provide counterpart funds for the aided projects and
to supply fringe benefits to experts, ranging in some countries from
free housing accommodation to free transportation. Apart from the
heavy budgetary costs of these obligations on the government, the

practice in fact makes the UN expert more or less a *functionary* of the government. As such, he is subject to the normal bureaucratic rules of accountability and reporting within his assigned ministry or agency while also carrying external responsibility toward the UN family. This dual accountability often causes confusion, friction and conflicting loyalties. In the process, the UN expert quickly develops a sense of frustration, indifference and inertia, given the inefficient rules and procedures which characterise the public service in most LDCs.[49] Terminating the practice of counterpart funding would be quite popular with the host governments since they would be relieved of financial contribution to UN-supported projects. UN aid would then be real aid, intended for those it is supposed to help: the target groups. The additional UN funds required to offset the resulting deficit could be raised under the Development Levy on MNCs proposed above. Thus, *direct* access to target populations by the UN would be feasible both financially and diplomatically. Functionally, the UNDP field office would become the nerve-centre of the country programme, enjoying financial independence and having direct access to the target populations who may, finally, begin to derive the main benefits of the UN aid system.

But perhaps the chief merit of the proposed system of direct access to target populations is that it would make the UN responsible for the UN aid operations. Strange as it may sound, this never existed before in view of the divided and confused lines of responsibility for field officials, as discussed above. When the UN technical assistance and aid programmes are conducted under full UNDP jurisdiction, the effectiveness of aid would become the direct responsibility of the UN personnel. Misuse and abuse of aid funds would no longer have to be covered for fear of exposing corrupt and self-seeking host-country politicians and officials.

The UNDP-managed direct aid system proposed above would fit in very effectively with the decentralised (pro-rural) planning advocated in Chapter 8, and elaborated in Chapter 11. In particular, the UN direct aid system could be extremely helpful in the context of the Integrated Rural Development strategy outlined in Chapter 11. Functional co-ordination with national planning efforts, however, should be only encouraged when and where it would clearly promote egalitarian objectives.

Admittedly, there will be some LDC governments that would object to the proposed method of UN technical assistance as a potential threat to their power over target populations. But the choice facing the UN is whether it should serve the ruling classes, as the present aid system tends to do, or whether it should help the masses, long denied their due share of the benefits of development. Surely, there are *some* LDCs whose leaders are willing to implement egalitarian development beneficial to the masses, and surely *they* should be the ones receiving first priority in the allocation of *scarce* aid funds. In a period of rising international focus on human rights it would indeed be regrettable if the UN itself lagged behind in this critically important issue of development with social justice.

Notes

1. Peter Townsend, 'Measures and Explanations of Poverty in High Income and Low Income Countries: The Problems of Operationalizing the Concepts of Development, Class and Poverty' in Peter Townsend (ed.), *The Concept of Poverty* (Heinemann, London, 1970). For a different view, see P.T. Bauer, 'Western Guilt and Third World Poverty', *Commentary* (January 1976).

2. P.N. Rosenstein-Rodan, 'The Have's and the Have-not's Around the Year 2000' in Jagdish N. Bhagwati (ed.), *Economics and World Order from the 1970's to the 1990's* (Free Press, New York, 1972), p.30.

3. Ibid., p.31.

4. A valuable collection of papers dealing with various issues of foreign aid is J. Bhagwati and R.S. Eckaus (eds.), *Foreign Aid* (Penguin Books, Harmondsworth, 1970). See also Goran Ohlin, *Foreign Aid Policies Reconsidered* (Development Center, OECD, Paris, 1966). On the problem of debt servicing, see Lester B. Pearson *et al.*, *Partners in Development, The Report of the Commission on International Development* (Praeger, New York, 1969).

5. Quoted by Rosenstein-Rodan, 'The Have's and the Have-not's', pp.39-42.

6. Ibid., p.32.

7. This is the major finding of Alasdair I. Macbean's study: *Export Instability and Economic Development* (George Allen and Unwin, London, 1966). Based on several country case-studies, Macbean did not find a significant correlation between instability in export earnings and domestic development, a finding which, while by no means implying that instability has *no* damage on development, points to the *relative* unimportance of this factor. In fact, Macbean argues (p.340) that other factors, especially education and training, may be more important determinants of development in LDCs. Macbean's findings have been challenged by others: for example, see Alfred Maizels, *Exports and Economic Growth of Developing Countries* (Cambridge University Press, Cambridge, 1968), and also Maizels' review of Macbean's book in *American Economic Review* (June 1968), and C. Glezakos, 'Export Instability and Economic Growth: A Statistical Verification', *Economic Development and Cultural Change* (July 1973), so that the issue remains a controversial one.

8. S. Golt, 'World Trade and the Developing Countries' in Harry G. Johnson (ed.), *The New Mercantilism* (Basil Blackwell, Oxford, 1974); E.K. Hawkins, *The Principles of Development Aid* (Penguin Books, Harmondsworth, 1970), Ch.8, 'The Role of International Agencies'.

9. The details of the establishment of UNCTAD are presented in Diego Cordovez, 'The Making of UNCTAD', *Journal of World Trade Law* (May-June

1967), and *idem, UNCTAD and Development Diplomacy From Confrontation to Strategy,* published by the Journal of World Trade Law.

10. A highly informative account is given in Wilbur F. Monroe, *International Trade Policy in Transition* (D.C. Heath, Mass., 1975), esp. Chapter 4, pp.51-77.

11. Robert S. Walters, 'UNCTAD: Intervener Between Poor and Rich States', *Journal of World Trade Law* (September-October 1973).

12. On the pre-Kennedy Round trade negotiations, see John Pincus, *Trade, Aid and Development, The Rich and Poor Nations* (McGraw-Hill, New York, 1967), especially p.259 *et seq.* For subsequent GSP system, see Monroe, *International Trade Policy,* Chapter 4.

13. Monroe, *International Trade Policy,* pp.54-5.

14. T. Murray, 'UNCTAD's Generalized Preferences: An Appraisal', *Journal of World Trade Law* (July-August 1973); *idem,* 'How Helpful is the Generalized System of Preferences to Developing Countries?', *Economic Journal* (June 1973). An additional weakness of the GSP arrangements is that they appear to discriminate against the least developed LDCs. Thus only about 19 per cent of the exports of these countries (as compared with 39 per cent of the other LDCs) actually qualify for GSP treatment in preference-giving countries. See J. Ahmad, 'The Least Developed Amongst the Developing Countries', *Journal of World Trade Law* (March-April 1974).

15. Monroe, *International Trade Policy,* pp.61-7.

16. C. Fred Bergsten, *Toward a New International Economic Order, Selected Papers of C. Fred Bergsten, 1972-74* (D.C. Heath, Mass., 1975); C. Fred Bergsten and Lawrence B. Krause (eds.), *World Politics and International Economics* (Brookings Institution, Washington, DC, 1975). An excellent analysis of the 1973-5 commodity boom is given in Edward R. Fried, 'International Trade in Raw Materials: Myths and Realities', *Science* (February 1976), pp.641-6.

17. Thus, exports of copper ore accounted for 90.6 per cent of Zambia's total exports in 1972; in the same year, copper ore represented 73.0 per cent of Chile's exports; cotton exports accounted for 61.2 per cent of Sudan's exports; copper ore made up 61.1 per cent of Zaire's exports; cocoa in Ghana 60.3 per cent of exports; tea in Sri Lanka 59.4 per cent; coffee in Uganda 59.3 per cent; coffee in Colombia 57.9 per cent; cotton in Egypt 57.7 per cent and bananas in Panama 57.3 per cent: Dietrich Kebschull, 'Raw Materials in the Foreign Trade of the LDCs', *Intereconomics,* No.12 (1975), p.373.)

18. G.K. Helleiner (ed.), *A World Divided* (Cambridge University Press, London, 1976); P. Streeten, 'Terms of Trade are not made on Paper', *CERES* (March-April 1972); H. Singer, 'The Distribution of Gains from Trade and Investment – Revisited', *Journal of Development Studies,* Vol.11, No.6 (July 1975).

19. Dhruba Gupta, 'The First Four Years of SDRs', *Finance and Development* (June 1974).

20. United Nations, *Multinational Corporations in World Development* (Department of Economic and Social Affairs, ST/ECA/190, New York, 1973); Raymond Vernon, *The Economic and Political Consequences of Multinational Enterprise: An Anthology* (Harvard University Press, Boston, Mass., 1972); Richard Barnet and Ronald Muller, *Global Reach* (Simon and Schuster, New York, 1975).

21. Augusto Curti, 'Bananas', *CERES, FAO Review on Development* (July-August 1976), p.7. See also *Fortune* (July 1976), pp.145-51.

22. United Nations Development Programme, 'The Latin American Banana Crisis', Development Issue Paper 1, New York (mimeo.), p.2.

23. Ibid., p.8.

24. Frederick F. Clairmonte, 'The Banana Empire', *CERES, FAO Review on*

Development (January-February 1975).

25. Ibid., p.34.

26. United Nations Development Programme, 'Bauxite: A Commodity in Dispute', Development Issue Paper 12, New York 4/76 (mimeo.). Also, see C. Fred Bergsten, 'A New OPEC in Bauxite', *Challenge* (July-August 1976).

27. Thus, Guyana took over ALCAN's bauxite operations in February 1971 with a compensation payment of $52 million payable out of future profits, and then in 1975 nationalised Reynolds Metal Co. of the USA paying the company $14.5 million compensation over a period of 13 years. Jamaica, another important producer of bauxite, after an unsuccessful negotiation with foreign mining concerns in the country, introduced legislation designed to impose additional royalty levies per ton of bauxite exported and locally processed. The legislated levy meant an approximate 700 per cent rise in the revenue realised by Jamaica from bauxite mining. UNDP, 'Bauxite'.

28. The following remark by Charles Bettelheim is extremely appropriate in this context: 'Actually, while the growth of inequality in standards of living – i.e. between nations – constitutes one of the elements explaining the rise of struggles for national independence in countries exploited or dominated by imperialism. . .What is really decisive is the development of internal contradictions (economic, political, and ideological) between the masses, subjected to increasingly unbearable exploitation, and the privileged minorities linked with imperialism and protected by it, who enrich themselves from the labor of "their own people" and are themselves dominated by the ideology and way of life of the "great" industrial and imperialist countries.' Commenting on Arghiri Emmanuel, *Unequal Exchange, A Study of Imperialism of Trade, with additional comments by Charles Bettelheim* (Monthly Review Press, New York, 1972), p.271.

29. United Nations, *Monthly Bulletin of Statistics*, Vol.XXX, No.6 (June, 1977), Table C, p.xx.

30. OECD, *1976 Review Development Cooperation* (Paris, November, 1976), Table 10, p.215.

31. For example, the late US Senator Robert Taft, when asked what he thought about the policy of 'Trade Not Aid', is reported to have replied, 'I agree with the second part of it.' Quoted by Hans Singer, 'An Elusive Concept', *CERES, FAO Review on Development* (July-August 1976), p.26.

32. T. Balogh, 'Multilateral versus Bilateral Aid', *Oxford Economic Papers,* new series, Vol.19, No.3 (1967), excerpted in Bhagwati and Eckaus *Foreign Aid.* Also, see John White, *The Politics of Foreign Aid* (Bodley Head, London, 1974); Raymond F. Mikesell, *The Economics of Foreign Aid* (Aldine, Chicago, 1968).

33. George Cunningham, *The Management of Aid Agencies* (Croom Helm, London, 1974); Bruce Dinwiddy (ed.), *European Development Policies* (Praeger, New York, 1973).

34. Maurice Domergue, *Technical Assistance, Theory, Practice and Policies* (Praeger, New York, 1968); White, *The Politics of Foreign Aid,* esp. pp.184-90.

35. For example, see Balogh, 'Multilateral versus Bilateral Aid'; Robert G.A. Jackson, *A Study of the Capacity of the United Nations Development System* (United Nations, Geneva, 1969) (2 vols.).

36. Douglas E. Hall and Alan E. Dieffenbach, 'Compensation of Foreign Advisers in Developing Countries', *International Development Review/Focus* Vol.XV (1973/3).

37. Alvin G. Edgell, 'Aid Encounter in Iboland', *International Development Review/Focus,* Vol.XV (1973/4); D. Seers, 'Why Visiting Economists Fail', *Journal of Political Economy,* Vol.LXX, No.4 (August 1962); Francis C. Byrne, 'Role Shock: An Occupational Hazard of American Technical Assistants Abroad', *Annals of the American Academy of Political and Social Science* (November 1966).

38. Rita Cruise O'Brien, 'Colonization to Co-operation? French Technical Assistance in Senegal', *Journal of Development Studies,* Vol.8, No.1 (October 1971); Steven F. Hochschild, 'Technical Assistance and International Development: A Need for Fundamental Change', *International Development Review/Focus,* Vol.XIV, No.4 (1972/4).

39. Jackson, *A Study of the Capacity of the United Nations Development System.*

40. Pearson, *Partners in Development.* Probably the most important recommendation of the Pearson Report was that each industrialised country should increase its 'resource transfers' to LDCs to a minimum of 1 per cent of their respective GNP, a proposal which has had practically no success.

41. Jeffrey M. Davis, 'The Fiscal Role of Food Subsidy Programs', *IMF Staff Papers,* Vol.XXIV, No.1 (March 1977).

42. Robin E.I. Poulton, 'Young Experts for Young Countries', *International Development Review/Focus,* Vol.XV, No.3 (1973/3).

43. In 1973, there were a total of 96,528 bilateral technical assistance personnel serving in LDCs from DAC countries, compared with 90,930 in 1965. Of the 1973 personnel, 40.4 per cent were educational experts, 25.6 per cent operational experts, 16.5 per cent advisers and 17.5 per cent were volunteers. (OECD, *1976 Review Development Cooperation* (Paris, November 1976), Table VII-9, p.161.)

44. To be sure, there are several obstacles here, ranging from the doctrine of national sovereignty and the UN principle of non-interference in the internal affairs of member states, to the bureaucratic vested interests dependent upon the present *status quo.*

45. Although decreasing relatively since 1965, bilateral aid from DAC countries accounted for 72 per cent of the total official aid in 1975.

46. Since 1965, the share of multilateral aid to LDCs from DAC countries has been increasing. In that year, disbursements of net Official Development Assistance aid amounted to a total of $5.9 billion, with only 5 per cent being challenged through multilateral agencies. In 1975, total ODA aid amounted to $13.6 billion, and the multilateral component accounted for 28 per cent. (OECD, *1976 Review,* Table 10, p.215, and OECD, *1974 Review,* Table 33, p.233.)

47. E.g. the Jackson Report. See also Brian Johnson, 'The Multilateral System: Approaching the Limits to Globalism' in Dinwiddy, *European Development Policies.*

48. This, of course, is the method used by private aid agencies, such as Oxfam, CARE, etc., and missionary groups.

49. James A.F. Stoner and John D. Aram, 'Effectiveness of Two Technical Assistance Efforts in Differing Environments', *Journal of Development Studies,* Vol.9, No.4 (July 1973); O. Mehmet, 'Administrative Machinery for Development Planning in Liberia', *Journal of Modern African Studies,* Vol.XIII, No.5 (September 1975).

13 SUMMING UP: EGALITARIAN PLANNING AS A NON VIOLENT REVOLUTION

Economic planning in LDCs is now in a state of crisis brought about by inappropriate prescriptions formulated during the post-war period. Alarming rates of unemployment, mass poverty and urban overcrowding are some of the visible consequences of faulty policies designed to drain rural areas of every possible surplus resource that could be squeezed out of agriculture in order to finance a process of industrialisation which has actually widened the socio-economic disparities between the elites and the masses.

A Crisis of Relevance?

But the crisis in planning is not a crisis of relevance. If anything, economic planning is more relevant and more urgently needed now than ever before. Rather the crisis is one of approach. It relates to the objectives and strategies of planning. The economic incentives generated by the price-market mechanism *can* be reconciled with egalitarian interventions for a new approach to planning based on social justice. If this is a valid assumption, egalitarian planning may be viewed as a non-violent revolution for promoting a more equitable socio-economic order in the Third World. The fundamental purpose of egalitarian planning is raising the income share of the poverty target groups — almost by definition, the bulk of the rural population. This would make future planning a heavily pro-rural approach with policy interventions designed for this purpose. In particular, it would aim at reversing the direction of investment resource flow so that development expenditures are channelled from urban to rural areas to launch a diversity of income-generating activities in, and for, the rural communities.

Egalitarian planning would also be a *decentralised* process. Projects to be included in development plans would be determined by the villagers, peasants and rural communities themselves in line with the decentralisation strategy outlined in Chapter 8. But decentralised planning requires both new policy interventions and new institutions. The planning agency, for example, must open offices at the regional and sub-regional levels in order to collect information on, and maintain regular links with, the target groups.

Peasant Revolts or Participation in the Planning Process?

How feasible is the decentralised, egalitarian planning process? Surely the entrenched elites, dominating the political and economic decision-making process, will put every possible obstacle against it? Given this type of resistance, isn't a revolution by violent means the only option available to get rid of the 'rascals' and *then* begin to build an egalitarian society?

Rebellions and uprisings seldom work *for* the masses; and they always entail heavy social costs, disproportionately borne by those who have the least to lose and the most to gain.

That is precisely why economic planning — as a regular, dynamic process — offers the best bet for the target groups. It is a non-violent option for an egalitarian revolution with active participation by the masses. Instead of being organised for uprisings against the bosses, landlords and exploiters, they (the masses) could be organised to take part in the making of choices and the ranking of priorities in the planning process. But who should organise the rural communities and the target groups for taking a part in the planning process? Independent urban intellectual leadership is no remedy: the social and ideological distance between the peasants and the radical intellectuals is too great to forge the necessary links of mutual trust.

The planning agency itself would be the logical place to initiate the decentralised process. In most instances, these initiatives can be expected to meet ready, willing and positive response from the rural communities eager to participate in the making of planning choices. This, of course, may be contrary to the widely held opinion in the post-war period about the irrational behaviour of villagers and their inability to specify their needs. But given a chance, even the most undereducated peasants can be articulate, well informed and rational about their needs and constraints. Even though the planners and economists of the planning agency are often urban intellectuals themselves, the fact is that the planning agency is almost always the most egalitarian-minded organ of any establishment in the Third World. It is not unrealistic to look at the planning agency, at least in several LDCs, as the source of the new egalitarian planning approach based on social justice. The importance of constructive support by external participants in Third World development must also be recognised (see below).

The Egalitarian Planning Agency

For such a planning agency, two principal short- and medium-term tasks can be delineated. The first is land reform. As we have seen in Chapter 11, post-war planners were generally indifferent to the complex issue of land reform. Because of the economist's long-standing professional disdain for institutional problems, land reform was generally regarded as 'unplannable'. But land reform *is* plannable and its implementation through the regular and orderly planning process constitutes perhaps the most important single determinant of future egalitarian development. Thus, the first task of an egalitarian planning agency should be the determination, on the basis of field studies, of the mean farm size in given regions, on which to base a programme of land redistribution, intended to maximise the number of self-employed and economically viable smallholders. The mean farm size in this context is a vitally important measure of success, and it must be determined very carefully on the basis of accurate studies of yield rates, income pay-off streams, suitability of crops, credit, marketing and the all-important matter of intermediate farm technology. All these elements are most effectively co-ordinated to achieve maximum impact through the Integrated Rural Development strategy outlined in Chapter 11. It is important to realise explicitly that the land redistribution scheme suggested here is diametrically opposed to capitalist farming techniques aimed at maximising marketable food production. The 'Green Revolution' provides ample evidence about the negative social effects of large-scale, plantation techniques of food production. It is precisely in order to avoid these negative effects that land redistribution must be tied to the objective of maximising the number of self-employed smallholders who are to be given sufficient holdings to operate efficiently. Experience from Taiwan and Japan, and more recently from Malaysia, demonstrates the practical feasibility of this type of land reform.

The second principal short-term task of an egalitarian planning agency would be to maximise job creation and employment income by submitting every proposed development project to a rigorous and careful *ex-ante* social benefit-cost evaluation. This was discussed in Chapter 9, where a planning approach was advocated under which jobs would be matched with workers on the basis of micro-manpower planning. In addition, fiscal, monetary, tariff and industrial policies would have to be rewritten in order to promote employment generation by getting rid of unnecessary reliance on capital inputs, especially imported capital goods.

Collectively, these two planning tasks represent the most feasible mix of measures that can be launched in the short and medium run to begin a process of income levelling among regions and social groups within LDCs.

As a longer-run objective, the egalitarian planning agency should aim at designing and implementing an 'infant industry' programme of investment in human capital formation (as discussed in Chapter 9) in order to raise the quality and productivity of its citizens and workers everywhere, based on equal and universal accessibility to schools and training institutions for all. This approach is an essential step in ensuring that future generations may be able to contribute to, and take full part in, the dynamic process of development. It is the only sure way of minimising the huge (human) capital loss going on in LDCs now, as reflected in alarming rates of unemployment. Investment in human capital formation is expensive, but there are several alternatives. For example, as discussed in Chapter 10, there are interesting possibilities of low-cost, informal types of education which may be appropriate for some LDCs faced with severe budgetary constraints. Even though human capital formation is a very slow process, it should be clear by now that there are no short-cuts in development, nor are there any magic solutions. There may be alternative theories of, and approaches to, development in LDCs, but investment in human resources is basic to all.

How feasible are these terms of reference, especially in those LDCs under strong elite domination? Will not an egalitarian planning agency be frustrated by a self-seeking and corrupt political leadership? It is precisely under such circumstances that the *type* of external intervention in the planning and development process in LDCs becomes so relevant.

The Role of External Parties

The prospects for egalitarian development in the Third World are vitally dependent upon supportive roles by the international community, especially the aid agencies and the rich countries. In extreme cases (e.g. Uganda), the intensity and extent of political or military tyranny may be so great as to rule out any possibility of economic planning — egalitarian or otherwise. International exposure and rebuke of the tyrannical leaders are probably the most meaningful contribution external parties can make in such cases. International public opinion may not be enough to end the tyranny and oppression directly, but silence and indifference, or worse still assistance given to the tyrannical leadership, would be totally unethical.

Under more normal circumstances, external parties can play important and constructive roles to promote egalitarian development. Economic philosophy and theory cannot be transplanted from other countries. This implies a different and restricted role for the future foreign adviser and expert involved in LDC planning. First of all, his duty station ought to be out in the field among the target groups — not in the capital city. While maintaining strict political neutrality, he should assist the target groups in their attempts to take part in the dynamic process of decentralised, egalitarian planning. However, every temptation to act as a 'leader' ought to be resisted with tact, patience and skill. The most successful foreign expert in the field is one who stimulates the target groups to define their needs and to convey these needs to the planning agency.

The supply of UN aid, especially capital assistance, should be designed to bring direct and visible benefit to target groups. This implies that schools, clinics, training centres, experimental farms etc., should be built in rural areas, away from capital cities, and the planning of these projects should be within the framework of the integrated rural development strategy outlined in Chapter 11. It is vitally important that these projects be designed to serve rural needs and impart rural values; there would be little advantage in building, say, a school for rural youth, if it did not offer a very large component of agrarian and community studies, aimed at producing educated farmers and farm-workers.

In Chapter 12, a UN Development Levy on multinational corporations was proposed in order to raise additional revenue to finance multilateral aid projects for egalitarian development in LDCs. This is potentially a highly effective instrument capable of bringing rapid benefits to target groups. But it should be supplemented with wide-ranging reforms within the existing UN aid system. In particular, the United Nations Development Programme (UNDP) should be depoliticised by placing its experts *outside* the agencies and Ministries of the host government and by stopping the practice of counterpart funding by LDCs. As discussed in Chapter 12, these reforms are required to overcome the existing built-in inefficiencies in the UNDP operations, and to gain direct access to target groups.

The rich and industrialised countries, too, can and should play a positive role in the promotion of egalitarian development in LDCs. Instead of tied and inappropriate forms of bilateral aid, meaningful trade concessions should be provided in order to increase and stabilise income flows to LDCs. But linear expansion of trade opportunities (i.e. without structural changes in the trade and monetary framework) is unlikely to help the LDCs since the oligopolistic activities of multinational corporations often range from production in the Third World to distribution and marketing in rich countries. Thus, even if trade liberalisation policies were to double LDC exports of manufactured goods, under the existing international framework most of the additional revenue would accrue right back to the multinational corporations rather than to the LDCs.

Thus structural reforms in the framework of international trade are necessary to promote greater global equity. Ways and means must be found in the north-south dialogues and NIEO debates in order to increase the income share of LDCs and finance future development. But these international reforms ought to be linked to, and be accompanied by, egalitarian internal reforms *within* LDCs themselves so that the benefits of increased income flows are not utilised for elitist income concentration in those countries. In this context, world public opinion, especially the news media, can play a useful and constructive role.

INDEX

Adelman, I. 39-42
administrative machinery 17, 32
Africa: élites in 48; illiteracy in 68,
  226-7; population growth in 81
agrarian movements 239-41
agricultural education 136, 223-4,
  226, 228
agriculture: co-operatives 131-2, 227;
  farm sizes 234-8, 245, 273;
  ignored by forecasting 203-4;
  in Liberia 129-30; in Pakistan
  142, 146-50; income redistributed
  to industry from 54-5; need for
  incentives to 208-10;
  productivity of 187-8; research
  into 234; technology of 232-4;
  two-sector growth models and
  26-8; youth employment and
  210-11; see also rural areas
Algeria 70, 78
Amin, General 160
Argentina: illiteracy in 67-8;
  industrialisation in 55; land
  reform in 237; peasants in 70
Asia: élites in 48

balance of payments 9
Baldwin, G. 225
banana trade 257-9
Bangladesh 151; poverty in 61
barefoot planner 11-12
Basic Needs Approach 10, 36n,
  178-9
Bauer, P.T. 104
Bedeau, Hugo A. 175
benefit cost analysis 207-8, 273
Bettelheim, Charles 24, 269n
Big Push theory 18, 231
Blaug, M. 225
Brazil 141, 151-60; balance of
  payments 154, 155; coffee in
  152; economic fluctuations
  152-3; economic growth of 155;
  élites in 153-5; fiscal policy 159;
  foreign investment in 154;
  foreign trade and 151, 152;
  government's role in 157; income
  distribution in 43-4, 157-9;

industry in 155-7; inflation in
  155; literacy in 67, 170n; multinational companies in 158; need
  for reform in 160; poverty in
  63, 155-7; public expenditure in
  159; urbanisation in 158; wages
  in 158-9
Brookins, O.T. 41

capital: accumulation 81-3; assistance 263-4; flight of 25, 163;
  human 82, 201-2, 220-2, 274
centrally planned economies 11
Chenery, Hollis 42
Chile 70
civil servants 85-6; Malaysian 98
class theories 47-8
Colombia 39; land tenure in 238;
  unemployment in 80
colonialism 25; effect on international trade 252-4; effect on
  Malaysia 95-106
commodities, primary 255-9, 268n
comparative advantage, theory of 83
Compensation Principle 30
comprehensive employment policy
  199-213 passim
conflict resolution 12, 181-2
consumption 178-80; in rural
  areas 213; investment and 182-3
corruption 186
Costa Rica 70

DRIPP project 12
Dahomey 85
decision-making 177, 184
Denti, Ettore 81
Desarrollismo 12
development: distinguished from
  economic growth 175-6; see also
  rural development
development banks 261
development plans see egalitarian
  planning and planning
Domar, E.D. 18, 35n
dual economies 252; Malaysia 95,
  95, 101-3; Uganda 160,
  161

277